OXFORDSHIRE FORESTS

The Oxfordshire Record Society

OXFORDSHIRE FORESTS
1246-1609

Edited by Beryl Schumer

VOLUME No. 64
2004

Produced for the Society by
Past Historic, Kings Stanley, Gloucestershire
Printed in Great Britain

TABLE OF CONTENTS

FOREWORD

Beryl Schumer has been the acknowledged authority on the royal forest of Wychwood in the Middle Ages since she published her researches in *The Evolution of Wychwood to 1400: Pioneers, Frontiers and Forests* (1984, reissued with revisions in 1999 as *Wychwood: Evolution of a Wooded Landscape*). In this volume Miss Schumer makes available to the public a translated transcript of the raw material of her research, the 13th- and 14th-century forest records in the National Archives. That material makes up the bulk of what is to be found here, but to it she has added medieval material relating to the forests of Shotover and Stowood, and a Jacobean survey of Wychwood.

The Society is grateful to Miss Schumer for undertaking this edition and for her patience during several delays that have slowed its preparation for the printer. We believe that *Oxfordshire Forests* will make an important contribution to our understanding not only of the administration of royal forests but also of the development of those communities that lay within forest boundaries and were subject to its law and customs.

Oxford, June 2004

Christopher Day
General Editor, O.R.S.

EDITOR'S PREFACE

Transcripts of many of the medieval documents in this volume had been prepared for and used by Mrs. Violet Wickham Steed in her studies of the forest. At her death they passed to the staff of the Victoria County History of Oxfordshire, and later were used in the preparation of this volume by the present editor who had already transcribed and translated the documents independently. Each transcript has been checked against the other and against the original documents.

EDITORIAL NOTES

The following editorial conventions have been used:

[ ]	editorial insertion
( )	interlineation
< >	words which had been crossed out
italics	words which also appear as marginal notes

Latin personal names and surnames have been translated except in those instances where the translation is uncertain. Place-names used as surnames have been modernised where the identification seems reasonably clear, and in those cases "de" has been translated "of". Where the identification is not clear the name has been left in the form in the document, and "de" has not been translated.

In some documents items have been numbered, to facilitate cross-referencing.

LIST OF ABBREVIATIONS

Boarstall Cartulary *The Boarstall Cartulary*, ed. H E Salter (Oxford Historical Society lxxxviii, 1930)

Cal. Chart. R *Calendar of the Charter Rolls preserved in the Public Record Office* (H.M.S.O. 1903-27)

Cal. Close *Calendar of the Close Rolls preserved in the Public Record Office* (H.M.S.O. 1892-1963)

Cal. Inq. Misc. *Calendar of Inquisitions Miscellaneous (Chancery) preserved in the Public Record Office* (H.M.S.O. 1916-68)

Cal. Inq.p.m. *Calendar of Inquisitions post mortem preserved in the Public Record Office* (H.M.S.O. 1904-87)

Cal. Pat. *Calendar of Patent Rolls preserved in the Public Record Office* (H.M.S.O. 1891-1986)

Cart. St. Frid. *The Cartulary of the Monastery of St. Frideswide at Oxford*, ed. S.R. Wigram (O.H.S. xxviii, xxxi)

Complete Peerage G.E.C[okayne] and others, *The Complete Peerage*

DB OXF *Domesday Book, Oxfordshire*, ed. John Morris (Phillimore, 1978)

D.N.B. *Dictionary of National Biography*

Des. Vill. Oxon. K. J. Allison, M. W. Beresford and J. G. Hurst, *The Deserted Villages of Oxfordshire*, Leicester Occasional Papers No. 17 (1966)

Eynsham Cart. *Cartulary of Eynsham Abbey*, ed. H.E. Salter, (O.H.S. xlix, li)

Feudal Aids *Inquisitions and Assessments relating to Feudal Aids preserved in the Public Record Office* (H.M.S.O. 1899-1920)

L. & P. Henry VIII *Letters and Papers, Foreign and Domestic, of the reign of Henry VIII* (H.M.S.O. 1864-1932)

Oseney Cart. *Cartulary of Oseney Abbey,* ed. H.E. Salter (O.H.S. lxxxix-xci, xcviii, ci)

Rot. Hund. *Rotuli Hundredorum temp. Hen. III & Edw. I* (Record Commission, 1812-18)

Rotuli Ricardi Gravesende *Rotuli Ricardi Gravesende 1258-79*, ed. F. N. Davis, Cant. & York Soc. x 1913 & L. R. S. xx, 1925

V.C.H. *Victoria County History*

INTRODUCTION

It has been estimated that at the beginning of the thirteenth century one-third of England was subject to the forest law,[1] and the lives of the inhabitants and the development of the landscape of almost every county would have been affected to a greater or less extent by this fact. While the whole of Oxfordshire was never in the forest, in 1200 the legal forest included all the land from the Thame northwards to the county boundary with Northamptonshire, and from the Thames to Great Tew, the town of Oxford alone being excepted. However, this was the greatest extent of the forest, and it was reduced in size at various dates in the following centuries, although it was not until the disafforestation of Wychwood in 1857 that the last traces of the Crown's forestal rights were abolished.

The documents transcribed in this volume are some of those arising from the operation of the forest law in the county, and they fall into two groups, firstly a collection of previously unpublished records relating to the forests in the thirteenth and fourteenth centuries, and secondly a survey of Wychwood made *circa* 1609. They have a value both in providing information about the landscape and people of Oxfordshire at various times, and in demonstrating changes in the administration of the forest law. The early documents show that administration at its height, the later ones the beginning of its decline; while the *c.* 1609 survey comes from the period of the attempts by the Stuart kings to revive that law.

The Oxfordshire forests

In Domesday Book five forests are named for Oxfordshire - Woodstock, Cornbury and Wychwood in western Oxfordshire, and Shotover and Stowood to the east of Oxford. In reality there were only two forests since Shotover and Stowood were jointly administered by one forester, and the western forests by another, although the parks of Woodstock and of Cornbury later came to be controlled by their own parkers.

In addition several vills further to the east of Oxford lay within the Forest of Bernwood, although the greater part of that was in Buckinghamshire.[2]

For most of the thirteenth century, the period during which the first three documents were written, Wychwood consisted of all the land bounded by the county boundary with Gloucestershire and the rivers Windrush, Thames, Evenlode, and Glyme, while the other forests lay between the rivers Thame,

---

[1]   Oliver Rackham, *Ancient Woodland, its history, vegetation and uses in England*, Edward Arnold, 1980, p. 179.

[2]   These were Waterperry, Ledhale, Horton, Woodperry, Upper and Lower Arncott and Piddington: *The Boarstall Cartulary,* ed. H. E. Salter (Oxford Historical Society lxxxviii, 1930), 181, No. 575.

Thames, Cherwell and Ray.[3] The list of manors whose woodwards are recorded on pages 45 to 49 confirms the fact that the greater part of central Oxfordshire was subject to forest law. Some manors to the north of the Ray are included in the list, and it is not clear to which forest they belonged. Possibly they were considered to lie within the Forest between the Bridges of Oxford and Stamford, a unique institution whose warden or keeper had jurisdiction over several forests in the counties of Oxfordshire, Buckinghamshire, Northamptonshire and Huntingdonshire.

The two manors of Lillingstone Lovell and Boycott, which are now in Buckinghamshire, were formerly detached parts of Oxfordshire, and they lay in the Forest of Whittlewood, which straddled the boundary between Buckinghamshire and Northamptonshire.[4] Since they were "in Oxfordshire", some references to those two vills are found among the Forest Pleas in this volume.

On the other hand, the manor of Widford was within the bounds of Wychwood and its woodward is recorded in one Oxfordshire eyre;[5] but it was, until 1844, a detached portion of Gloucestershire, so that any forest offences in that manor were presumably presented at the forest eyres for that county.

The forests included land and woods which belonged to lords other than the King, and by the end of the thirteenth century those lords were pressing for their disafforestation. Edward I was eventually forced to order perambulations which would define the area to remain within the forest, and perambulations of Bernwood were made in 1294 and 1298, and of Wychwood and Shotover and Stowood in 1298 and 1300. The county boundary became the new boundary of Bernwood, so that its Oxfordshire vills were disafforested, as also were almost all of the private woods in the other forests so that only the king's own manors and woods, and the Bishop of Winchester's Chase of Witney (over which he already had control), remained within the forest.[6] Some local lords in the Wychwood area took advantage of this situation and proceeded to assart some of their woodland (see p. 146, **4**), but others did not. This may have been because the lords and tenants of the former forest vills wished to retain their rights of common in the large tract of royal demesne woodland, rights which

[3] Beryl Schumer, *The Woodland Landscape of the Wychwood region in the centuries before AD 1400*, M. Phil. thesis, University of Leicester, 1980, 11-13.

[4] *V.C.H. Buckinghamshire* ii, 131. Boycott was in the parish of Stowe: *op. cit.* iv, 232.

[5] See p. 48.

[6] *Boarstall Cartulary* 181 No 575 and 182 No. 576; Schumer, *op. cit.,* 13-15. One undated perambulation for Shotover and Stowood is transcribed in both the *Boarstall Cartulary*, 179-180, and in the *Cartulary of Eynsham Abbey*, ed. H. E. Salter (Oxfordshire Historical Society li 1908), 96, but the Public Record Office lists two, in 1298 and 1300: C205/17 No 3 and C67/6A m. 7.

they would have lost if they claimed complete freedom from the Forester's control.[7]

Edward I refused to accept the new bounds and obtained the Pope's sanction to revoke them. However the perambulations remained an issue between the crown and the lords, and it is generally agreed that they were accepted in 1327.[8] It was presumably as a result of this that in the Wychwood inquisition of 1332 (p. 145) all twenty-four members of the jury are said to live outside the forest; there would have been few free men, qualified to sit on the jury, living on those parts of the king's or the bishop's estates which still lay within the forest. However the documents in this volume suggest that both forests did not remain in this state for long, since in inquisitions in and after 1337 the juries usually consisted of men living both within and outside the forest bounds, and the presentments relate to woods in the whole of the previously disafforested areas. In 1370 the men of Eynsham stated that the Forester, Thomas of Langley, had enlarged the bounds of Wychwood eighteen years earlier,[9] but the inquisitions in this volume suggest that the reversion to the pre-perambulation bounds had happened earlier still. It is not clear what the state of the forests was later since there are no surviving records of forest courts or inquisitions for Wychwood or Shotover and Stowood between 1370 and the sixteenth century.

In the fifteenth century a 'New Forest' was instituted which consisted of the woods in the vicinity of Woodstock Park which transferred the responsibility of keeping them from the Keeper of Wychwood to a new Keeper who was also usually the custodian of the Park.[10] Otherwise there were no further major alterations in the extent of the forests until the seventeenth century.

Forest Administration and Justice[11]

The person responsible for the administration of the forest law throughout England or, after 1241, for England either north or south of the Trent,[12] was the Justice or Keeper of the Forest.

---

[7] See *Cal. Close 1302-1307*, 323, No. 135.

[8] Charles R. Young, *The Royal Forests of Medieval England*, pp. 140,147; *Statutes of the Realm I*, 255.

[9] *Eynsham Cartulary ii*, 107.

[10] *Cal. Pat. 1476-1485*, p. 177.

[11] No detailed account of the forest law will be given here. Apart from the standard work on that subject by G. J. Turner, excellent summaries can be found in *A Calendar of New Forest Documents, 1244-1334*, ed. D. J. Stagg, Hampshire Record Series iii, 10-12. and *Collections for a History of Staffordshire 4th series, XVIII, The Forests of Cannock and Kinver*, ed. Jean Birrell, Staffordshire Record Society 1999.

Other Justices were appointed by the king at intervals to conduct the forest eyres, that is to hear presentments and pass sentence on men brought before them for offences against the forest law committed within a county.

The day-to-day administration of, and justice within, an individual forest was the responsibility of its Forester or Keeper, and in Oxfordshire this was originally a hereditary office.[13] He presumably had a staff of under-foresters, although these are rarely mentioned in the records before the fourteenth century. Unpaid local freeholders who had been elected in the county court acted as agisters, regarders or verderers. The agisters held courts three times a year to regulate the use of the forest as common pasture for the villages in the vicinity and collect any payments for pannage,[14] while the regarders made a triennial perambulation to detect any assarts (clearances for agriculture), purprestures (encroachments), or waste (excessive cutting of trees) within the forest.[15] The verderers' duties were more onerous for they, with the Forester, held regular courts of attachment, where any persons who had been detected committing offences against the vert (trees and underwood) or the venison (the beasts of the chase) were tried. Those who had committed minor offences against the vert were fined at that court, but the more serious offences against the vert and all other offences were recorded on the verderers' rolls which would be presented later at the higher court, the forest eyre.

Another form of local jurisdiction was the inquisition or inquest held following the wounding or death of a deer.[16] This was held under the supervision of the Forester and verderers, and the men of the four vills nearest to the place where the offence occurred were summoned to determine the facts. Their findings were also referred to the eyre.

The forest eyre must always have been a cumbersome procedure, involving as it did not only the presence of the sheriff, the bailiffs of the appropriate Hundreds, all the forest officials and the woodwards of the private woods within the forest, but also all freeholders whose land lay within the forest

---

[12] Jurisdiction over the Forests was divided in a north-east/south-west fashion in 1229, with the boundary following the Cherwell so that the eastern half of Oxfordshire was in one jurisdiction and the western in the other. However this innovation was short-lived and by 1241 the Trent had become the dividing line. *Cal. Pat. 1225-1232,* 273; *Cal. Pat. 1232-1247,* 261.

[13] From the 12th century until 1361 the forestership of Wychwood was held by members of the Langley family. The Mymekan family held that of Shotover and Stowood until 1309 when the office was bought by John de Haudlo, who had married the heiress of the forester of Bernwood, and from that time until its disafforestation in 1660, the forest of Shotover and Stowood was administered with Bernwood. See p. 137 fn.

[14] see p. 84.

[15] see pp. 36-38, 71-78, 90-94, 110-119.

[16] see pp. 18-19, 21-22, 24, 66, 87, 97.

bounds and the representatives of the forest vills. It is not surprising that many were amerced for non-attendance at the eyre of 1272, the list including the names of Edmund, earl of Cornwall, Matilda, countess of Gloucester, and Roger, earl of Norfolk, whose Oxfordshire manors can have been only an insignificant part of their estates.[17]

The object of the eyre was not to try offenders, since that had been done at the lesser forest courts, but to impose the sentence which, by the thirteenth century, took the forms of outlawry for offenders who had fled and could not be found and imprisonment or the payment of a fine for those who had been caught or gave themselves up. Fines could be imposed not only on offenders against the vert and the venison or persons who broke any of the other clauses of the forest law,[18] but on their sureties if they failed to appear, on freeholders who failed to attend the forest eyre and on officials convicted of dereliction of duty.[19] Forest justice was a major source of royal revenue,[20] and the fines imposed in the Oxfordshire eyres of 1256 and 1272 amounted to £93 and £144.

Great lords presented as having committed offences were not sentenced at the eyre, but referred to the king for judgement.[21] However other lords of quite high status could be fined or sentenced to imprisonment by the Justices.[22]

Clerics were subject to the forest law and could be imprisoned, but there seems to have been a distinction between beneficed clergy and others. If a parson or vicar had committed an offence and did not appear before the Justices, his bishop was instructed to ensure his appearance at the next eyre, although if he had fled he was exacted and outlawed in the same way as lay persons were.[23] Other *clerici* (usually these were "clerks" at Oxford) were not attached as the laity were, but if they did not appear before the Justices were exacted and outlawed without reference to any person higher in the church hierarchy.[24]

The only people who had any sort of immunity were married women, who were held to be under their husbands' orders and so could not themselves be guilty of any offence. Widows, however, were responsible for their own actions and those of their household members.[25]

---

[17] see pp. 94-5.
[18] e.g., failing to raise a hue and cry, pp. 20,23,24.
[19] e.g., p. 24, **24, 25**.
[20] Young, *Royal Forests of Medieval England*, 39.
[21] see pp. 71, 86, 93 and 95.
[22] see p. 70, **38**.
[23] see pp. 67, **27** and 27, **36**.
[24] see p. 16, **6**.
[25] e.g., p. 18, **8**, 25 **30**.

In the interval between eyres offenders against the vert were freed if they could produce two men to act as sureties that they would appear at the eyre. Offenders against the venison who had been caught were initially committed to prison, in either the Forester's prison or Oxford Castle.[26] Here they would stay to await the coming of the Justices unless released on bail and with sureties, by writ of the King or the Justices.[27]

If any offenders against the venison had managed to escape, the Justices ordered the sheriff to distrain their goods, or those of their relatives or their lord, until the person appeared. Failing this, they were exacted and outlawed.[28]

In the thirteenth century the eyres were held so irregularly that some offenders, or forest officials, died before the Justices' arrival, hence the lists of those "excused by death" in the records.[29] When an official died, his heir had to appear before the eyre and produce his roll of record.[30]

Forest justice is often depicted as merciless, but these documents record several occasions when offenders were pardoned because of youth, old age, or poverty.[31]

No eyres are recorded for Oxfordshire after 1272,[32] although in some other counties eyres continued to be held in the fourteenth century. The general eyre for the county was replaced by an inquisition into the state of one forest, held by the Keeper of the Forest south of Trent or his deputy in the presence of all the officials of that forest and a jury of local freeholders, a procedure which had been laid down by Edward I in 1306.[33] These took place more frequently than the eyres, sometimes yearly or even twice in a year. The inquisition appears to have been less a court of law than a record of what was happening in the Forest, since no amercements are recorded although the Keeper had the power to accept fines without waiting for an eyre.

By this date the use of the forests was changing. Coppicing is recorded for the first time (although it may have been practised earlier), and in Wychwood woodland was increasingly being cleared for agriculture. The king himself was

[26] see pp. 66 **24**, 17 **7**.
[27] see pp. 16, 26fn., 66, 67.
[28] e.g. p. 28 **39**.
[29] see pp. 13-14, 18, 21, etc..
[30] see pp. 65, 69.
[31] see pp. 25, 21, 28.
[32] An inquisition described as a forest eyre was held in Oxford in 1637 (P.R.O. C99/91 and C99/92), and Edward Marshall, in *The early history of Woodstock Manor and its environs in Bladon, Hensington, New Woodstock and Blenheim, with later notices,* 177, records another "Justice Court" for the forest held at Woodstock, but these dealt only with Wychwood, not with the whole county.
[33] *Statutes of the Realm* I, 148.

involved in this process, as shown by the extensive assarts in the royal manor of Combe.[34] Records of assarts were kept by the crown so that the rents arising from them, which were intended to compensate for the crown's loss of feed for the deer, could be collected. However, with the growth of other means of taxation, forest justice became no longer of great financial importance to the crown, and the forest system decayed so that only scattered records, usually relating to the king's own woods, have survived from the fifteenth and sixteenth centuries.

Interest in the forests as a source of revenue revived in the seventeenth century, when James I tried to increase the profits from them.[35] It was proposed that this should be done by two different means.

The first was to obtain more money from the royal demesne woodland, which was divided into a number of coppices separated by areas of open forest. The coppices were used mainly for the growth of timber and underwood, although they were open for pasture for part of the coppice cycle, and the open forest was permanent pasture not only for the deer but also for the animals belonging to the tenants of the neighbouring vills. By the sixteenth century the coppices in the royal demesne woodland were leased out as a group to a private person, usually the man who was keeper of the forest at the time, who paid so that he could have the crop of underwood which was obtained at their periodic felling; it was suggested that the payment for this should be increased.

The other proposal was to attempt to gather more revenue from assart lands, either by selling them to the occupiers in fee farm, or by forcing the occupiers to compound (pay a fine) or to raise the annual rent of that land. The king's agent in this was Otho Nicholson, who in 1605 was appointed as Receiver of all the money raised in this way. He commissioned surveys of many forests, of which the Wychwood survey transcribed in this volume was one, and it, with others, was reported by him as being completed by February 1609. It was presumably made by Robert Treswell, Surveyor-General of Woods south of Trent,[36] although it may have been based on an earlier document since in 1590 it was said that 'Mr Agas and his sons' had spent ten weeks in Wychwood surveying the forest.[37]

The survey is based on the three sections which had been retained within the forest by the 1300 perambulation, but also includes the adjoining woods, as

[34] p. 106, **4**.
[35] Good accounts of this period are found in Phillip A. J. Pettit, *The Royal Forests of Northamptonshire*, Northamptonshire Record Society XXIII, 1968, Chapter 4, and in Stephanos Mastoris and Sue Groves, *Sherwood Forest in 1609: a Crown Survey by Richard Bankes*, Thoroton Society Record Series 40, 1998, xxxvi-xxxvii.
[36] He is named as "Surveyor of Whichwood Forest" in *Cal. S P Dom. 1603-1610*, 649.
[37] P.R.O. CRES 40/10 p. 115.

well as places like Ascott and Leafield which by inheritance had become attached to the manor of Langley and Wychwood Forest. The attempt to raise money from the assarts in this area was not well received, especially in the vills near Woodstock Park where owners believed their land to be "within the olde precincte of the forest of Whichwood but not used or reputed as parcell of the said forest within the memory of man".[38] The Attorney-General had to draw up bills against men such as Sir Henry Lee, Sir William Pope, Sir Rowland Lacy and others who refused to pay, and eventually most did pay the sums demanded from them.[39] Charles I went further and re-imposed the forest law on these and other forests, but following the Act for the Certainty of Forests of 1641 the local jury declared that Wychwood consisted only of the area of royal demesne woodland, and so it remained until its disafforestation in 1857. The Forest of Shotover and Stowood had also been reduced to the two areas of royal woodland, and it was disafforested in 1660.[40]

The Documents

The first of the medieval documents, E32/135, is the roll of an attachment court, listing offenders against the vert, and it had been prepared, presumably by the verderers, in anticipation of a forest eyre. At first sight it is an uninteresting series of names, but closer examination reveals an Oxfordshire landscape which differs considerably from that found later. For example, in 61 of the 194 offences the offender came from Walcot, and 22 men are named as living in that village. By 1609 Walcot had dwindled to "one faire house with gardens" surrounded by its fields.[41] Other settlements named in the document, such as Cote, Boriens and Slape, no longer existed.

The names in the first document also appear in the next, E32/251, which records the eyre of 1256. It also lists many offenders whose names must have appeared in similar attachment rolls which have been lost.

The eyres of 1256 and of 1272 are the only forest eyres for Oxfordshire to survive, although it is known that others had been held, including one in the intervening period, in 1262.[42]

---

[38] Edward Marshall, *The Early History of Woodstock Manor and its environs in Bladon, Hensington, New Woodstock and Blenheim (1873-4)*, p. 177, citing a document of 1585.
[39] *Cal. S.P. Dom. 1623-1625, Addenda 1603-1625* pp. 571-2; Otho Nicholson's Roll of Accounts (1610), P.R.O. E351/405 m 3d and 5d., records payments by Wychwood men totalling £337.
[40] P.R.O. C205/17; *V.C.H Oxfordshire v*, 280
[41] See **318**, p. 204.
[42] G.J. Turner, in *Select Pleas of the Forest*, lvi, states that most of the records of the eyres held in 1262 have been lost. It is significant that the earliest date recorded in the 1272 eyre for Oxfordshire is 1263 [**92** p. 84, **96** p. 85]. Another eyre held by Robert Passelewe in 1244-5 is mentioned on p. 52. Previous Oxfordshire eyres are recorded in the Pipe Rolls for 1163 (*Vol. 6*, 48), 1167 (*Vol. 11*,14-15), 1169 (*Vol. 15*, 169), 1175 (*Vol 25*, 30-34), 1178 (*Vol. 28*, 960), 1184 (*Vol. 34*, 108), 1212 (*NS Vol. 30*, 18), and 1230 (*NS Vol. 4*, 258).

E32/251, the record of the eyre of 1256, is possibly incomplete, and E32/137, which records that for 1272, gives a better idea of the scope of the forest eyre. The various items which appear are the names of those attending on the first day, essoins (excuses for non-appearance), a list of the woodwards (keepers) of the manorial woods within the forests, presentations for vert and for venison, the regarders' report on assarts, purprestures, and waste, the agisters' report on payments for pannage, and the list of fines to be paid. The presentations and reports for each forest are given separately. An additional feature of the 1272 eyre is the list of charters of privileges, which is now labelled as m. 1, but probably came later in the original sequence.

The other medieval documents transcribed here are of various types. C47/11/5(4) and C47/11/6(8) are each inquisitions on one particular topic. The extract from E36/75 lists wastes and assarts in Wychwood which were arrented *circa* 1300, and E32/138 also records assarts there, while E32/306/12 lists purprestures. An assart is usually taken to be an inclosure from the woodland which was intended to be used as arable, with a purpresture being an inclosure for another purpose. Most of the purprestures in E32/306/12 are smaller in size than the assarts and it seems likely that they were used as gardens or enclosures for animals. Some are specifically said to be curtilages or to have houses on them. These lists again may seem to be uninteresting collections of names, but they record the creation of much of the arable land of Charlbury, Fawler and Combe, and many of the purprestures may relate to the expansion of Combe village on its present site, rather than its presumed original site beside the river Evenlode.[43]

The remaining medieval documents are those which survive of the general inquisitions into the state of a forest which replaced the forest eyre. They take two forms. The first consists of a single parchment membrane, originally bearing the seals of those present, on which is transcribed the record of one inquisition. Transcripts of some of these, and of others where the original has been lost, are found in the second type of document, a roll in which the records of inquisitions into the Oxfordshire forests are mingled with those of other forests taken in the same year or years, by the same Justice.

The last of the documents is the Survey of Wychwood made *circa* 1609. As has been stated, this survey was produced as a result of renewed royal interest in the forests as a means of raising revenue during the reign of James I. It is a written description only and there is no record of any contemporary map such as that which accompanies the 1609 Survey of Sherwood Forest.[44]

---

[43] *V.C.H. Oxfordshire xii*, 78-9.

[44] Stephanos Mastoris and Sue Groves, eds., *Sherwood Forest in 1609: a Crown Survey by Richard Bankes,* Thoroton Society Record Series 40, 1998.

The document consists of a number of individual sheets of paper which have been pasted into a large book, together with surveys of other royal estates of the Stuart period. There is an incomplete contemporary index. Three lists of the royal coppices in Wychwood are bound with the Survey, but they do not appear to have formed part of it originally. The first of them is the only document to bear a date, 1609, but, although the Survey must also date from that period, the two documents cannot be directly related. The acreages given in that list are proportional to, but not the same as, those in the Survey, indicating that the measurements were made using perches of different sizes. It is clear that part of the Survey has been lost, since the first surviving sheet is numbered f. 2, and, although it is headed *Whichwood Forest cum membris Com. Oxon,* this is in a different hand and the original heading is *Adhuc Witney* ('Still Witney') while the land in the first entry is said to adjoin that described earlier.

The Survey is in three parts or 'plotts', which correspond to the three sections of the perambulations of the bounds of the forest made in 1298 and 1300, although they are not given in the same order. However the Survey includes not only the land which had been retained within the forest at that date but also areas which had been disafforested. Some, at least, of this additional land was still subject to residual rights of herbage for the deer in the nineteenth century (the purlieu woods), and most of the rest was presumably on record as having been woodland within the covert of Wych-wood at one time, and so liable to pay assart rents to the Crown. However, most of the common arable fields, closes and meadows of the townships of the thirteenth-century forest as described on page xi are not included in the Survey, since they were not liable to such payments. Some of those fields and settlements which are included, Hanborough, Combe, Stonesfield, Hailey and Crawley and parts of North Leigh and of Finstock, appear in the Survey because they had been retained within the forest by the perambulations; but the survey also includes some vills which had been excluded from the forest in 1300 - the hamlets of Leafield, Ramsden, Ascott, Chilson, Walcot and Shorthampton, of which the last four are stated to be outside the forest. It seems probable that some of these are included only because, in the early seventeenth century, they were held by the Crown, having been acquired by escheat at the same time as the Forestership.[45]

The woods of Eynsham, Cogges and Stanton Harcourt had been within the forest in the thirteenth century, but in contrast to the other woods disafforested by the perambulations they do not appear in the Survey. This may relate to the

---

[45] They were listed together in the public records as 'part of the possessions of the earl of Warwick', and had escheated to the Crown on the death of Anne, countess of Warwick, in 1588: P.R.O. LRRO3/82, Receiver's Accounts (transcript); *Complete Peerage* 6, 400.

fact that in the twelfth century a separate forest called Stanton or Piriho is recorded in the Pipe Rolls, for which an annual census of £3 was to be paid by the lord who then held Stanton Harcourt manor. This payment is too great to be merely for the woods in Stanton itself, and it presumably included those of Eynsham and Cogges. It is not found after 1170,[46] and the woodland was clearly administered after that date by the Forester of Wychwood, but it is possible that the area retained some sort of separate identity in the crown records.

The first 'plott' of the Survey corresponds to the land within the bounds of that section of the 1298/1300 perambulation which consisted almost entirely of the northern part of the Bishop of Winchester's manor of Witney (Hailey and Crawley), but included part of North Leigh. As stated earlier, the first page of this 'plott' is lost, but information which would have appeared there can be reconstituted in part from an associated contemporary (although also undated) document, SP12/276/87,[47] which consists of two lists of assart lands in Wychwood arranged under the name of the owner, rather than topographically as in the Survey. Both lists, however, are incomplete and it is not possible to reconstruct f.1 of the Survey fully.

The first section of the 1300 perambulation had outlined the royal woods and vills around and including Woodstock Park, and the second 'plott' of the Survey describes both that area and other woods and land in the vicinity. Since this was the location of active assarting *circa* 1300, both in the royal and non-royal manors, it includes much of the land which had been recorded as the site of assarts in earlier documents.

All of the land described in the first two 'plotts' ceased to be forest in 1641, but the greater part of the third 'plott' of the Survey corresponds to the area which remained as Wychwood Forest and its purlieus until the final disafforestation in 1857. For this there are later records with accurate descriptions and maps, so that any errors in the Survey can be easily detected. The most important are the omission of two coppices, Smallstones and Kingswood, and the confusion between Wastage and Nuttridge Copses.[48] Otherwise the description of the area agrees well with the later maps and records, and clearly shows the compartmented nature of the forest. The survey records four of the forest lodges, Batten's Lodge (now Ranger's Lodge), Hills Lodge (High Lodge), Bowman's Lodge (now Brizes Lodge) and the lodge in

---

[46] *Pipe Rolls* 4,26; 16,66. In some years the Pipe Roll entry names the forest for which the £3 census is to be paid as Cornbury, the name also applied to the Forest (Wychwood) for which a census of £7 was paid.

[47] see p. 161.

[48] see p. 217.

South Lawn, but it omits Newell Lodge and Potters Hill Lodge, both of which had been recorded in 1591.[49]

Both the Survey and the associated SP12/276/87, referred to above, must have been working documents, since in many places entries have been crossed out, and *compounded* or some abbreviation of that word has been added in the margin.

In some entries in SP12/276/87 the acreage has been rounded up, and occasionally different names are found, probably implying, in some cases at least, the death of a holder and inheritance by his heir. Otherwise there are few discrepancies between the two documents, the most significant being that **232** and **235** are said to belong to the King in LR2/202, but to William Castill and Jerome Nashe respectively in SP12/276, while **217** (Sharswell's Copse) is entered under Sir Henry Lee in the latter, not Ralphe Sheldon, and **342** under John Harris, not Sir Francis Fortescue. A discrepancy as to the ownership of land in North Leigh is noted on p.176.

SP12/276/87 has clearly been prepared by taking extracts from another document, since a folio number appears beside each entry. In most cases this is the same as that in the Survey, but some are not, suggesting that the writer of SP12/276/87 was working from another document very similar to, but not identical with, that in LR2/202.

[49] P.R.O. CRES40/10, p. 255.

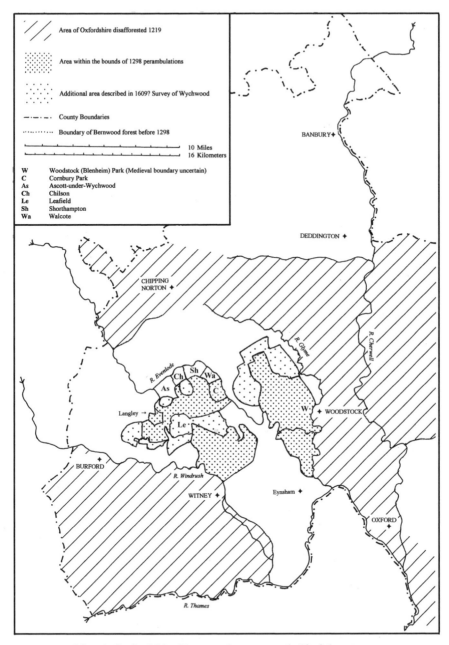

Map 1 Oxfordshire Forests: the western half of the county
(Oxford was not within the Forest)

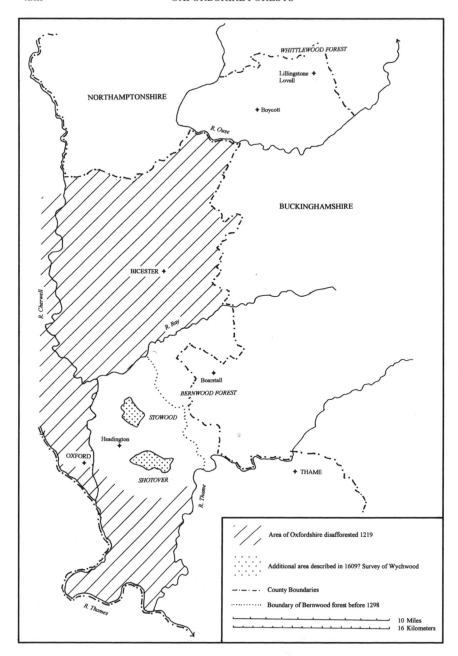

Map 2 Oxfordshire Forests: the eastern half of the county
(Oxford was not within the Forest)

Attachments for Vert, Forest of Wychwood, [1246 x 1256]

[The document is in the form of a long roll.]

Pleas to be held regarding attachments of vert in the Forest of Wychwood since the last pleas, held at Oxford in the thirtieth year of the reign of king Henry who now is [1245-6] before the lords Robert Passelewe and G[eoffrey] of Langley, then Justices in Eyre of the lord King.[1]

1   Thomas son of Gilbert Sweyn of Charlbury was taken with oak outside the lord king's demesne.[2] He found Nicholas attegrene of Charlbury and William Harald of Cote[3] as sureties that he would appear before the Justices.

2   Walter son of Stephen of Fawler, taken with oak outside the demesne, found as sureties John Capel and William Coleman of Fawler.

3   Richard le Frere of Cote, taken with oak outside the demesne, found as sureties Richard carboner and Geoffrey Salebern of Charlbury.

4   Geoffrey Salebern of Charlbury, taken with oak outside the demesne, found as sureties Richard le Frere and Gilbert Sweyn of Cote.

5   Auncell son of Hugh Young of Walcot, taken with thorn in Cornbury, found as sureties Richard le Frere and Gilbert Sweyn of Cote.

6   Walter son of Salomon of Leafield, taken with oak outside the demesne, found as sureties Richard Salomon of Leafield and Lawrence of the same.

7   Hugh of Bampton of [North] Leigh, taken with oak outside the demesne, found as sureties Hugh reeve of Wilcote and Robert le Lepar of [North] Leigh.

---

[1]   Robert Passelewe and Geoffrey of Langley were appointed to hear Pleas of the Forest in all counties at an unknown date before Christmas 1245: *Cal. Pat. 1232-47* 472.

[2]   Offences noted as being outside the King's demesne would have taken place within the bounds of the Forest but in woods belonging to lords other than the king. Those "in demesne" took place in the king's own woods and parks.

[3]   This document names several settlements which were later to be wholly or largely deserted. These are (with the number of the entry where the name first occurs):

Boriens	58	In Glympton and Kiddington. See *The Deserted Villages of Oxfordshire*, K J. Allison, M W Beresford, J G Hurst et al., 32; and *V.C.H. Oxfordshire xi*,122.
Cote	1	In Charlbury at its boundary with Spelsbury: *Des. Vill. Oxon.* 35.
Ditchley	10	In Spelsbury and Enstone: *op. cit.* 37.
Dornford	21	In Wootton: *op. cit.* 37.
Ludwell	86	In Wootton: *op. cit.* 40 and *V.C.H. Oxfordshire xi*, 122.
Radford	15	In Enstone.
Slape	11	In Glympton & Wootton: *V.C.H. Oxfordshire xi*, 122.
Tilgarsley	22	In Eynsham: *V.C.H. Oxfordshire xiii*, 115-6.
Walcot	5	*Des. Vill. Oxon.* 45.
Wilcote	7	*ibid.* 46.

8   Richard le Frere of Cote, taken with oak outside the demesne, found as sureties John son of Richard of Cote and Reginald son of Richard of Cote.

9   William Russel of Wootton, taken with oak outside the demesne, found as sureties Richard Hurel and Matthew the scribe of Wootton.

10   John le Fox of Ditchley, taken with oak outside the demesne, found as sureties Adam of Ditchley and William Crispus of Walcot.

11   Geoffrey Terry of Slape, taken with oak outside the demesne, found as sureties John Terry and Godfrey of Slape.

12   Adam of Slape, taken with oak outside the demesne, found as sureties Walter le Frere of Stonesfield and Geoffrey Terry of Slape.

13   Maurice Danvers of Fawler, taken with green wood by night, and he had a horse of the value of 3 shillings and 8 pence, found as sureties William Coleman and Adam Damary of Fawler.

14   Adam Damary of Fawler, taken with vert at night-time, and he had a horse of the value of 3 shillings, found as sureties William Coleman and Maurice Danvers of Fawler.

15   Adam Coleman of Radford, taken with green thorn, found as sureties Fray Punchard of Kiddington and Adam de Cace in Kiddington.

16   Adam le Frere of Stonesfield, taken with oak outside the demesne, found as sureties William le Mayster of Wilcote and Richard of Hanborough of Ramsden.

17   Stephen Paucok of North Leigh, taken with oak outside the demesne, found as sureties William Wyd and Sewale Wyd of North Leigh.

18   Sewale Wyd of North Leigh, taken with oak outside the demesne, found as sureties Stephen Paucok and William Wyd of North Leigh.

19   Geoffrey Terry of Slape, taken with oak outside the demesne, found as sureties Nicholas Young of Stonesfield and Geoffrey Gorwy of Stonesfield.

20   Reginald of Cote, taken with oak outside the demesne, found as sureties Gilbert Swein of Charlbury and Richard de Swynden of Wilcote.

21   John Terry of Slape, Simon of Slape and Roger son of Simon of the same were taken with an apple tree outside the demesne. They found as sureties Adam Ruffus of Slape, Walter son of William, Thomas of Slape and William of Dornford.

22   William Jope of Tilgarsley, taken with underwood by night, and he had a horse of the value of 3 shillings, found as sureties Adam Le Frere of Tilgarsley and Richard of Hanborough of Ramsden.

23   Ralph Levesune of Wootton, taken with oak outside the demesne, found as sureties Peter son of Hugh and William Ruffus of Wootton.

24   Hugh Young of Walcot, taken with oak in Cornbury, found as sureties Thomas Palmer of Walcot and Richard of Mollington of Chadlington.

25   Auncell son of Hugh of Walcot, taken with hazel in Cornbury, found as sureties Thomas Palmer of Walcot and Richard of Mollington of Chadlington.

26   Adam at Well of Charlbury, taken with oak outside the demesne, found as sureties Robert de Slade of Charlbury and Richard miller of Cote.

27   Isaac Wybet of Chilson, taken with oak outside the demesne, found as sureties Hugh Young and William Wace of Walcot.

28   Walter smith of Ascott, taken with oak outside the demesne, found as sureties Robert Ysaac and Geofrey Ysaac of Chilson.

29   Robert Musat of North Leigh, taken with oak outside the demesne, found as sureties Peter of Wilcote and Thomas Eadwyn of North Leigh.

30   John de Welde of North Leigh, taken with oak (towards Oxford), found as sureties Thomas Eadwyn of North Leigh and Peter of Wilcote.

31   Robert Harald of Cote, taken with oak outside the demesne, found as sureties Henry of Cote and William Toky of Charlbury.

32   Ralph Gode of Ramsden, taken with oak outside the demesne, found as sureties Richard of Hanborough and William son of Richard of Ramsden.

33   William Harald of Finstock, taken with oak outside the demesne, found as sureties Richard Le Prest of Wilcote and Ralph Gode of Ramsden.

34   William Crispus of Walcot, taken with hazel in Cornbury, found as sureties William Wace and Ralph Cubbel of Walcot.

35   Hugh Young of Walcot, taken with oak in Cornbury, found as sureties Thomas Palmer and William Eve of Walcot.

36   Adam Coleman of Fawler, taken with oak outside the demesne, found as sureties William of Cote and Henry of Cote.

37   Geoffrey Ysaac of Chilson, taken with oak outside the demesne, found as sureties Roger de Rumely and Richard Forester of Chilson.

38   Peter Furel of Kidlington, taken with oak outside the demesne, found as sureties Adam at Well of Wilcote and Robert Eadwyn of Stonesfield.

39   Henry son of the smith of Chilson, taken with oak outside the demesne, found as sureties Richard son of Roger and Richard son of Kane of Chilson.

40   Walter son of Hugh Young of Walcot, taken with hazel in Cornbury, found as sureties Thomas Palmer and Hugh Young of Walcot.

41   Thomas of Slape, taken with oak outside the demesne, found as sureties Walter of Stonesfield and William of Dornford.

42   Henry Wallensis of Wilcote, taken with oak outside the demesne, found as sureties Adam smith of Wilcote and Robert Coy of the same.

43   Ralph Hurel of Wootton, taken with oak outside the demesne, found as sureties William Burel of Wootton and John Terry of Slape.

44   John Terry of Slape, taken with oak outside the demesne, found as sureties William Burel and Ralph Burel of Wootton.

45   Robert Black of Chilson, taken with oak outside the demesne, found as sureties Thomas of Chilson and Thomas buventon of the same.

46   Roger le Cupere of [North] Leigh, taken with oak outside the demesne, found as sureties Roger swineherd of Finstock and Gilbert Gerebode of [North] Leigh.

47   Stephen Le Bule of Walcot, taken with oak within the demesne, found as sureties Hugh Young and Thomas Palmer of Walcot.

48   William of North Leigh, taken with oak outside the demesne, found as sureties Thomas de Haddon of North Leigh and Walter Yngelys of the same.

49   Roger le Cupere of North Leigh, taken with oak outside the demesne, found as sureties John le Cupere of Wilcote and Roger swineherd of Finstock.

50   Richard of Hanborough of Ramsden, taken with oak towards Oxford, found as sureties Robert de Wytenhulle of Ramsden and Peter son of the reeve of North Leigh.

51   Stephen Coy of Wilcote, taken with oak outside the demesne, found as sureties Adam smith and Walter Wybur of Wilcote.

52   Hugh Young of Walcot, taken with oak within the demesne, found as sureties Stephen Lebule and Thomas Palmer of Walcot.

53   Auncell son of Hugh Young, taken with hazel in Cornbury, found as sureties Thomas Palmer and William son of Eve of Walcot.

54   Thomas Palmer of Walcot, taken with oak outside the demesne, found as sureties William son of Eve and Hugh Young of Walcot.

55   William son of Eve of Walcot, taken with oak outside the demesne, found as sureties Thomas Palmer and Hugh Young of Walcot.

56   John Terry of Slape, taken with oak outside the demesne, found as sureties Geoffrey Terry and Alan Eadwak of the same.

57   William son of Pagan of Glympton, taken with oak outside the demesne, found as sureties Hugh of Boriens and William Jordan of Glympton.

58   Roger of Boriens, taken with oak outside the demesne, found as sureties Richard Boneyr and John Terry of Slape.

59   Hugh Young of Walcot, taken with oak in Cornbury, found as sureties Thomas Palmer and William son of Eve of Walcot.

60   John Terry of Slape, taken with oak outside the demesne, found as sureties Walter Gilebert and William Le Frere of Stonesfield.

61   Adam Coleman of Fawler, taken with oak outside the demesne, found as sureties Walter Clement of Cote and Henry son of Roger of the same.

62   Geoffrey Ysaac of Chilson, taken with oak outside the demesne, found as sureties Roger de Rumely and Richard forester of Chilson.

63   Peter Furel of Kidlington, taken with oak outside the demesne, found as sureties Adam smith of Wilcote and Robert Aldwyn of Stonesfield.

64   Roger son of Thomas de Lega, taken with oak outside the demesne, found as sureties William Hurel of Wootton and Geoffrey Terry of Slape.

65   Walter Walle of North Leigh, taken with a large thorn bush, found as sureties Walter Notebem and Gilbert Gerebode of North Leigh.

66 Norman Coy of Wilcote, taken with oak outside the demesne by night, and he had a horse of the value of 2 shillings, found as sureties John Le Gek and Adam smith of Wilcote.

67 John Le Cupere of Wilcote, taken with oak within the demesne, found as sureties Robert Coy and Henry le Bule of Wilcote.

68 Walter in angulo⁴ of Finstock, taken with oak outside the demesne, found as sureties Geoffrey Harald of Finstock and John le Cupere of the same vill.

69 John le Cupere of Wilcote, taken with oak outside the demesne, found as sureties Walter de angulo of Finstock and Geoffrey Harald of the same.

70 Geoffrey Harald of Finstock, taken with oak within the demesne, found as sureties Walter in angulo and John le Cupere of Wilcote.

71 Walter son of Hugh Young of Walcot, taken with thorn in Cornbury, found as sureties Warin of Shorthampton and Thomas Palmer of Walcot.

72 Auncell son of Hugh Young of Walcot, taken with hazel in Cornbury, found as sureties Hugh Young and Walter Cok of Walcot.

73 Roger Ruge of Ascott, taken with thorn, found as sureties Robert le Freman and Walter marshall⁵ of Ascott.

74 William Devereus of Walcot, taken with hazel in Cornbury, found as sureties William Le Bule and Ralph Cubbel of Walcot.

75 William Duke of Wootton, taken with oak by night, found as sureties Hugh Russel and Kemel of Wootton.

76 John of Ramsden, taken with oak outside the demesne, found as sureties William de Wytenhulle of [North] Leigh and John Le Cupere of Finstock.

77 Walter of Ramsden of Finstock, taken with hazel, found as sureties Adam Schort of Finstock and Walter Aylward of the same.

78 Henry de Evereus of Walcot, taken with hazel, found as sureties William son of Eve of Walcot and Randolph le Bule of Shorthampton.

79 John le Cupere of Wilcote, taken with hazel, found as sureties William de Wytenhulle and Randulph Lebule.

80 Hugh Wyber of Ascott, taken with oak within the demesne, found as sureties Geoffrey Ysaac of Chilson and Walter marshall of Ascott.

81 William shepherd of Chilson, taken with vert outside the demesne, found as sureties [found as sureties *repeated*] Roger shepherd and Richard of Chilson.

---

⁴ *In, de angulo* is almost certainly the Latin form of the name atte Hurne (see records **113** and **114,** William atte Hurne of Walcot, and **170, 174-6** and **179-181,** William *in angulo* of Walcot. However, the name Corner is also found (see p. 139, Alan atte Corner). See also Richard McKinley, *The Surnames of Oxfordshire,* 42 and 55.

⁵ *Marescallus* is here translated as Marshall, since presumably it is the name recorded on pages 14 and 43 as le Mareschal and Marschall.

82   Walter Walle of Wilcote, taken with oak by night within the demesne, and he had a horse of the value of 12d, found as sureties Hugh swineherd and Gilbert Gerebode of Le Lega [North Leigh].

83   < Walter Walle of Wilcote, taken with oak by night within the demesne, and he had a horse of the value of 12d, found as sureties Roger le Swon and Gilbert Gerebode> [This entry crossed out]

84   Walter of Finstock, taken with vert outside the demesne, found as sureties Richard Le Prest and John reeve of Ramsden.

85   Adam smith of Wilcote, taken with vert outside the demesne, found as sureties Richard Le Prest and John reeve of Ramsden.

86   Adam of Slape, taken with oak outside the demesne, found as sureties Ralph de Radeweye and Thomas at Well of Ludwell.

87   Richard Dyrray of Chilson, taken with oak outside the demesne, found as sureties William and Roger Dyrray of Chadlington.

88   Walter son of Hugh of Walcot, taken with oak in Cornbury, found as sureties William Le Bulle and Thomas at Well of the same.

89   Auncell son of Hugh, taken with vert in Cornbury, found as sureties Thomas Palmer and Richard Le Bule of the same.

90   Roger son of Thomas of Slape, taken with oak outside the demesne, found as sureties John Terry and Richard le Cupere of Glympton.

91   Walter le Cres of Walcot, taken with vert from Cornbury, found as sureties Thomas Palmer of Walcot and Geoffrey Ysaac of Chilson.

92   Gilbert Bouquer of Glympton, taken with vert outside the demesne, found as sureties Ralph de Radeweye and Henry of Boriens.

93   John Terry of Slape, taken with oak outside the demesne, found as sureties Richard le Cupere of Glympton and Ralph of Stonesfield.

94   Roger son of Thomas of Slape, taken with oak outside the demesne, found as sureties John Terry of Slape and Richard Cupere of Glympton.

95   Auncell son of Hugh Young of Walcot, taken with oak within the demesne, found as sureties Thomas Palmer and Walter Cres of the same.

96   William of Cote, taken with oak outside the demesne, found as sureties Richard miller of the same and Robert Sweyn of Fawler.

97   Henry de Evereus of Walcot, taken with oak within the demesne, found as sureties Ralph Cubbel of Walcot and Waryn of Shorthampton.

98   Richard of Hanborough of Ramsden, taken with oak within the demesne, found as sureties William White of Ramsden and Hugh reeve of Wilcote.

99   Joel of Finstock, taken with oak outside the demesne, found as sureties Hugh reeve of Wilcote and William Harald of Cote.

100 William Blundus of Ramsden, taken with oak within the demesne, found as sureties Hugh reeve of Wilcote and Richard of Hanborough of Ramsden.

101 William Cumeleffman of Ditchley, taken with oak outside the demesne, found as sureties Ralph de Radeweye and William Choppe of Asterleigh.

102 William Bule of Shorthampton, taken with oak within the demesne, found as sureties Randulph Bule and Warin of the same.

103 William Crispus of Walcot, taken with oak outside the demesne, found as sureties William son of Eve and Walter Cres of the same.

104 Stephen Coy of Wilcote, taken with vert from Cornbury, found as sureties William Blund and Richard of Hanborough of Ramsden.

105 Roger of Slape, taken with oak outside the demesne, found as sureties Richard Bouquer of Glympton and William of Boriens.

106 Thomas Paumer of Walcot, taken with vert from Cornbury, found as sureties Stephen Bule and Ralph Cubbel of the same.

107 Richard le Serise of Hanborough, taken with oak within the demesne, found as sureties Richard de Wake of Stonesfield and Nicholas Hawyse.

108 John le Capiar of Wootton, taken with oak outside the demesne, found as sureties Robert Aldon and John Waleraund of Stonesfield.

109 William Hereward and Walter Hall were taken when assarting in the wood of the Hospitallers of Jerusalem.[6] He [sic] found as sureties Gilbert Gerebode of Wilcote, Walter son of Stephen of Fawler, Robert Aldewyn and Nicholas Taylard of Charlbury.

110 Walter Lowy of Wootton, taken with oak within the demesne, found as sureties Geoffrey of Slape and John Terry of the same.

111 Robert de Wytenhulle of Ramsden, taken with oak outside the demesne, found as sureties Gilbert Godefray of North Leigh and William White of Ramsden.

112 Gilbert Gerebode of Wilcote, taken with oak within the demesne, found as sureties Martin Frig and Robert Coy of Wilcote.

113 Thomas Palmer of Walcot, taken with hazel in Cornbury, found as sureties William atte Hurne and William Crespus of Walcot.

114 William Crisp of Walcot, taken with hazel in Cornbury, found as sureties Thomas Palmer and William atte Hurne of Walcot.

115 Richard Kemel of Wootton, taken with oak outside the demesne, found as sureties Geoffrey and John Terry of Slape.

116 Robert Le Colyar of Ditchley, taken with oak outside the demesne, found as sureties Robert le Wyte and Robert cobet of the same.

117 William Carter of Spelsbury, taken with oak outside the demesne, found as sureties Richard Boventun and Nicholas miller of the same vill.

---

6   The only wood in Wychwood known or presumed to have belonged to the Hospitallers is Friars' Wood in Stanton Harcourt: *V.C.H. Oxfordshire xii,* 269, 279-80.

118 William Cumeleffman of Ditchley, taken with oak outside the demesne, found as sureties Geoffrey miller of Fulwell and Robert Cobet of Ditchley.
119 William le Wyte of Ramsden, taken with hazel in Cornbury, found as sureties Robert Coy and Roger le Cupere of Wilcote.
120 Adam of Cote, taken with vert outside the demesne, found as sureties Richard attewatere and Reginald of Cote.
121 Gilbert Raysun of Leafield, taken with oak outside the demesne, found as sureties Roger Tril of Leafield and Ralph Godes of Ramsden.
122 Roger Tril of Leafield, taken with vert outside the demesne, found as sureties Gilbert Raysun and Ralph Godes of Ramsden.
123 Stephen Pynnok of Wilcote, taken with vert, found as sureties Adam smith and John le Cupere of the same.
124 John Bene of Ramsden, taken with oak within the demesne, found as sureties Robert Coy and Adam smith of Wilcote.
125 Ralph Levesone of Wootton, taken with oak outside the demesne, found as sureties Nicholas son of Hawyse of Stonesfield and Richard son of Stephen of Wootton.
126 Roger Tril of Leafield, taken with vert within the demesne, found as sureties Thomas Tobich of Leafield and Ralph Godes of Ramsden.
127 Richard of Hanborough of Ramsden, taken with oak within the demesne, found as sureties Roger of Ramsden and Ralph Godes of the same.
128 Hugh Russel of Wootton, taken with oak outside the demesne, found as sureties Nicholas Cut and Jordan smith of Glympton.
129 Jordan smith of Glympton, taken with oak outside the demesne, found as sureties William of Boriens and Nicholas Cut of Glympton.
130 Thomas Palmer of Walcot, taken with oak within the demesne, found as sureties Ralph Cubbel and Richard Lebule of the same.
131 Walter Tocye of Charlbury, taken with vert in Cornbury, found as sureties Walter of Ramsden and Richard Swein of Finstock.
132 Ralph Levesone of Wootton, taken with oak outside the demesne, found as sureties John de Hulle and William Russel of Wootton.
133 Stephen le Blay of Walcot, taken with vert in Cornbury, found as sureties Thomas Palmer and William Crisp of the same.
134 Thomas Palmer of Walcot, taken with vert in Cornbury, found as sureties William Crisp and Stephen bule of the same.
135 Hugh Russel of Wootton, taken with oak outside the demesne, found as sureties John Capyar and William Le norreys of the same.
136 Walter marshall of Dean, taken with vert in Cornbury, found as sureties Robert Barun and John smith of Chad[lington].
137 John Le Capyar of Wootton, taken with oak towards Oxford, found as sureties Henry de Hull of Wotton and Adam son of William of Glympton.

138 Walter son of Hugh Young of Walcot, taken with oak in Cornbury, found as sureties William Bule and Hugh Young.

139 Walter Tocye of Charlbury, taken with oak within the demesne, found as sureties William Devereus and Stephen pynnoc of Wilcote.

140 Richard of Hanborough of Ramsden, taken with vert within the demesne, found as sureties William White and John le Cupere of Wilcote.

141 Richard son of Roger of Ramsden, taken with oak within the demesne, found as sureties Lawrence of Leafield and Richard of Hanborough of Ramsden.

142 Roger Tril of Leafield, taken with oak within the demesne, found as sureties William Tril and Walter porcher of the same.

143 Richard Raysun of Leafield, taken with oak within the demesne, found as sureties Roger Tril and Alexander of Leafield.

144 Richard son of Roger of Ramsden, taken with oak outside the demesne, found as sureties Roger of Ramsden and Lawrence of Leafield.

145 Thomas son of Adam Le Capiar of Wootton, taken with oak outside the demesne by night and he had a horse valued for the lord king's work at 18d. Sureties for the value William Russel of Wootton and Ralph Levesone.

146 Walter Tocye of Charlbury, taken with vert within the demesne, found as sureties William Deverews and Stephen pynnoc.

147 Thomas Palmer of Walcot, taken with oak within the demesne, found as sureties William Devereus and Stephen le Blay of Walcot.

148 Walter Forester of Bloxham,[7] taken with vert outside the demesne, found as sureties Elias reeve and John Leverich of Bloxham.

149 Walter son of Hugh Young of Walcot, taken with oak in Cornbury, found as sureties William Bule and Stephen Bule of Walcot.

150 Stephen Le Bule of Walcot, taken with oak within the demesne, found as sureties Richard bule and Ralph Cubbel of the same.

151 Thomas Palmer of Walcot, taken with oak within the demesne, found as sureties Ralph Cubbel and Richard Bule of the same.

152 Henry Deverews of Walcot, taken with vert in Cornbury, found as sureties Ralph Cubbel and Richard bule.

153 Roger Le Cupere of Wilcote, taken with oak towards Oxford, found as sureties Walter Le Gek and Robert Coy of the same.

154 Jordan smith of Glympton, taken with vert outside the demesne, found as sureties William of Boriens and Hugh reeve of Glympton.

155 John of Kingham of Ascott, taken with oak outside the demesne, found as sureties Robert Charles and Hugh Wyber of the same.

---

[7] Bloxham's wood was within Wychwood Forest, many miles away from the village: *V.C.H. Oxfordshire ix, 66*. The V.C.H. reference is not correct in recording two woodland areas as if they had always existed. Originally there was only one wood, but it was divided in 1232 after two manors had been created. See p. 23 fn. 14.

156 Walter son of Hugh of Walcot, taken with vert within the demesne, found as sureties Thomas Palmer and William Devereus.

157 Henry Deverews of Walcot, taken with oak in Cornbury, found as sureties Ralph Cubbel and Thomas Palmer of the same.

158 Richard of Hanborough of Ramsden, taken with oak within the demesne, found as sureties Robert de Wytenhull and William Le Wyte of Ramsden.

159 Walter son of Hugh of Walcot, taken with oak in Cornbury, found as sureties William Devereus and Thomas Palmer of the same.

160 Henry Deverews of Walcot, taken with oak in Cornbury, found as sureties Ralph Cubbel and Thomas Palmer of Walcot.

161 Hugh Young of Walcot, taken with oak in Cornbury, found as sureties William and Henry Devereus.

162 Thomas Palmer of Walcot, taken with oak in Cornbury, found as sureties William and Henry Devereus of the same.

163 Henry Devereus, taken with thorn in Cornbury, found as sureties Hugh Young and William Devereus.

164 John Devereus of Walcot, taken with hazel in Cornbury, found as sureties Hugh Young and William Devereus of the same.

165 Nicholas Abelyn of Ditchley, taken with green oak outside the demesne, found as sureties Walter of Ditchley and John Le Fox.

166 Walter Tocy of Charlbury, taken with green thorn in Cornbury, found as sureties Robert of Brailes of the same and William Aldwyn of Fawler.

167 Stephen Le Blay of Walcot, taken with green oak outside the demesne, found as sureties Thomas Palmer and Gilbert Bule of the same.

168 Walter son of Hugh of Walcot, taken with green maple in Cornbury, found as sureties Henry Devereus and William Devereus of Walcot.

169 Henry Devereus of Walcot, taken with green oak outside the demesne, found as sureties Thomas Palmer and Stephen le Bule of the same.

170 Thomas Palmer, taken with green oak outside the demesne, found as sureties William in angulo and Stephen le Bule of the same.

171 John Furel of Ascott, taken with green oak in the demesne, found as sureties Thomas Pride and Thomas Bulloc of Ascott.

172 Thomas Pride of Ascott, taken with green oak outside the demesne, found as sureties John Furel and Hugh Ruge of Ascott.

173 Hugh son of Hugh clerk of Ascott, taken with green oak within the demesne, found as sureties Thomas Bulloc and Hugh clerk of the same.

174 Henry Devereus of Walcot, taken with green oak outside the demesne, found as sureties William in angulo and Thomas Palmer of the same.

175 Stephen Le messer of Walcot, taken with oak outside the demesne, found as sureties William In Angulo and Thomas Palmer.

176 Thomas Palmer of Walcot, taken with oak outside the demesne, found as sureties William in angulo and Henry De Everewes of the same.

177 William Deverews of Walcot, taken with oak within the demesne, found as sureties Ralph Cubbel and Thomas Palmer of Walcot.

178 Walter son of Hugh of Walcot, taken with oak in Cornbury, found as sureties William Devereus and Stephen Bule.

179 William Crispus of Walcot, taken with thorn in Cornbury, found as sureties William in angulo and William Bule of the same.

180 Stephen Le Blay of Walcot, taken with oak in Cornbury, found as sureties Thomas Palmer and William in angulo of Walcot.

181 Henry Deverews, taken with green maple within the demesne, found as sureties William Devereus and William in angulo.

182 Walter son of Hugh of Walcot, taken with thorn in Cornbury, found as sureties William Devereus and Ralph Cubbel of the same.

183 Henry Devereus, taken with oak in Cornbury, found as sureties William son of Roger Shorthampton and William Devereus of Walcot.

184 Richard of Hanborough of Ramsden, taken with oak within the demesne, found as sureties Robert Coy and Adam smith of Wilcote.

185 John Devereus, taken with oak in Cornbury, found as sureties Thomas Palmer and Stephen Le Blay of Walcot.

186 Stephen Le Blay of Walcot, taken with oak within the demesne, found as sureties Henry Devereus and Thomas Palmer of Walcot.

187 John Devereus, taken with green oak within the demesne, found as sureties Stephen Bule and Henry Devereus of Walcot.

188 Henry Devereus, taken with vert within the demesne, found as sureties Stephen le Bule and William of Walcot.

189 Gilbert reeve of Shipton, taken with oak within the demesne, found as sureties Ralph Cubbel and William Devereus.

[dorse of roll]

Oxon. Wychwood

190 William Harald had two yearling pigs found within the covert of the Forest in the forbidden month, and they are valued at 2 shillings; wherefore he found Richard Sweyn and Ralph Godes of Ramsden as sureties that he would have that price before the Justices.

191 Sewald Wyd of North Leigh had one sow and 4 piglets found within the covert of the forest in the forbidden month and they are valued at 2 shillings; for which he found William de Wytenhull and William Anphray of [North] Leigh as sureties.

192 Nicholas Young of Stonesfield had 5 pigs found within the covert of the forest in the forbidden month and they are valued at 2 shillings and six pence;

and he found William Nicholas of Stonesfield and Robert Aldon of the same as sureties for the value.

193 Robert Le Frere had a sow in the forest in the forbidden month, of the value of 12 pence. He found Nicholas Young and Robert Aldon of Stonesfield

194 William Le Bule of Walcot had three pigs found in Cornbury at three impoundings, to the value of 2 shillings and 8 pence; and Ralph Cubbel and Thomas Palmer of Walcot are sureties for the value.

[Document endorsed in a later hand]
Attachments for Vert in the Forest of Wychwood in the County of Oxford in the 30th Year of Henry 3.[8]

---

[8]   The date in the endorsement presumably results from a hasty reading of the heading. The document could be of any date between 1246 and 1256 when the Forest Pleas were next held. Several of the wrong-doers named in it are recorded in *E32/251* (see pp. 13-14 & 42-45) although the essoins in that document show that some of them had died before 1256 (Gilbert Raysun who is recorded in **121**, Thomas of Slape **41**, Sewald Wyd **18** and Auncell son of Hugh of Walcot **25** and **89**).

[The document comprises 8 membranes tied together. It seems probable that it is not a complete record of the Pleas, and almost certainly the membranes are not in the original order. Membrane 1 has no general heading and was presumably not the beginning of the record (and see below, fn. 4, p. 16), while m. 5d was probably the end, with the words at the bottom of the page appearing on the outside of the roll and indicating its contents.

It is clear that parts had been prepared in advance, as some entries are interlined, and fines or the names of sureties are sometimes added in different ink.]

m. 1]

1   Essoins taken at Oxford on Monday next after the octave of St. Hilary in the 40th year of the reign of king Henry [24 January 1256]

[* indicates an offender recorded in *E32/135*]
Henry of La Thirn[1] [because] of death by Robert of Fulwell.
Adam de Amber' of Fawler of the same for the same by William Coleman.
Henry of Chilson of death by William le Bole.
Henry Wyber of death by Henry son of William.
Alan le Cupere of Woodstock of the same, by William de Blachingeleg.
Thomas son of Ralph of Elsfield of death by Richard son of Thomas.
Alan of Combe of death by James of the same.
Walter Wudeward of Combe of death by Robert le Mei.
Simon of Paris of death by Walter Mareschallus.
William Turry of death by John Turry.
William son of Harold of Cote* of death by Richard miller of Cote.
Adam atte Welle of Charlbury* of death by Robert Swein of Fawler .
Wulf de Le Leye of death by Robert Aylmer of North Leigh.
Geoffrey de la Pirye of death by William Long.
John son of Geoffrey de la Pirye of death by Thomas le Nappar.
Gilbert Raysun of Shipton* of death by Ralph Gode.
Thomas of Slape* of death by Roger son of Thomas.
Roger le Fraunceis of Woodstock of death by Simon le Fraunceis.
Sewald son of Wido* of death by John de Lee.
Robert Wifmon of Combe of death by Robert Streme

[1]   La Thirn (Thern, Thurn) was a lost hamlet, often associated with Chilson in Eynsham Abbey records: *Eynsham Cart. ii,* ix-x. It was almost certainly in Pudlicote since a dispute regarding 2½ hides in La Thirn is recorded in 1231 and 1233 between Henry de Penbroc and William de Rumelly who was lord of Pudlicote: *Cal. Close 1227-1231* 583 and *Cal. Close 1231-34* 302. It was probably sited at SP308199 where appropriate earthworks have been recorded: *C.B.A. Group 9 Newsletter 7, 1977,* 46. A field name Thorn Green is found nearby.

Juliana widow of capiar of death by John Capiar.
Walter le Frere of Stonesfield of death by Nicholas of Stonesfield.
Hugh le Lung of Walcot of death by Walter Young of the same.
Auncell son of Hugh of Walcot* of death by Stephen le Bule of the same.
Walter Penduc of Lillingstone by Hugh son of Walter of the same.

2   Names of those who presented themselves on the first day

Walter le Mareschal of Woodstock
John le Turner of the same
Richard Skilful of the same
Walter of Tackley of the same
Stephen of Walcot
Nicholas his brother
William his brother
William of La Thirne
Walter Inge of the same
William of St. Cross
Nigel le Herd
Ralph del Hilwerk
John le Fox of Ditchley
William Tril of Leafield
Robert his son
William his brother
Hugh of Ditchley
Peter Punchard
Richard of Godestowe
Alice who was the wife of
   Thomas son of Ralph
Ralph de Preawes
John le Capiere
Robert de Chandur
William of Enstone

Hervey of Slape
Roger of the same
William Turry of the same
Walter Swein of Fawler
Robert de la Wiche of Combe
John de la Hethe of the same
William of Combe
Peter le Fevre of Kidlington
Ralph Iuaus of Newington
Robert of Pishill
Geoffrey Joye of Stonesfield
Stephen Frefecent of the same
Nicholas le Kat of the same
Siward le Frere of the same
Robert son of Aldwin of the same
John Herbert of Combe
Colin Cut of Wootton
John Russel of the same
William of Burford
Walter le Mert of North Leigh
Robert Museht of the same
Hugh Russel of Wootton
Roger de Stape [Slape]

3   Names of the Hundreds[2]

Hundred of Bampton
John of Bampton   Bailiff   Sworn

[2]   The hundreds named are those which included manors with land or woods within one or other of the Forests. Surprisingly, Bloxham hundred is not included, although the wood belonging to Bloxham manor was in Wychwood.

Hundred of Chadlington
r'   William Baldewine   Bailiff
     Robert of Broadstone   } Sworn
r'   Ralph of Ditchley

Hundred of Wootton
r'   John of Eynsham   Bailiff
     Robert of Leigh   } Sworn
r'   William of Combe

Hundred of Banbury
     Richard Omnibon   Bailiff
     Nicholas Danvers   } Sworn
     Oliver of Fawler

Hundred of Ploughley
r'   Thomas Stakssil   Bailiff
     Walter de Alnet   } Sworn
     Ralph son of William de Hemford

Hundred of Bullingdon
r'   Thurstan of Marston   Bailiff
     Nicholas clerk   } Sworn
     Thomas at Well

m. 1 dorse]
4   [The following paragraph is crossed through]
Whereas it is found, in the Roll of the lord Ernald du Boys,[3] Justice of the
Forest, regarding an inquisition held by the same Ernald, by the verderers,
namely by Peter de Lye, James le Blund, Robert de Ellesford, Robert of
Sarsden, verderers, and by twelve good and worthy men of the vill of
Woodstock on Tuesday next after the feast of St. Lucy in the 39th year [15
December 1254], who say that on the day when Walter le Marshal of
Woodstock was taken with a certain doe, Hubert clerk son of the parson of
Hanborough was at Woodstock waiting for that doe so that he could have it and
carry it away with him to Oxford. And that the aforesaid Hubert habitually did
wrong in this way. They also say that around the feast of the Assumption of the
Blessed Mary [15th August] Nicholas de Brokedis, clerk, was an associate of
the said Hubert and the son of Hugh Brun of Hanborough and five other

---

3   Ernald du Boys (Arnold du Bois, de Bosco) was appointed Justice of the Forest south of Trent on 16
February 1253, and was still Justice in January 1255 although dead before 1 March 1255: *Cal. Pat.
1247-1258* 178, 394, 432.

unknown men [when] they entered Woodstock Park with bows and arrows, and that all the aforesaid clerks and their followers and Hugh Brun of Hanborough also on Wednesday next after the feast of All Saints [4 November] took seven bucks and five does in the aforesaid park. And Hubert [and] Nicholas did not come and were not attached since they are clerks. Therefore *to be exacted and outlawed*. And Hugh Brun was imprisoned elsewhere and now is still in *prison*. And Richard his son did not come etc. Therefore *to be exacted and outlawed*. And William of Tackley, John Turner and Richard Skilful were im*prison*ed in another place and having been freed by the Lord King's writ, now came. And Walter le Marschal and Nigel le Hert similarly came and being convicted of an offence to the venison were committed to *prison*.

Because [written] below [therefore crossed out]

5   It was presented by the same and found that Richard Churchyard of Charlbury and Geoffrey parson of Stonesfield are evildoers to the Lord King's venison, as is shown above.[4] And now they have taken venison again since the arrival of the Lord King at Woodstock;[5] and that the same Geoffrey is the harbourer of clerks of Oxford, whose names are not known, who are accustomed to hunt the Lord King's venison. And Richard did not come therefore *to be exacted and outlawed*. And the Bishop of Lincoln is *commanded* for the same Geoffrey.

6   It was presented by the same and found by an inquisition which Ernald du Boys held, when he was Justice of the Forest, in the presence of the verderers, namely Peter de La Lye, James le Blund, Robert de Eylesford and Robert of Sarsden, that Walter le Mareschal of Woodstock took a certain doe in Woodstock park and that William of Tackley, John le Turner and Richard Skilful and Nigel le Hert were guilty of hunting the said doe, and the said Walter [was] an accomplice; who came and were committed to *prison*.

It was also found by the same that Hubert clerk, son of the parson of Hanborough, Nicholas de Brokedis and five unknown clerks with their followers are guilty of taking seven bucks and five does in Woodstock park. And Hubert [and] Nicholas did not come and were not attached because they are clerks. Therefore *to be exacted and outlawed*. Afterwards Walter le Mareschall paid a fine of 40s. through his sureties John le Poure of Woodstock and Stephen le Mareschall of the same. And William of Tackley fined for half a mark, and John le Turner fined for 2 marks, and Richard Skilful fined for half

[4]   These men are recorded in **24** and **36** on m. 3 and 3d, which presumably preceded m. 1 when the document was created.
[5]   The king was at Woodstock from June 1st to 24th in 1255, and from January 30th to February 20th in 1256: *Cal. Pat. 1247-1258* 412, 414, 460, 463.

a mark through sureties William Pudding of Woodstock and William Brun of the same.

m. 2]

Pleas of the Forest at Oxford before William le Breton, Nicholas of Romsey, Geoffrey of Lewknor and Simon de Throp[6] on Monday next after the octave of St. Hilary in the 40th year of the reign of king Henry son of king John [24 January 1256]

Shotover

7   It was presented by the foresters and verderers and found that on Saturday in the Vigil of St. Gregory in the 35th year [11 March 1251] Roger de la Punfaud of Stanton [St. John] was taken with the hide of a certain brocket [young stag] whose flesh was afterwards found in the house of the same Roger. The said Roger was imprisoned in the Castle of Oxford in the time of Nicholas de Hanred[7] who says nothing about his release, therefore he himself is in *mercy*.

Afterwards the said Roger came and was committed to *prison*. The hide of the said brocket was handed over to the vill of Stanton, and *one mark* from the value of his chattels, and now they do not have that mark, therefore the vill is in *mercy*, and Nicholas the sheriff answered for it.

Afterwards Roger de la Punfaud fined for half a mark through sureties William son of Bernard of Stanton and Thomas le Frankelayn of the same.

8   It was presented by the same and found that on St. Andrew's day in the 39th year etc. [30 November 1254] Alice wife of Thomas son of Ralph of Elsfield was found with a certain shoulder from a stag which the aforesaid Thomas her husband and Hugh of the Ditch of Elsfield brought to her, and they caught the said stag with devices, at which capture William Skilling of Fritwell and Henry cook of the same and Richard le vachur, servant of the Prior of St. Frideswide, and Walter Cullemere were present, and had their part of it. And Richard le vachur and Walter Cullemere were caught and sent to prison at Oxford, and Richard came and was committed to prison. And Walter Cullemere did not come. And Nicholas de Hanred truly acknowledged that he received him and the other prisoners and handed them over to the Constable of

---

6   These men were appointed as "justices in eyre … for pleas of the forest in the counties of Huntingdon, Northampton, Buckingham and Oxford" on 1 June 1255: *Cal. Pat. 1247-1258* 412.
7   Nicholas de Hanred was sheriff of Oxfordshire from 5 October 1250 to November 1258: *Cal. Pat. 1247-1258*, 75, 655.

Oxford Castle, who was with the lord Imbert Pugeys[8] to whom the Lord King had committed the custody of that castle. And he handed over to him all the prisoners on the instructions of the Lord King, and showed the warrant for this.

And John le Walays, who was the Constable of Oxford Castle, did not come to *answer* regarding the release of the prisoners. And it was testified that he had land at Kimble in the County of Buckingham. Therefore the sheriff is *commanded* etc.

Afterwards it was acknowledged and testified by the Foresters and Verderers that Richard le vachur and Walter Cullemere were not guilty of this. Therefore they are quit of it. And Thomas son of Ralph and Hugh of the Ditch, William Skilling and Henry Cook did not come. Thomas died in prison and the others were not attached because they were not found, therefore to be exacted and outlawed. And Alice came and since it was found that Thomas, her husband, whom she could not refuse in his lifetime, brought the said venison to her, and Alice was not guilty, therefore she is quit of it. And Nicholas de Hanred, sheriff, answered for half a mark from the goods of Hugh of the Ditch. And since the vill of Elsfield did not have the foot of the said shoulder of the said stag before the Justices as it had been given to them to have, therefore the vill is in mercy.

Afterwards Hugh of the Ditch came and was committed to *prison*. And afterwards he fined for *1 mark* by sureties of Thurstan of Marston and William of Finmere.

9   It was presented by the same and found that on Tuesday in the feast of the beheading of St. John the Baptist in the 39th year etc. [31 August 1255] around midday, a certain deer was brought down between the wood of Shawe and the wood of Chille.[9] An inquisition [was] held by the four vills nearest to [the place] where the said deer was felled, namely Holton, Wheatley, Forest Hill and Stanton [St. John] who say on their oath that certain clerks of Oxford, namely David de Curcy of Ireland, Nicholas de la Repentine and Robert Long of Ireland, caught the said deer with greyhounds in the wood of Schawe and carried it away with them to Oxford; but they do not know whose the deer was. So because they did not come fully to hold the inquisition, therefore in *mercy*. And David Nicholas and Robert did not come and were not attached because they are clerks. Therefore *to be exacted and outlawed.*

---

[8]   The keeping of Oxford Castle was granted to Imbert Pugeys on 3 June 1253. He was no longer its custodian by 8 June 1256: *Cal. Pat. 1247-1258*, 195, 479.

[9]   Shawe was a wood belonging to the manor of Cuddesdon, but detached from it and in Holton parish: *Rot. Hund. ii* 718; *L. & P. Henry VIII 17*, No. 1912, 40, p. 566; and see p. 54, **10**. Chille was the wood belonging to Holton: *Rot. Hund. ii* 718. This offence is also recorded in that volume, p. 41.

10 Lord Aymer, Bishop-elect of Winchester,[10] took a doe in Shotover without warrant on Monday next after Palm Sunday in the 33rd year [29 March 1249].

11 Lord John de Plescy, earl of Warwick, took a doe in the same place without warrant on Tuesday next before the feast of the blessed Mary Magdalene in the 35th year [18 July 1251]
 before the king [marginal note only]

12 Lord Peter of Savoy took a stag without warrant in the vigil of the Blessed Mary in Autumn in the 37th year [14 August 1253]

Bernwood

13 It was presented by the Foresters and verderers and found that on Friday next before the feast of St. Clement in the 35th year etc. [18 November 1250] a certain deer was taken in the Forest of Bernwood. Therefore an inquisition was held by the four nearest vills, namely Arncott of the Abbott of Osney, Arncott of the Prior of Bicester[11] and Piddington who say on their oath that certain men of the Temple of Merton, namely Walter Forester of Cranehull and Hugh Miller of the Temple,[12] Martin, reeve of the lord earl Richard at Ambrosden,[13] and William Shepherd of Arncott in the same took that deer, that is to say, a brocket, with greyhounds, within the limits of the Forest. And because they did not come fully to hold the inquisition, therefore in *mercy*. And the vill of Murcott, of the Abbot of Westminster, being summoned to the said inquisition, did not wish to come, therefore in *mercy*. And Walter Forester and Hugh Miller did not come and were not attached because they were not found. Therefore *to be exacted and outlawed*. And the Sheriff was *instructed* to distrain the Preceptor of the Temple of Merton so that he should appear before the Justices to answer for the aforesaid Walter and Hugh, a member of his household. And that the sheriff should cause Martin the reeve and William Shepherd to come from day to day to *answer* etc.

---

10 Aymer de Valence, half-brother of the king. He was elected as Bishop of Winchester in 1250, but not consecrated until 1260; *D.N.B. 2*, 286-8.

11 The Abbott of Osney held Upper Arncott, the Prior of Bicester Lower Arncott; *V.C.H. Oxfordshire v*, 19.

12 The Knights Templar held Merton; Cranehull may be a misreading of the name of their wood, Gravenhull: *Rot. Hund. ii*, 715.

13 Ambrosden was held by Richard, earl of Cornwall, the king's brother: *V.C.H. Oxfordshire v*, 17, 61.

And afterwards the Master of the Knights Templar came and was convicted regarding the offence, therefore in *mercy*.

m. 2 dorse]

Wychwood

14   It was presented by the Foresters and verderers and found that Hugh Brun of Hanborough, who was caught within the covert of the Forest with a bow and arrows, is a wrong-doer to the venison. And now he came and was committed to *prison*. And Stephen in La Hale of Hanborough, Walter at Well of the same, Walter Boverye of the same, Richard Levesone of the same, Martin Houndleye of the same, [and] Robert Wunge of the same bailed to have the same before the Justices etc. And they did not have him on the first day, therefore in *mercy*. And Hugh Brun made a fine, below.

15   Hugh son of Nicholas of Ditchley was an associate of evildoers to the venison in the forest and their accomplice. Now he came and was convicted of this. Therefore he was committed to *prison*. Afterwards the same Hugh paid a fine of *half a mark*, by sureties of Ralph of Ditchley and John Fox of the same.

16   It was presented by the Foresters and verderers that Stephen le messir and Peter Maundevil caught a doe in the croft of William of Rotherfield in South Leigh and carried that doe away through the middle of the house of the afore-said William. And Stephen and Peter did not come, and were not attached, because they were not found. Therefore *to be exacted [and] outlawed*. And because the said William did not raise a hue on the aforesaid evildoers, nor cry out according to the assize of the Forest, etc., therefore *in mercy*. And because Richard de Huvill in South Leigh and Geoffrey Bele of the same bailed that they would have the same William etc., and did not have him, etc., therefore *in mercy*.

17   It was presented by the same and found that Walter Sweyn of Fawler was the harbourer of Thomas son of Henry of Ascott, clerk, an evildoer to the Lord King's venison. And Walter came now and was committed to *prison*. And because William Coleman of Fawler, Thomas Poue of the same, Richard Swein of the same and Robert of Brailes bailed that they would have etc., sixteen shillings of the value of the chattels of the said Walter, and now they did not have it etc., therefore *in mercy*. And he [sic] answered for the aforesaid 16s. And Thomas son of Henry did not come because he was not attached since he was not found. Therefore *to be exacted [and] outlawed*. Afterwards Walter Sweyn fined for *16s.* for which N[icholas] the sheriff answered. Afterwards in the County of Essex a certain man came on behalf of the said Thomas asking that he might find sureties to be before the Justices at Reading in 15 days from the day of St. John Baptist [12 September], wherefore the Sheriff of Oxford was ordered that on receiving sufficient security from him as is aforesaid, he should delay his outlawry; and now the said Thomas did not come, therefore to be exacted as above. And Ysac son of Walter of Ascott, Henry son of Stephen of the same, Walter Culling of the same and Richard Chark of the same bailed him etc. and now they did not have him, therefore in mercy. Afterwards Thomas came and paid half a mark through the sureties of William le Viniter of Reading and William Alan of Rotherfield.

18   Syward le Frere of Stonesfield, Robert son of Aldwin of the same and Stephen Herbert of the same, found to be evildoers to the venison, came and were committed to *prison*. And Geoffrey son of Hugh of Stonesfield, John Codel de Manebyr [sic: Hanborough], Richard Churchyard of Charlbury, Geoffrey his brother, Geoffrey brother of Savary of Walcot, Stephen, Richard, Geoffrey and Nicholas, sons of Savary of Walcot, were associates of the aforesaid Syward and Stephen and Robert, and their accomplices. And Walter le Frere of Stonesfield was the harbourer of all the aforesaid malefactors. And John Cadel, Stephen and Nicholas sons of Savary came and were committed to *prison*. And Richard Churchyard, Geoffrey son of Hugh, Geoffrey brother of Richard, Richard and Geoffrey sons of Savary of Walcot did not come and were not attached because they were not found. Therefore *to be exacted [and] outlawed*. And Richard Churchyard and Geoffrey his brother were harboured in the vill of Charlbury and now they do not have them as by right [they should]. Therefore *in mercy*. And Richard and Nicholas sons of Savary were [members] of their brothers' household, and now they do not have them, therefore *in mercy*. And Geoffrey son of Savary and Walter le Frere did not come because they are dead. And Walter le Frere had chattels worth 5 shillings for which Nicholas de Hanred, the sheriff, answered. Afterwards Savary came and made a fine for himself and Stephen and Nicholas his sons, for 5 marks, by the sureties of Robert Wainer of Shipton and Nicholas Noreys of the same. Afterwards Robert son of Edwin made a fine of *1 mark* by the sureties of Walter son of Emma of Stonesfield and John son of Emma of the same. And Syward le Frere who is very poor and feeble came and was *pardoned* by the King.

19   It was presented by the same and found that a certain stag was felled in the forest, and therefore an inquisition was held by the four nearest vills, namely Glympton, Slape, Wootton and Kiddington, who said that two strangers with greyhounds felled it, and they fled when a hue and cry was raised. And because the said vills did not come fully to hold the inquisition, therefore in *mercy*. And that the men [*homines,* an error for Johannes, John] de Haddon, Eustace le Eyre, Robert de Elseford, Robert of Sarsden and James Blund and Peter de Ley, the verderers, made no mention in their roll of the year, day and place of the taking of the said deer nor the names of the vills by which the inquisition was made, therefore in *mercy*.

20   It was presented by the same and found that William in Angulo of La Therne, Henry son of Agenild of the same, Hugh Ive of Chadlington and Walter Inge of La Thirne caught a doe in the forest and it was divided between them. And William and Walter came and were committed to *prison*. And Henry did not come because he is dead [marginal note *Marc'* instead of *mortuus*]. And Hugh did not come but Henry of Pudlicote, bailiff of Shipton for the lord earl of Gloucester, bailed to have him etc. The inquisition into this was held by the four nearest vills, namely Ascott (*40s.*) Chadlington (*50s.*) Pudlicote (*40s.*) and Leafield (*1 mark*), and because they did not come fully etc., therefore *in mercy*. Afterwards Hugh came and was commited to prison. Afterwards he fined for *20s.* by sureties of Geoffrey le Paumer of Chadlington and William son of Reginald of the same. Afterwards William in Angulo in La Thirne fined for *1 mark* by sureties Henry of Pudlicote and Ralph of Shipton, clerks; and Walter Inge fined for *1 mark* by the same sureties.

21   It was presented by the same and found that Geoffrey of Little Barton, servant of Peter Punchard of Kiddington, caught a hind in the forest with a snare and Geoffrey himself felled the hind and threw himself on it until the said Peter approached and released him and finally killed the hind and carried it away to his house. And now Geoffrey did not come, nor was he attached because he was not found. Therefore *to be exacted [and] outlawed*. And Peter Punchard came and the four nearest vills, namely Stonesfield (*40s.*), Combe (*4 marks*), Ditchley (*20s.*) and Wootton (elsewhere). And because they did not come fully to the inquisition etc. therefore *in mercy*.

22   It was presented by the same and found that Richard de Hameberg [sic: Hanborough] in Ramsden, John his brother, Roger le Wyte of the same, Alexander his son and Robert Coy of Wilcote are evildoers to the Lord King's venison and Richard, John and Roger and Robert came and were committed to *prison*. And Alexander did not come and was not attached because he was not found, therefore *to be exacted [and] outlawed*. And the inquisition was held by the four nearest vills, namely Finstock, North Leigh, Charlbury and Leafield. And because they did not come fully etc. therefore *in mercy*. Afterwards Richard came and fined for *half a mark* by sureties of Gilbert reeve of Shipton and Peter at Well of the same. And John fined for *half a mark* by sureties of William Saleman of Leafield and William Tril of the same. And Roger fined for *half a mark* by sureties of Walter In Angulo of Finstock and Walter son of William of Stonesfield. Afterwards Alexander came and was committed to *prison*. Afterwards Robert Coy of Wilcote came and was committed and fined for *half a mark* by sureties of Adam Smith of Wilcote and Stephen Coy of the same. After Alexander came and was committed and fined for *half a mark* by sureties of William Saleman of Leafield and Robert Tril of the same.

m. 3]

Still Wychwood

23 It was presented by the same and found that Hervey son of Alice, widow, of Slape, Nicholas Cat of the same, William son of William Terry of Dornford and Roger son of Thomas of Slape caught a doe, and it would have escaped in the water below the vill of Slape, where it was hunted by mastiffs who throttled it; and Hervey and the others came and were committed to *prison*. And Alice did not come but her chattels were valued at *5s.* for which the sheriff, Nicholas de Hanred, answered. And Ralph Terry of Slape, Juliana wife of Adam of Slape and Matilda his daughter saw the aforesaid evildoers and did not raise a hue on them, and they were attached by Geoffrey Terry of Slape, Simon of Slape, John Terry of the same and William Terry of the same, and now they do not have them, therefore all are *in mercy*. And afterwards Hervey and Alice his mother came and fined for *10s.* by sureties of Walter Forester of Slape and Adam le Rus of the same. Afterwards Nicholas Cat fined for *half a mark* by sureties of Adam le Rus of Slape and Ralph Terry of the same. And William son of William Terry fined for *half a mark* by sureties of William his father and Walter son of Alice of Slape. And Roger son of Thomas fined for *half a mark* by sureties of John son of Emma of Stonesfield and Walter Gothird of the same.

24 It was presented by the same and found that Richard Churchyard and two unknown men brought down a certain doe in the wood of lord Amaury of St. Amand,[14] which malefactors Walter of Slape, the Lord King's forester, and a certain William his associate first perceived and found, and they attacked them and raised a cry, but because of the darkness of the night and the thickness of the wood the said malefactors escaped. And Richard Churchyard did not come and was not attached since he was not found, therefore *to be exacted* [and]

---

[14] Amaury of St. Amand held one of the two manors which had been created in Bloxham: *V.C.H. Oxfordshire ix*, 60. Bloxham Wood, however, remained "in common" between the lords of those manors until 1232 when Thomas of Langley, then Forester of Wychwood, was ordered to divide it, and in 1235 the Sheriff of Oxford was ordered to deliver seisin of one part to Amaury of St. Amand: *Cal. Close 1231-1234*, 117; *Cal. Close 1234-1237*, 57. Other evidence locates this wood in the northern part of Stonesfield parish.

outlawed. And Ralph of Bloxham, woodward of the aforesaid wood, came, and because the said offence was discovered by the Lord King's foresters earlier than by him, therefore he was committed to *prison*. And the wood is *to be taken* into the Lord King's hand.

25 It was presented by the same and found that when Philip de la Hull, the Lord King's forester, saw some evildoers between the Abbot of Eynsham's wood[15] and the Lord King's forest, he caught one of the aforesaid malefactors and when he wanted to take the said malefactor away with him, the aforesaid evildoers, namely John de Bakepuz of Kingston [Bagpuize] in Berkshire and Guy son of Robert and fifteen of their associates whose names are not known, took the aforesaid malefactor away from the aforesaid Philip, and they fled and escaped. And John and Guy did not come, nor were they attached because they were not found. Therefore the sheriff is instructed to distrain John through his lands etc. on Friday etc. and that he should distrain etc. Guy son of Robert so that he should have his son Guy etc. on that same day etc. And since Stephen of Fawler, the Abbot of Eynsham's forester who ought to keep his bailiwick well and faithfully and be quick to raise a cry and to catch evildoers of this sort, did not [do this], now he came and was committed to *prison*. It was found by the same that John Fox and Adam his brother were harbourers and leaders of all the aforesaid evildoers, and now they came and were committed to *prison*. Afterwards the aforesaid John Fox came and made a fine of *10s.* by sureties of Thomas parson of Woodstock, and Roger of Radford in Enstone. Afterwards John de Blakepuz came and was committed to *prison*. Afterwards he fined for *1 mark* by sureties of Roger de Peauton and John son of Guy son of Robert.

26 It was presented by the same and found that Walter Prat of Enstone and John his brother were evildoers to the Lord King's venison and now they did not come, nor were they attached because they were not found. Therefore *to be exacted [and] outlawed*. An inquisition on this was held by four vills, namely Enstone, Spelsbury, Asterleigh [and] Charlbury, and because they did not come fully to the inquisition therefore *in mercy*.

27 It was presented by the same and found that Alan Eadwaker of Combe and John Querdeleon, chaplain of Master William parson of Spelsbury, were evildoers to the venison etc. And Alan did not come because he is dead. And John did not come because he is a clerk; therefore the Bishop of Lincoln is *commanded* to cause etc. An inquisition was held by the four nearest vills,

---

[15] This cannot have been the wood in Eynsham itself, which did not touch any royal woodland. Since Stephen of Fawler was the forester, and John and Adam Fox lived in Ditchley, it was presumably the Abbot's wood in Charlbury and Fawler, which bordered on Bloxham Wood.

namely Hanborough etc. And because they did not come fully, therefore *in mercy*.

28   It was presented by the same and found that Ralph de Holwerk, the forester of the lord earl of Gloucester,[16] Ralph son of Shepherd of Minster [and] John son of John of Crawley were evildoers to the venison, etc. And Ralph of Holwerk came and was committed to *prison*. Afterwards he made a fine for 1 mark by sureties of Walter de la Hill of Shipton and Nicholas le Noreys of the same. And Ralph son of Shepherd and John son of John did not come and were not attached because they were not found. Therefore *to be exacted [and] outlawed*. And elsewhere the sheriff was instructed by Ernald du Boys, Justice of the Forest, to seize the same John for the aforesaid offence; which sheriff made a report to the Bailiff of lord William de Valence's liberty of Bampton,[17] namely to John, Bailiff of Bampton, who is present and cannot deny this, and did nothing about it; therefore *in mercy*. Afterwards Ralph son of Beatus [sic, error for *Bercarius, shepherd*] came and was committed to *prison*.

29   It was presented by the same and found that Nicholas le Colier was the harbourer of John and Hugh his sons and Stephen Frethecent, evildoers to the venison etc., And Nicholas came and was committed to *prison*. And John his son did not come and the sheriff was *instructed* to cause him to come etc. And Stephen and Hugh, as written above, were committed to *prison*. Afterwards the said John came and was committed to *prison*. Afterwards he fined for half a mark by sureties of Ralph of Ditchley and John Fox of the same.

30   It was presented by the same and found that Philip Longhals of Hensington, John Herbert of Combe, John atte Heythe of the same, Hugh Russel of Wootton and William his brother [no offence stated]. And John Herbert, John atteheithe, Hugh Russel and John his brother came and were committed to *prison*. And Philip and William brother of Hugh did not come and were not attached because they were not found, therefore *to be exacted and outlawed*. And the sheriff was *instructed* to distrain Agnes mother of the aforesaid Philip to cause her son to come etc. Afterwards the aforesaid William Russel came and was committed to *prison*. Afterwards John Herbert fined for *4s.* by sureties of William de Edon of Combe and William attehethe. And because John attehethe is very poor and under age he was *pardoned* by the King. Afterwards Hugh Russel and William Russel made a fine for 20s. [4s. in

---

[16]   The earls of Gloucester held Shipton-under-Wychwood: *Rot. Hund. ii,* 734.

[17]   Both Minster and Crawley were in Bampton Hundred. Jurisdiction over that Hundred had been granted to William de Valence, so that his bailiff was responsible for law and order there: *Rot. Hund. ii,* 30.

margin] by sureties of William of Ludwell in Wootton and Thomas le Capier of the same.

m. 3 dorse]

Still Wychwood

31 It was presented by the same and found that William Sleye of Asterleigh, Gilbert Cheppe of the same and Walter Culhar of the same are evildoers to the venison etc. And Gilbert Chippe came and was committed to *prison*. And William and Walter did not come therefore *to be exacted and outlawed*. And William was imprisoned elsewhere and freed on bail,[18] namely by Elyas Achard of Asterleigh, Gilbert Chippe of the same, Richard son of John of the same, Robert Cullehar of the same, Walter Choppe of the same, John Cullehar of the same, Henry Widesham, William Choppe of Kiddington, Gilbert reeve of the same, Walter Dogge, William Tesselin [and] Ralph Tesselin, and now they do not have him, therefore *in mercy*. Afterwards Gilbert Choppe fined for *half a mark* by sureties of John carter of Asterleigh and John le Lunge of the same.

32 It was presented by the same and found that Nicholas attegrene of Charlbury and John Sterthup and Hugh son of Ralph clerk of the same are evildoers to the venison etc. and Nicholas and John came and were committed to *prison*. And Hugh did not come and was not attached because he was not found. Therefore *to be exacted [and] outlawed*. Afterwards Hugh came and was committed to *prison*. Afterwards John Sterthup [and] Nicholas attegrene came and were committed to *prison*. Afterwards Nicholas attegrene fined for *10s.* by sureties of Richard Durdent of Charlbury and Richard of Stonesfield of the same. And John Sturthup fined for *10s.* by sureties of Reginald attedik [and] Roger of Cote of the same. And Hugh son of Ralph clerk fined for *10s.* by sureties of Reginald attewode of Charlbury and Henry Norman of the same.

33 It was presented by the same and found that Walter Wymark of Hanborough, Walter le Bern of North Leigh and Robert Muset of the same are evildoers to the venison etc. Now they came and were committed to *prison*. And William [sic] Wymark did not come and was not attached because he is a clerk. Therefore *to be exacted [and] outlawed*. Afterwards Walter le Bern came and fined for *half a mark* by sureties of Thomas Edon of North Leigh and Ralph attegrene of the same. Afterwards Robert Muset came and fined [for]

---

[18] A writ dated 3 May 1255, which freed William Sley from prison and put him on bail, is recorded in *Cal. Close 1254-56*, 75.

half a mark by sureties of John son of Gilbert of North Leigh and William son of Gilbert of the same.

34 It was presented by the same and found that Elyas le Noreis of Witney and Crispus his brother, Lorekin le Noreys and Richard his brother are evildoers to the Lord King's venison. They did not come and were not attached because they were not found. Therefore *to be exacted [and] outlawed.* Afterwards it was testified that Elyas and Crispus live at Witney in the liberty of the lord Bishop-elect of Winchester. Therefore the sheriff was *instructed* to take their lands and tenements etc. and to have their bodies etc.. Afterwards Elyas le Noreys came and fined for 10s. by sureties of Walter de la Bruera and Richard Hilde. And Walter Crispus fined for *10s.* by sureties of Richard Forester and Robert Frankelyn.

35 It was presented by the same and found that John Goman of Hailey, Walter Mundelgum of the same, Ralph de Dyve, Bay of Crawley, Alexander le Lord of the same, Richard Wymark of Hailey, Hugh le Wyne of Crawley, Doleman of the same, Richard le Schireve of Hailey and Henry le Cupere of the same are evildoers etc.. They did not come and were not attached because they were not found. Therefore *to be exacted [and] outlawed.* Afterwards it was testified that all are inhabitants of the liberty of the lord Bishop-elect of Winchester: therefore the sheriff was *instructed* to take their lands and tenements etc. and to *have* their bodies etc.. Afterwards John Goman, Alexander Louerd, Richard Wymund, Doleman and Richard Schireve came and were committed to *prison.* Afterwards John Goman fined for *10s.* by sureties of Walter Cupar [and] William de Garefford. And Alexander fined for *10s.* by sureties of Robert Jacob and Geoffrey of Poffley. And Richard Wymund fined for *10s.* by sureties of William Wyking and John Wymark. And Doleman fined for *10s.* by sureties of Walter Wyth and Robert Jacob. And Richard Schireve fined for *10s.* by sureties of Walter Edwine [and] Geoffrey of Poffley. Afterwards Ralph de Dyve came and was committed to *prison.* Afterwards he fined for *half a mark* by surety of Thomas of Williamscot.

36 It was present by the same and found that Geoffrey, parson of the church of Stonesfield, Geoffrey Joye of the same and Walter his brother are evildoers to the venison, etc.. And Geoffrey Joye came and was committed to *prison.* And Geoffrey did not come and was not attached because he was not found. Therefore *to be exacted [and] outlawed.* And because Geoffrey Joye remained in prison for a long time and is very poor, he was *pardoned by the king.*

37   It was presented by the same and found that Nicholas King of Tapwell[19] in Finstock [and] Thomas son of Henry Clerk of Ascott are evildoers to the venison etc. They did not come and were not attached because they were not found. Therefore *to be exacted [and] outlawed*. Afterwards Nicholas came and was committed to prison. Afterwards he was *pardoned by the king* because he is very poor.

38   It was presented by the same and found that Robert de Chandos, Ralph de Preawes and Ralph Iuwas are evildoers to the venison etc. They came and were committed to *prison*. Afterwards Robert de Chandos made a fine for *2 marks* by sureties of William de la Hill of Swinbrook and Joceus Mussel of Shipton. And Ralph de Preawes fined for *40s.* by sureties of Thomas de Breure and Hugh of Tew. And Ralph Iuaus made a fine for *100s.* by sureties [sic] of Roger de Amar'.

39   It was presented by the same and found that James son of Robert del Broc of Tew, Henry son of James Terstane [and] Richard son of Thomas le Prest of the same are evildoers to the venison etc. They did not come and were not attached because they were not found. Therefore *to be exacted [and] outlawed*. And Robert del Broc, father of the aforesaid James, harboured the aforesaid James his son etc.. Therefore the sheriff is *instructed* to distrain the said Robert etc. so that he causes the aforesaid James his son to come from day to day etc. Afterwards James son of Robert came and was committed to *prison*. Afterwards he made fine for *40s.* by sureties of Robert del Broc and William del Brok.

Examined

m. 4]

40   **Amercements for defaults**

Hundred of Chadlington

From lord Richard earl of Gloucester for default
From Brian de Brampton Huntingfield[20]
From Saer de Huntingfeld, he holds in dower

---

[19] The hamlet of Tapwell is yet another of West Oxfordshire's deserted settlements. *Des.Vill. Oxon.* 45 and *V.C.H. Oxfordshire x* ,138.
[20] Brian de Brampton (the "Huntingfield" is presumably a clerical error) held a fee in Idbury, which would have been within the bounds of Wychwood as defined in 1219: *Book of Fees pt 2*, 828; BL Stowe MS 79887. His manor had no woodland within the covert but freeholders with tenures within the Forest bounds were expected to attend the Forest Eyre, and were amerced for non-attendance.

From Geoffrey Cross for the same	½ mark
From Savary of Walcot for the same	½ mark
From John parson of Brampton for the same	2s.
From Roger of Carswell for the same	½ mark
From William Warin de Lanore for the same	½ mark
From Stephen Parmentarius of the same for the same	2s.
From Alexander de Andevill for the same	1 mark
From John Por of Chilson for the same	3s.
From Mayn son of Richard in Heythrop for the same	½ mark
From Nicholas de Noers of Churchill for the same	½ mark
From Reginald Forester of Lyneham for the same	½ mark
From John son of Alan for the same [marginal note only]	*before the king*

Hundred of Bullingdon

From John of Elsfield for default	5 marks
From Roger de la Wente of Thomley for the same	2s.
From Walter Gamel of the same for the same	2s.
From Peter Folyot in Albury for the same	100s.
From the vill of Wheatley for the same	1 m.

Hundred of Ploughley

From Miles son of Robert Abselon in Lillingstone[21] for default	2s.
From Robert de Heye in the same for the same	2s.
From Robert le Cuidur of the same for the same	2s.
From Adam Oysel of the same for the same	½ mark
From the Abbot of Cirencester[22] for the same	5 marks

Hundred of Wootton

From Hugh le Butelir of Wilcote for default	10s.
From the Prior of Cogges for the same	40s.
From Robert de Twit in Cogges for the same	20s.

[21] Lillingstone Lovell and Boycott (see next fn.) are now in Buckinghamshire but were then detached portions of Oxfordshire and regarded as being in Ploughley Hundred. They were within the boundaries of Whittlewood Forest, which lay mostly in Northamptonshire but included part of Buckinghamshire. In the Pleas of the Forest held at Northampton between 20th and 30th June 1255 the justices dealt with the Northamptonshire section of Whittlewood, and presumably these two vills had also been excluded from the Buckingham Pleas, which were held on 26th April 1255; *V.C.H. Northamptonshire ii*, 343; *V.C.H. Buckinghamshire ii*, 135.

[22] The Abbey of Cirencester held Boycott, which had been granted to it by Henry II; *Rot. Hund. ii*, 44.

41 It was presented by the foresters and verderers, namely John de Haddon, Eustace le Eyr, John [sic, error for James] le Blund and Robert de Elleford, and by the regarders, that Peter de Leya,[23] after he had received the Lord King's manors at farm, supported evildoers to the vert in Combe and Stonesfield against his faith and fealty done to the lord, and, as much as he could, hindered their appearance before the Foresters and Verderers at the Swanmote according to the assize of the forest, and they were not attached because of money which he took from them, by estimation 1 mark or more, which the same Peter received. And that the same Peter, as much as he could, supported Robert de Channdos, a frequent evildoer to the Lord King's hunting when he was bailiff of Shipton, and he helped the said Robert by supporting him against William of Langley[24] and the verderers, when he ought to have assisted and supported them and the rights of the Lord King; in which he was an accomplice of the said Robert and his offences against the venison. And that the same Peter made a certain John de Lech Forester of the Lord King's wood of Bloxham and did not present the said John before the Foresters and verderers at the swanmote in accordance with the assize and custom of the Forest; which John sold oaks and branches from the said wood on the orders of Peter himself, to the value of thirty shillings which the same Peter received, to the injury of the King. And that the same Peter also, after the said John was removed, made a certain other man forester, namely Adam Fox, who was suspected and proved by an earlier inquisition to be a wrong-doer to the venison, and he retained him in his bailiwick for half a year or more after the inquisition concerning him [which had been] held by the verderers and foresters. And the same Peter as much as he was and could suborned the verderers to delete the name of the same Adam from their roll, and the name [sic] of John le Fox and Robert Muset of North Leigh, who were convicted by the inquisition of doing harm to the venison; in respect of which he was their associate in their wrong-doing and their harbourer. And the same Peter caused charcoal to be made in the aforesaid wood while the said Adam was his forester, from which he gave 2 cart-loads of charcoal to Philip de Sancto [sic] Helena, 3 oaks to William de Riston, 1 oak to Roger Fuller of Cleveley, 1 oak to R. de Mauverdin and 1 oak to William King and 1 cart-load of charcoal to Nicholas de Hanred, the sheriff. And that the same Peter had men with him, namely Hugh Schitehol, Ralph Pilon and John clerk, who had not been presented before the foresters and verderers nor made fealty to the Lord King in accordance with the assize of the Forest, and the same un-pledged men were accustomed to do harm to the vert in the aforesaid

[23] Peter de Legh (Leya), with John of Hanborough, was granted the king's "towns" of Bladon, Combe, Bloxham, Hanborough and Stonesfield for six years in 1251: *Cal. Pat. 1247-1258*, 87.

[24] William of Langley was the hereditary Forester of Wychwood. He had been deprived of his bailiwick for trespasses, but regained it in 1246: *Cal. Pat. 1232-1247*, 472.

wood with the aforesaid Ralph and John. And Peter came and being convicted of this was committed to *prison*. Afterwards he paid a fine of *5 marks*. Afterwards Roger le Folun of Cleveley came [and] paid a fine of *4s*.

42 The Mayor and Burgesses of Oxford, summoned to appear before the Justices, came and, being asked about certain roe-bucks appertaining to the forest, said that they did not have to answer to any Justice about any pleas outside the walls of Oxford, and they asked for a postponement so that they could approach the Lord King and petition for immunity regarding this; and a day was given, the Friday next after the Purification of the Blessed Mary [4 February 1256], at which day they came and brought with them letters from the Lord King by which the Lord King commanded the Justices to allow the burgesses of Oxford to enjoy those liberties and customs which they were [accustomed to] use and enjoy. And because the said burgesses were before the King's Court on the same day and came, it seemed to the Justices that the said letters of the King were not a warrant for them; and since they ought to come before the justices and answer to them a day was given for them to do this, the following Saturday, on which day they did not come nor did they send anyone in their place. Therefore in *mercy*.

m. 4 dorse]
43 [No heading]

From William son of Robert de Stocke of Combe for vert and for breaking into the Lord King's park of Bladon[25]	½ mark
From Reginald Sewet of Combe for the same	he is pardoned
From William Sewet of the same (and John his son) for the same	8s.
From William de Wytenhull of North Leigh for a surety for the same William	12d.
From Stephen of East End of the same for the same	12d.
From Robert Cubham of Eynsham for the same	poor
From William Cef of the same for the same	12d.
From John Sewet of Combe for breaking into the aforesaid park of the Lord King	[blank]
From Richard Bonvallet of Witney for a surety for the same John	12d.
From Robert le Porchir of Eynsham for the same	nothing
From John son of Robert de la Hethe for breaking into the said park	[marginal note only] *he did not come*

---

[25] In *V.C.H. Oxfordshire xii*, 441 it is implied that this event took place in Hensigrove, a wood which was in Bladon parish but belonged to Hensington. However, the men named as taking part in the incursion come from Stonesfield and Combe, making it more likely that it was actually in Bladon wood, which adjoined Combe, rather than in Hensigrove which was further away and on the far side of the river Glyme.

From John le Frere of Kiddington for a surety for the said John
    son of Robert   12d.
From John Punchard of the same for the same   12d.
From Adam Smith of Combe for the same   poor
From William Gilbert of the same for the same   elsewhere
From John, servant of Emma of Stonesfield, for breaking into
    the said park   ½ mark
From William of Stonesfield of Thorp for a surety for the same
    John   2s.
From William Achard of the same for the same   2s.
From William Crisp of Combe for the same   2s.
From Simon le Iofne of Thorp for the same   2s.
From Robert le Lung of Combe for breaking into the said park ½ mark
From Robert attestock of the same for a surety for the said
    Robert le Lung   2s.
From William Edon of the same for the same   12d.
From Robert Northman of the same for the same   12d.
Fom John Popel of the same for the same   poor
From Robert Fesant of Combe for breaking into the said park elsewhere
From Reginald attegrene of Combe for a surety for the same elsewhere
From Thomas Cross of Combe for breaking into the said park 4s.
From John le Iofne of Bladon for a surety for the same Thomas 4s.
From William at Water of Thorp for the same   2s.
From Robert Cross of the same for the same   2s.
From Richard of Kiddington for a surety for the same   12d.
From Walter Alfroine of the same for the same   12d.
From Richard atte Elme for the same   12d.
From William of Kiddington for the same   12d.
From William attestreme of Combe for breaking into the said park uͭ
From William Willnoht of the same for a surety   uͭ
From Robert attehethe   12d.
From John attewod of the same for the same   poor
From Reginald son of John of the same for the same   12d.
From Richard le Frok of the same for the same   12d.
From Walter son of Emma of Stonesfield for breaking into the
    said park   4s.
From Godric of Fawler for a surety for the same Walter   12d.
From William Aldon of the same for the same   12d.
From William Coleman of the same for the same   elsewhere
From [tear and blot] of the same for the same   12d.
From John son of Reginald Crisp for breaking into the said park 4s.
From Adam le Franceys of Yarnton for a surety   ½ mark

From John of Kiddington for the same   in prison, elsewhere
From <Walter of North Leigh> for the same   elsewhere
From William Crips for the same   elsewhere
                                                                   Examined

m. 5]
44   Fines and Amercements before W. Briton [Breton] and his fellows, Justices in Eyre of the pleas of the Forest at Oxford in the 40th year of the reign [1255-6]

[The number in brackets is that of the corresponding presentment]

From Roger de La Punfaud of Stanton [St John] for an offence against the venison	[7]	½ mark
by sureties of William son of Bernard of Stanton and Thomas le Frankelyn of the same.		
From William [sic; Willata, vill] of Stanton because it did not have etc. And because it did not come	[7]	1 mark
From Nicholas de Hanred, sheriff, of the chattels of Roger de la Punfaud	[7]	1 mark
From the same Nicholas, sheriff, of the chattels of Hugh of the Ditch because they were used to redeem the same Hugh	[8]	<½ mark>
From the Vill of Holton because it did not come	[9]	1 mark
(From Hugh of the Ditch for an offence against the venison by sureties of Thorstan of Marston)	[8]	1 mark
From the Vill of Wheatley for the same	[9]	elsewhere
From the Vill of Forest Hill for the same	[9]	½ mark
From the Vill of Elsfield because it did not have etc.	[9]	½ mark
From the Abbott of Osney's Vill of Arncott because it did not come	[13]	elsewhere
From the Prior of Bicester's Vill of Arncott for the same	[13]	elsewhere
From the Vill of Piddington for the same	[13]	elsewhere
From the Abbot of Westminster's Vill of Murcott because it did not come	[13]	40s.
From Martin, reeve of the lord earl Richard of Ambrosden, for an offence against the venison	[13]	[blank]
From William Shepherd of Arncott for the same	[13]	[blank]
From Hugh le Brun of Hanborough for the same	[14]	[blank]
From Stephen in La Hale of the same who did not have [the man] for whom he was surety	[14]	½ mark
From Walter at Well of the same for the same	[14]	2s.

From Walter Boneyre of the same for the same	[14]	elsewhere
From Richard Levesone of the same for the same	[14]	4s.
From Martin de Hunderleye of the same for the same	[14]	4s.
From Robert Winge of the same for the same	[14]	dead
From Hugh son of Nicholas of Ditchley for an offence against the venison	[15]	½ mark
by sureties of Ralph of Ditchley and John Fox of the same.		
(From William of Rotherfield in South Leigh for an offence	[16]	12d.)
From Richard de Howill in South Leigh because he did not have [the man] for whom he was surety	[16]	12d.
From Geoffrey le Bere of the same for the same	[16]	12d.
From Walter Sweyn of Fawler for an offence against the venison	[17]	16s.
for which Nicholas the sheriff answers		
From William Coleman of the same because he did not have [the man] for whom he was surety	[17]	12d.
From Thomas Pole of the same for the same	[17]	2s.
From Richard Sweyn of the same for the same	[17]	12d.
From Robert of Brailes of the same for the same	[17]	2s.
<From Nicholas de Hanred>, sheriff, for the chattels of Walter Sweyn of Fawler	16s.	(elsewhere)
<From Syward> le Frere of Stonesfield for a hunting offence	[18]	[blank]
From Robert son of Aldwin of the same for the same	[18]	1 mark
From Stephen Herbert of the same for the same	[18]	elsewhere
From William [sic, Willata, vill] of Charlbury because it did not have etc.	[18]	40s.
From Nicholas de Hanred for the chattels of Walter le Frere	[18]	5s.
From William [Willata, vill] of Glympton because it did not come	[19]	2 marks
From William [Willata, vill] of Slape for the same	[19]	½ mark
From William [Willata, vill] of Wootton for the same	[19]	1 mark
From John de Haddon, verderer, for concealment and other offences	[19]	100s.
From Eustace le Eyr, verderer for the same	[19]	6 marks
From Robert de Elesford, verderer, for the same	[19]	4 marks
From Robert of Sarsden, verderer, for the same	[19]	5 marks
From James Blund, verderer, for the same	[19]	5 marks
From Peter de Leye, verderer, for the same	[19]	[blank]

From Hugh le Brun of Hanborough for an offence against the venison		
by sureties of William Blund of Ramsden and William in la Hale of Headington		1 mark
From William [Willata, vill] of Ascott because it did not come	[20]	40s.
From William [Willata, vill] of Chadlington for the same	[20]	50s.
From William [Willata, vill] of Pudlicote for the same	[20]	40s.
From William [Willata, vill] of Leafield for the same	[20]	1 mark
From William [Willata, vill] of Stonesfield for the same	[21]	40s.
From William [Willata, vill] of Combe for the same	[21]	4 marks
From William [Willata, vill] of Ditchley for the same	[21]	20s.
From Richard of Hanborough in Ramsden for the same by surety of Gilbert reeve of Shipton	[22]	½ mark
From John his brother for the same by surety of William Saleman of Leafield	[22]	½ mark
<From Roger le Wyte of Ramsden for the same	[22]	½ mark>
From Alexander his son	[22]	½ mark
From Robert le Coy of Wilcote for the same	[22]	½ mark
From William [Willata, vill] of Finstock because it did not come	[22]	1 mark
From Hervey son of Alice of Slape and his mother for an offence against the venison	[22]	10s.
From Nicholas Cat of the same for the same	[23]	½ mark
From William son of William Terry of Dornford for the same	[23]	½ mark
From Roger son of Thomas of Slape for the same	[23]	½ mark
From Ralph Terry of Slape for an offence	[23]	12d.
From Geoffrey Terry of the same because he did not have [the man] for whom he was surety	[23]	2s.
From Simon of Slape for the same	[23]	elsewhere
From John Terry of the same for the same	[23]	2s.
From William Terry of the same for the same	[23]	elsewhere

m 5. dorse]
Regard of Wychwood in the County of Oxford for the 34th year [1249-50]

[In the original, the following three sections are entered in columnar form, e.g.
Vill   person's name   acreage   crop   sum to be paid.
Lack of space does not allow that format to be used here.]

45

Ascott	From Roger Douly for 2 acres of winter wheat	2s.[26]
	From Adam le Fulur of Ditchley for 1½ roods of oats	2¼d.
	From Alice widow of Reginald of Fulwell	
	for ½ acre and 1 rood of oats	4½d.
	From John Fox for ½ acre & ½ rood of oats	3¾d.
Asterleigh	From Ralph de Saucey for 1 acre & 1 rood of oats	7½d.
	From the same Ralph for ½ acre of oats	4d.
	From Gilbert Jop for 1 rood of oats	3½d.
	From Roger Pass' for 2 acres of oats	12d.
	From Henry War for 2 acres of oats	12d.
Charlbury	From John son of the reeve for ½ rood of oats	3¾d.
Fawler	From Nicholas de Anvers for 1 acre of oats	6d.
	From Richard Schireve for 1 rood of oats	3½d.
	From James le Blund for ½ acre of oats	3d.
Finstock	From the Abbot of Eynsham for 2½ acres & 1 rood of oats	16½d.
	From Adam Schort, Agnes Nod, Alice Sprot, Edward King,	
	Cecilia Nod and Hugh Newman for 3 acres of oats	18d.
	From Richard of Hanborough for ½ acre of winter wheat	6d.
	From Walter Aylward and John Leky for 1 rood of oats	3½d.
	From Edward King and Cecilia Nod for 1½ roods of oats	9d.
	From William of Pachesdich, Elias Swein and Matilda	
	Wylot for 1½ acres of oats	9d.
	From Stephen of Hanborough for 1 rood of oats	3½d.
North Leigh	From the Abbot of Locus Sancti Edwardi[27] for ½ acre of oats	3d.
Tilgarsley	From Peter carbonarius for ½ acre of winter wheat	6d.
	From Simon le Viniter for 1 acre of oats	6d.

46	**Regard for the 37th year** [1252-1253]	
Spelsbury	From Roger Doyli for 2 acres of oats	12d.
	From Adam le Fulur for 1½ roods of oats	2¼d.
	From Reginald of Fulwell for ½ rood of oats	¼d.
Enstone	From John le Fox for ½ acre ½ rood of oats	3¾d.
Asterleigh	From Ralph de Saucey for 1 acre & 1 rood of oats	7½d.

---

[26] These sums are the "rents" paid to the king for crops grown on assart land; 1/- per acre for wheat, 6d.
per acre for oats.
[27] Netley Abbey, which owned the manor of North Leigh. *V.C.H. Oxfordshire xii*, 220.

	From Peter Punchard, William Josselin, Gilbert reeve, Elias Achard, Fray Punchard, Henry son of Ralph of Kiddington, Henry de la Mar, William Tesselin, Walter Jap, Gamel & Hugh parson for 1 rood of oats	3½d.
	From the heirs of Ralph de Saucey for ½ acre of oats	3d.
	From Gilbert Jop for 1 rood of oats	1½d.
	From Roger Pass' for 2 acres of oats	12d.
	From Henry War for 2 acres of oats	12d.
Charlbury	From John son of the reeve for ½ rood of oats	¼d.
Fawler	From Nicholas de anvers for 1 acre of oats	6d.
	From Richard Schireve for 1 rood of oats	1½d.
	From James le Blund for ½ acre of oats	3d.
Finstock	From the Abbot of Eynsham for ½ acre and 1 rood of oats	4½d.
	From the same Abbot for 2 acres of oats	12d.
	From Adam Schort, Agnes widow, Alice Wrot, Edward King, Cecilia Mody for 3 acres of oats	18d.
	From Richard of Hanborough for ½ acre of oats	3d.
	From Walter Aylward and John Leky for 1 rood of oats	1½d.
	From Edward King and Cecilia widow for 1½ acres of oats	9d.
	From William of Pachesdich for 1½ acres of oats	9d.
	From Stephen of Hanborough for 1 rood of oats	1½d.
North Leigh	From the Abbot of Locus Sancti Edwardi for 1½ acres of oats	3d.
	From Peter carbonarius for ½ acres of winter wheat	6d.
Tilgarsley	From Walter le Viniter for 1 acre of oats	6d.

47	**Regard of the 39th year** [1254-55]	
Ascott	From Roger Doyli for 2 acres of oats	12d.
Spelsbury	From Adam le Fulur for 1½ roods of oats	2¼d.
	From John Fox for ½ acre and ½ rood of oats	3¾d.
Asterleigh	From Joan de Saucey for 1 acre and 1 rood of oats	7½d.
	From Peter Punchard, William Josselin, Gilbert reeve, Elias Achard, Fray Punchard, Henry son of Ralph of Kiddington, Henry de la Mar, Walter Josselin, Walter Gamel and John of St. Giles for 1 rood of oats	3½d.
	From Thomas of Williamscot for ½ acre of oats	3d.
	From Gilbert reeve for 1 rood of oats	1½d.
	From Richard Cusic for 2 acres of oats	12d.
	From Henry War for 2 acres of oats	12d.
Charlbury	From John son of the reeve for ½ rood of oats	¾d.
Fawler	From James le Blund for ½ acre of oats	3d.
Finstock	From the Abbott of Eynsham for 2½ acres and 1 rood of oats	10½d.
	From Adam Schort, Agnes widow, Alice Sprot, Cecilia Nod, and Hugh Norman for 3 acres of oats	18d.
	From Richard of Hanborough for ½ acre of oats	3d.
	From Walter Aylward for 1 rood of oats	1½d.

From Cecilia widow for 1½ acres of oats	9d.
From Walter de Angulo, Elias Swein, Matilda Wilot for 1½ roods of oats	2¼d.
From Walter of Ramsden for 1 rood of winter wheat	3d.
From Walter viniter for 1 acre of wheat	12d.

Pleas of the Forest at Oxford before William le Breton, Nicholas of Romsey, Geoffrey of Lewknor and Simon de Throp on Monday next after the octave of St. Hilary in the 40th year of the reign of King Henry son of King John.

[The above is written in a hand similar to that in the rest of the document. The following paragraph is written in a later hand.]

These rolls were examined and [matters] touching the forest copied, but nothing found regarding a perambulation.

Oxon.   Oxon.   Examined

m. 6]

48   **Of Vert in Shotover**

	From William le Paumer of Horspath for vert in demesne	2s.
	From Hugh Fabian of the same for a surety of the same	2s.
	From Walter Fud of the same for the same	2s.
	From Richard le Waterman of the same for vert	2s.
	From Henry Colhyne of Wheatley for a surety	2s.
Demesne	From Robert son of John of the same for the same	2s.
	From Robert Medicus of Forest Hill for acorns taken without warrant	2s.
	From Richard de la Wose of the same for a surety	2s.
	From William Hereward of the same for the same	2s.
	From William of Losethorn because he did not have the acorns	2s.

49   **Of Vert in Bernwood**

From Hugh son of Osmund of Bicester for vert	2s.
From William of Arncot for a surety	2s.
From Gilbert Walenc' for the same	2s.
From Ralph Carpenter of Studley for vert	12d.
From Nicholas reeve of the same for the same	2s.
From Nicholas son of Emma of the same for the same	2s.
From Walter Letice of Boarstall for vert	12d.
From Nicholas reeve of the same for a surety	elsewhere
From John, man of Robert le Lung of the same for vert	12d.
From Robert son of Alice as his surety	12d.
From Roger Patun for the same	12d.
From Walter Swandulf of Boarstall for vert	12d.
From Stephen Beforn as his surety	12d.
From Roger of Stowe for the same	2s.
From Robert of Holton for vert	2s.

From William Forester of Bedhal [error for Ledhale]
    as his surety   12d.

50   **Of Vert in Wychwood**

From Alan le Heyward of Combe for vert	2s.
From John Waleraund of Stonesfield for the same	2s.
From William son of Nicholas of the same for the same.	2s.
From Reginald (son of Richard) of the same for the same	2s.
From John Rad' of the same for the same	2s.
From Nicholas (le Iufne) of the same for the same	12d.
From Nicholas Hawys of the same for the same	12d.
From William son of Cecilia of the same for the same	2s.
From Robert attehethe of Combe for the same	12d.
From William Crisp of the same for the same	4s.
From John Terry of Combe for the same	4s.
From William Sprot of the same for the same	poor
From William son of Emma of Stonesfield for the same	2s.
From William Sewet of Combe of the same for the same	2s.
From John Cuphar of Stonesfield for the same	½ mark
From William Edon of Combe for the same	2s.
From William Pape of Stonesfield for vert	12d.
From Robert Norman of Combe for the same	12d.
From Robert le Frere of Stonesfield for the same	elsewhere
From Alan West of Combe for the same	12d.
From Henry Sprot of the same for the same	poor
From Henry Mang' of Woodstock for the same	12d.
From William of Boriens for a surety	2s.
From Henry of the same for the same	2s.
From Robert fesant of Combe for vert	poor

Prison   From William Terry of the same for the same against bail 2s. 6d.
         for which the sheriff answers
And from the same half a mark, by sureties of William
clerk of Combe and Thomas West of the same

From Walter son of William of Stonesfield for the same	2s.
From Robert Sewet of Combe for the same	12d.
From Richard le Gerisse of Hanborough for the same for	½ mark

         which the same sheriff answered, namely Nicholas
         de Hanred.

From Walter le Gothird of Stonesfield for the same	12d.
From John son of Ralph of the same for the same	5s.

         For which the same sheriff answered etc.

From Reginald son of Richard of the same for the same   2s.
         for which [the same sheriff answered]
From Reginald Faukes of Combe for the same   12d.

	From John Attewod of the same for the same	12d.
	From William Gilbert of the same for the same	12d.
Prison	From Robert de la Hacche of the same for the same and because he was against his bail	½ mark

m. 6 dorse]

51   **Still of the Vert of Wychwood**

From Humphrey reeve of Combe for vert	2s.
From William attehethe of the same for vert	2s.
From William Ferbras of the same for the same	2s.
From John le Frere of Stonesfield for the same	2s.
From William attewiche of Combe for the same	4s.
From Thomas son of Alan clerk of the same for the same	12d.
From William son of John Terry for the same	dead
From Robert attestock' of Combe for the same	2s.
From James son of Alan of the same for the same	2s.
From Thomas son of Geoffrey of the same for the same	not found
From William Kynne of the same for a surety	2s.
From Humphrey Baker of Woodstock for vert	2s.
From Richard le Turnour of the same for the same	2s.
From Thomas le Mercir of the same for the same	2s.
From Thomas son of Matilda of Combe for vert	12d.
From Robert Cross of the same for the same	12d.
From John son of Roger attehethe of the same for the same	2s.
From Robert son of Richard of the same for the same	12d.
From Nicholas Sewet of the same for the same	no chattels
From Osbert Botte of the same as his surety	12d.
From William Fauk of the same for the same	12d.
From Thomas son of Carpenter of Stonesfield for vert	12d.

Demesne {
From Thomas West of Combe for vert in demesne	2s. 6d.
From Henry Sprot of the same for the same	elsewhere

From Reginald son of Robert of Hanborough for vert	elsewhere
From John Herbert of Combe for the same	elsewhere for venison
From Robert of Combe of North Leigh for the same	12d.

Demesne {
From Geoffrey attewod (of Stonesfield) for the same	2s.
From John le Chaunceler for the same	2s.

From John son of Emma of Stonesfield for the same	2s.
From William atteheche of Combe for vert at night for which Nicholas the sheriff answered	2s.
From Robert Cross, William Edwine, Hugh of la Boxe for which the same [sheriff] answered	4s.
From William Ferbras for the same	elsewhere
From Robert Northman of Combe for the same	elsewhere
From Richard le Wohel of Stonesfield for the same	elsewhere
From Robert Aldun of Combe for a surety	elsewhere for venison

From Richard Haral of Cote for vert   12d.
From William de Bonerye of Hanborough for a surety   12d.
From the vill of Stonesfield because they did not have
    William le Frere for whom they were sureties   elsewhere

52   **Of Vert in Wychwood outside the demesne[28]**

From Thomas son of Gilbert Sweyn for vert   12 d
From William son of Stephen of Fawler for the same   2s.
From John Capel of the same for the same surety   12d.
From William Coleman of the same for the same   12d.
From Richard le Frere of Cote for vert   12d.
From Geoffrey Salberd' of Charlbury for the same   12d.
From Walter son of Salomon of Leafield for the same   4s.
From Richard Saleman of the same for a surety   4s.
From Laurence of Leafield for the same   2s.
From Geoffrey Terry of Slape for vert   2s.
From Adam le Rus of the same for the same   elsewhere
From Maurice de Anvers for the same   3s.8d.
    for which Nicholas the sheriff answered
From Oliver Damor' for the value of his horse   3s.
for which the same Nicholas, sheriff, answered
From Adam Coleman of Baddefford [Radford] for vert   12d.
From Adam le Frere of Wilcote for the same   12d.
From Stephen Pokoc of Notle [North Leigh] for the same   2s.
From Richard de Swinden in Charlbury because he did
    not have [the man] for whom he was surety   2s.
From Simon of Slape for the same vert   12d.
From John Terry of Slape for the same   12d.
From William of Dornford for the same   elsewhere for venison
From William Joye of Tilgarsley for vert   poor
From Ralph Levesone of Wootton for the same   2s.
From Isac Wibet of Chilson for the same   12d.
From Walter Smith of Ascott for the same   12d.
From John de Weld of the same for the same   2s.
From Robert Harold of Cote for the same   12d.
From Ralph God of Ramsden for the same   poor
From William Thorold of Finstock for the same   2s.
From William Crispe of Walcot for the same   2s.
From Peter Furel of Kidlington for the same   2s.
From Geoffrey Isak of Chilson for the same   12d.
From Robert son of Roger of the same for the same   12d.
From Richard son of Cristina for the same   2s.

---

[28] The amercments in this section and in **53** and part of **54** correspond to the attachments recorded in the previous document, pp. 1-17.

From Walter son of Hugh of Walcot for vert   2s.
From Henry le Waleys of Wilcote for the same   12d.
From Ralph Hurel of Wootton for the same   12d.
                                                        Examined

m. 7]
53   **Still of Vert in Wychwood**

From Robert le Blake of Chilson for vert   12d.
From Thomas of Chilson for a surety   2s.
From Thomas Abuveton for the same   12d.
From Roger le Cupere of North Leigh for vert   12d.
From Stephen le Bule of Walcot for the same   2s.
From William of North Leigh for the same   2s.
From Thomas de Heddon for a surety   12d.
From Walter Ingelys for the same   2s.
From Stephen Coy of Walcot for vert   2s.
From Thomas le Pamer of the same for the same   4s.
From William son of Eva of the same for the same   12d.
From William son of Pagan of Glympton for the same   12d.
From Roger of Boriens for vert   elsewhere
From William Jordan of Glympton for a surety   12d.
From Richard of Boriens for the same   2s.
From Roger son of Thomas de Leye for vert   12d.
From William Hurel of Wootton for a surety   no chattels
From Norman Coy of Wilcote for the same by   2s.
     sureties of Thomas Coy and Adam Smith of the same.
From Thomas Coy for a surety   12d.
Demesne   From John le Cupere for vert in demesne   2s.
From Walter in le Hirne of Finstock for vert   2s.
From Geoffrey Harald of the same for the same   2s.
From Robert Ruge of Ascott for the same   12d.
From William Evereus of Walcot for the same   4s.
Demesne   From Richard Kemel of Wootton for the same   poor
From Walter of Ramsden in Finstock for vert   elsewhere
From Henry de Evereus in Walcot for the same   12d.
Demesne   From Hugh Wycher' of Ascott for the same   12d.
From John Shepherd of Chilson for vert   12d.
From Roger Shepherd of the same for the same   12d.
From Richard of Chilson for the same   12d.
From Richard de Dyrai of Chilson for vert   12d.
From Richard son of Thomas of Slape for the same
                                        elsewhere for venison
Demesne   From Walter Grus of Walcot   4s.
From Gilbert Bouquer of Glympton for vert   12d.
From William son of Roger of Cote for the same   12d.

	From Richard miller of the same for a surety	12d.
	From Robert Sweyn of Fawler for the same	12d.
	From Joel of Hanborough [of] Finstock for vert	12d.
Demesne	From William le Wyte of Ramsden for the same	2s.
	From William le Bule of Shorthampton for vert	12d.
	From William Herward of Tilgarsley who assarted in	
	the wood of the Hospital of Jerusalem without warrant	2s.
Demesne	From Walter Lowy of Wootton for vert	12d.
Demesne	From Robert de Wytenhull for the same	12d.
	From William Carter of Spelsbury for the same	12d.
	From Richard Buveton of the same for a surety	12d.
	From Nicholas Maynard of the same for the same	12d.
	From Reginald of Cote for a surety	12d.
	From Walter AtteWater of Spelsbury for the same	12d.
	From Roger Tril of Leafield for vert elsewhere for venison	
	From Stephen Pynnock of Wilcote for the same	12d.
	From John Bene of Ramsden for vert	12d.
	From Jordan Smith of Glympton for the same	12d.
	From Walter Thoky of Charlbury for the same	12d.
	From Walter of Ramsden for a surety	12d.
Demesne	From Walter Marschall de Done [?Dean] for vert	2s.
	From Walter Choye of Charlbury for the same	12d.
Demesne	From Richard son of Roger of Ramsden for the same	
	elsewhere for venison	
	From Alexander of Leafield of the same for a surety	2s.
	From Thomas Capier of Wootton for vert	18d.
	by sureties of Hugh Russel and Ralph Levesone	
	From Walter Forester of Bloxham for the same	2s.
	From Elias reeve of the same for a surety	12d.
	From John Leuerk' of the same for the same	12d.
	From John of Kingham in Ascott for vert	12d.
Demesne	From John de Evereus of Walcot for vert	2s.
Demesne	From John Forel of Ascott for the same	12d.
	From Thomas Pride of the same for the same	12d.
Demesne	From Hugh son of Hugh of the same for the same	12d.
Demesne	From Gilbert reeve of Shipton for the same	2s.

m. 7 dorse]

54   Of Pigs found within the Covert in the forbidden month[29]

From William of Finstock for the value of two pigs	2s.
by sureties of Richard Swin and Ralph Godis	
From Nicholas le Iofne of Stonesfield for the value of 6 pigs	2s.6d.
by sureties of William Nicholas [and] Robert Alden of Stonesfield	

[29] The forbidden, or fence, month was 15 days before and following 24th June.

From Robert le Frere of Stonesfield for the value of 1 pig   12d.
   by sureties of Nicholas le Iofne [and] Robert Alden
   of Stonesfield
From William le Bule of Walcot for the value of 3 pigs   2s.6d.
   by sureties of Ralph Cubbil and Thomas Palmer of Walcot
From William le Bule for the value of 4 pigs   4s.
   by sureties of Ralph Bule of Walcot and Thomas Palmer
   of Walcot
From William Wace of Walcot for the value of 8 pigs   4s.
by sureties of Richard Bule and Ralph Cubbyl of Walcot

55 Still of Vert in Wychwood

From Gilbert son of John of Combe for vert   6d.
From Henry Sprot for the same   12d.
From Robert le Frere of Stonesfield for the same   6d.
From Robert Walnaht of the same for the same   6d.
From John Herbert of the same for the same   6d.
From Walter le Frere for the same   2s.
From Hugh of la Boxe for the same   2s.
From Alan Edon for the same   6d.
From John Terry for the same   2s.
From William le Frere for the same   12d.
From Robert atte Withege for the same   12d.
From Alan Clerk of Combe for the same   12d.
From Hugh of Boxe for the same   2s.
From John Terry for the same   2s.
From John le Frere for the same   2s.
From Robert de la Wythege for the same   2s.
From Robert Crisp for the same   2s.
From Robert de la Hatteleg' for the same   12d.
From Henry Sprot for the same   12d.
From William Nicholas for the same   12d.
From John Ralph of Stonesfield for the same   6d.
From John Popel for the same   2s.
From Robert de la Hecche for the same   2s.
From John Waleraund for the same   12d.
From Robert Handel for the same   3s.
From Hugh de Boxe for the same   5s.
From William son of Matilda for the same   6d.
From John son of Emma for the same   2s.
From Henry Sprot for the same   6d.
From Reginald de la Grene for the same   6d.
From Robert le Frere for the same   3s.
From William son of Matilda for the same   6d.

m. 8]

Names of the Woodwards in the County of Oxford

56   The Prioress of Studley presents John of Forest Hill as woodward for her wood of Binhal in Shotover; who was sworn.

57   William Cullebulloc, the woodward of John de Strafford for his wood of Acremel, had been presented at Headington before Geoffrey de Langley; he came and was sworn.[30]

58   Richard le Breton, Margery de Clifford's woodward for her wood of Lillingstone in Wychwood [error for Whittlewood], was presented at Heyburn before the lord Hugh de Goldingham by Walter le Brune, reeve of Peter Chasepork.[31]

59   Daniel of Cogges, woodward of the lord Walter de Gray for his wood of Cogges, was presented by his lord at Woodstock before the lord Ernald du Boys; now he came and was sworn.

60   William de Bray presents John of Boriens, woodward of his wood which is called le Freth.[32] And earlier he had been presented before the lord William of Langley, Forester of Wychwood, after the feast of Saint Michael last past, in the 39th year [29 September 1255]; who was sworn.

61   Roger de Amory presents Hugh Ansketil as woodward for his wood of Woodperry. And earlier he had been presented by his lord before William of Northampton, steward of the forest;[33] who was sworn.

---

[30]   This wood presumably belonged to the Musard manor in Horspath. See fn 43, p 48. Geoffrey de Langley was appointed keeper of all the forests of England in 1250, but on the occasion recorded here he was probably acting as Keeper of the Forest between the Bridges of Oxford and Stamford, a position he occupied from 24 April 1250 to 24 October 1252: *Cal. Pat. 1247-1258*, 61, 63, 154.

[31]   Margery de Clifford was the tenant of the manor of Lillingstone (Lovell) in 1254, at which date Hugh Chaceporc was the overlord, his father Peter having bought the lease of the overlordship sometime after 1247: *Rot. Hund. ii*, 44; *V.C.H. Buckinghamshire ii*, 192. The presentation of the woodward may have taken place at an inquisition regarding Whittlewood Forest which is recorded as being held by Hugh de Goldingham, Seneschal of the Forest between the Bridges of Oxford and Stamford, at Le Heybarn in May 1252: *Cal. Inq. Misc. I*, No. 148. Heybarn/Heyborn/Heyburn is a lost place-name which occurs as a boundary point in the Northamptonshire and the Oxfordshire-Buckinghamshire Perambulations of Whittlewood Forest *circa* 1299. It lay on the county boundary, between Leckhamstead and Lillingstone Dayrell, and is presumably related to Heyborn Fields, in the parish of Leckhamstead, which is recorded by George Lipscomb as having been a separate manor in the fifteenth century: George Baker, *The History and Antiquities of the County of Northampton, ii*, 75-6; George Lipscomb, *The History and Antiquities of the County of Buckingham iii*, 26.

[32]   Le Freth was a wood in the southern part of Glympton, but at the date of this document it did not belong to Glympton manor. *V.C.H. Oxfordshire xi*, 125-6.

[33]   William of Northampton was bailiff of the Forest between the Bridges of Oxford and Stamford from 1246 to 1249: Raymond Grant, *The Royal Forests of England*, 98.

62　The Abbot of Abingdon presents Robert le Messir as woodward for his wood of Schawe.[34] And earlier he was presented before William de Northampton, steward of the Forest, by Brother Henry of Frilford, monk; who was sworn.

63　Roger de Oyla presents Simon Potter as woodward for his wood in Bakinhal.[35] And earlier he was presented at the lawn near Northampton by his lord; who was sworn.

64　Sampson Foliot presents Richard le carpenter [as woodward] for his wood of Bakenhal; who was sworn.

65　The Abbot of Eynsham presents William AnetheWardetune as woodward for his wood of Woodeaton. And earlier he was presented at Headington before Hugh de Goldingham by his lord; who was sworn.

66　The same Abbot presents <Thomas> Stephen Alex' as woodward for his wood of Charlbury, and he was presented by his lord at another time before William of Langley, the aforesaid Forester, at the lawn near Shorthampton; who was sworn.

67　The same Abbot presents Richard le Mouner [as woodward] of the said wood,[36] and earlier he had been presented by his lord at the aforesaid place before the aforesaid [William of Langley]; who was sworn.

68　The same Abbot presents Walter Ithehurn as woodward for his wood of Finstock, and he was presented at another time before the said William by his said lord at the said lawn; who was sworn.

69　The same Abbot presents Robert of Thame as woodward for his wood of Tilgarsley,[37] who had been presented at another time before the said William in the said place; who was sworn.

70　The lady Joan de Saucey presents Thomas Le Petit as her woodward for her wood of Asterleigh and he had been presented at another time before the said William of Langley at the aforesaid Lawn by William de Ruyston her steward, at the feast of the apostles Simon and Jude in the 40th year [28 October 1255]; who was sworn.

71　Thomas of Williamscot presents Henry of Kiddington as woodward for his wood of Kiddington, and earlier he had been presented by his lord before the said William at the aforesaid Lawn on Lammas Day in the 39th year [1 August 1255]; who was sworn.

---

[34]　Abingdon Abbey held Cuddesdon, to which Schawe wood belonged: *Rot. Hund. ii,* 718.

[35]　The location of this wood is not known.

[36]　It is not clear why two woodwards were needed, unless one had the responsibility for the wood in Charlbury, and the other looked after that in Fawler.

[37]　Presumably this name was used for the woodland belonging to Eynsham manor.

72 John of St. Valery presents Pagan de Mobray for the first time as woodward for his wood of Fulbrook, and he had not been presented earlier. He came and was sworn. Therefore for Judgement.

73 Henry de la Wade presents Robert le Parmenter as woodward for his wood of Pyriho,[38] and he had been presented earlier before the lord Ernald du Boys at Woodstock by his lord; who was sworn.

74 William FitzEllis presents as woodward for his wood of Waterperry William le Waleis, who had been presented earlier at Brill[39] before Hugh de Goldingham by his lord; who was sworn.

75 Henry Pipard presents as woodward for his wood of Puriho Robert de la Wade, who had been presented earlier at Brill before Hugh de Goldingham by his lord; who was sworn.

76 The Prior of Deerhurst presents as woodward for his wood of Taynton Pagan de Mobray, who had been presented earlier before all the Justices of the forest and before Ernald du Boys, then Justice of the forest; who was sworn.

77 The Chancellor of Salisbury presents as woodward for his wood of Stockley[40] Thomas de Stoleg', who had been presented earlier before William of Langley, forester, by his bailiff, William de Briklesworth, at the aforesaid lawn; who was sworn.

78 Roger Gulafre presents as woodward for his wood which belongs to Sarsden Thomas abovetun, who had earlier been presented by his lord before William of Langley; who was sworn.

79 Angaret Beauchamp[41] presents as woodward for her wood of Spelsbury Walter of Fulwell, who had been presented earlier before Thomas of Langley, then forester of Wychwood, by Simon of Merton her bailiff; who was sworn.

80 Lady Katherine Lovel presents as woodward for her wood of Minster Ralph Pyle, who had been presented earlier before the said William of Langley at the aforesaid Lawn by lord John Lovell; who was sworn.

---

[38] Pyriho/Puriho was the name of the woodland in Stanton Harcourt and South Leigh (which then was a hamlet of Stanton), and it was divided between the Stanton manors. See also **75** and **84**. *V.C.H. Oxfordshire xii*, 269, 274, 276 and 277.

[39] There were two woods belonging to Waterperry, but the one held by William FitzEllis was Ledhale Wood: *Rot. Hund. ii*, 725. It was in Bernwood Forest, of which Brill was the administrative centre.

[40] Stockley Wood belonged to the Chancellor of Salisbury Cathedral as part of the Prebend in Shipton and Swinbrook. The estate of Stockley is recorded separately in Domesday Book and was granted to Salisbury by Henry I in 1107x16: *DB OXF* 1, 6; *Regesta Regum Anglo-Normannorum II*, ed. H. A. Cronne and R.C.Davies, 138, No. 1163.

[41] Angaret Beauchamp, second wife of Walter Beauchamp who died in 1235, held Spelsbury in dower; *The Beauchamp Cartulary Charters 1100-1268*, ed. Emma Mason, Pipe Roll Society NS 43, xxxiij and lviij; *Rot. Hund. ii*, 746.

81   Reginald of Asthall presents as woodward for his wood of Widley Richard son of Pagan, who had been presented earlier before the said William the Forester at the aforesaid Lawn by the same Reginald; who was sworn.

82   James le Blund presents as woodward of his wood of Stockey[42] William son of Stephen, who had been presented earlier before the said William [of Langley] at the aforesaid lawn; who was sworn.

83   Lord William de Lungespee presents as woodward of his wood of Bicester William attewode, who had been presented earlier before lord Ernald du Boys at Brill by his steward; who was sworn.

84   Lord Richard de Harcourt presents as woodward of his wood of Pyriho John Stokeman, who had been presented earlier before the said lord Ernald at Woodstock by the same Richard; who was sworn.

85   The Abbot of Osney presents as woodward of his wood of Kidlington[43] Hugh Dirra, who had been presented earlier before William of Langley at the aforesaid Lawn by his lord; who was sworn.

86   The same Abbot presents as woodward of his wood of Arncott Simon le Vorn, who had been presented earlier at Brill before Walter de Derneford by the Abbott; who was sworn.

87   The same Abbot presents as woodward for his wood of Forest Hill Peter le Vouhel, who had been presented earlier before the lord Hugh de Golding-ham at Headington by the same Abbot; who was sworn.

88   The Prior of Bicester presents as woodward of his wood of Arncott Hamo, who had been presented earlier at Brill before William of Northampton then steward of the forest by the same prior; who was sworn.

89   The Prior of St. Frideswide of Oxford presents as woodward of his wood of Thomley Robert de Maydewell, who was sworn for the first time.

90   Walter de Wahull presents Osbert Cobbe as woodward of his wood of Chadlington, and he had been presented at another time before the lord Geoffrey de Langley at Asterleigh ; who was sworn.

91   The Master of the Temple presents as woodward of his wood of Puri-hale[44] Robert le Mey, who had been presented at another time at Brill before Hugh de Goldingham by the said Master; who was sworn.

---

[42] James le Blund held an estate in Fawler: *V.C.H. Oxfordshire x*, 138. Stockey is recorded as a boundary point in the 1298/1300 Perambulation of Wychwood Forest: *Eynsham Cart. ii*, 93.

[43] Osney's "wood of Kidlington" is that which had belonged to Kidlington in 1086, but was separated from the rest of the manor and given to Osney Abbey by Henry d'Oilly *circa* 1200. It was not in Kidlington, but situated at Osney Hill, now in North Leigh but formerly extra-parochial: *V.C.H. Oxfordshire xii*, 188.

[44] Purihale and Acremel (see **92**) were in Horspath, in the forest of Shotover, where their names survived in the Tithe Map of 1847 as The Perils and Acre Mead: *V.C.H. Oxfordshire v*, 181-2. The Templars are recorded as having a wood called Pirehale in Horspath in 1279, but woods called Akermel are recorded only for the manor there held by Edmund, earl of Cornwall, and the Musard fee manor held by John de Scaccario: *Rot. Hund. ii*, 716-7.

92   The same Master presents as woodward of his wood of Akermel William Gardener, who at another time had been presented at Oxford before lord Geoffrey de Langley by the Preceptor of the Temple at Cowley; who was sworn.

93   The Prioress of Littlemore presents Robert Burdun as woodward of her wood of Swalehull,[45] and at another time he had been presented before Geoffrey de Langley at Oxford by Adam her chaplain; who was sworn.

94   The Prior of St. Frideswide presents as woodward of his wood of Gery[46] Henry Coyfin, who at another time had been presented before the aforesaid Geoffrey by the same Prior; who was sworn

95   John FitzNigel presents as woodward of his wood of Perry[47] William Buchel, who at another time had been presented by the same John; who was sworn.

96   John of Elsfield presents Richard son of Ralph of Elsfield as woodward of his wood of Sydele, and at another time he was presented at Headington before Geoffrey de Langley; who was sworn.

97   The Abbott of Winchcombe presented as woodward of his wood of La Boxe[48] John de Neuton who at another time had been presented before William of Langley, the aforesaid forester, at the aforesaid Lawn; who was sworn.

98   Elias son of Robert of Thomley presents Stephen Aelfrith as woodward for his wood of Thomley; who was sworn.

99   The Abbot of Winchcombe presents John de Neuton as woodward of his wood of la Hyde; who was sworn.

m. 8 dorse]

Names of the Regarders of Wychwood

[No names entered]

---

[45]   This wood is recorded as being within Shotover in 1337, and was possibly the wood belonging to Littlemore which in 1246 was said to adjoin the wood granted at that date to the Hospital of St. John without the East Gate of Oxford: *Boarstall Cartulary,* 172, No. 565, *Cal. Chart. R. I 1226-1257,* 307. However Littlemore also held land at Minchincourt Farm, now in Forest Hill but formerly in Stanton St. John, where some wood still stood in 1788: *V.C.H. Oxfordshire v,* 125, 288.

[46]   Gery was in Bernwood. See p. 55, **12**.

[47]   This was the wood belonging to the smaller, Beaufeu, manor in Waterperry, which is recorded as being held by John FitzNigel in 1254: *Rot. Hund. ii,* 725; *V.C.H. Oxfordshire v,* 296.

[48]   La Boxe and La Hyde (see **99**) were in Enstone, which was held by the Abbey of Winchcombe. See p.190, No. **219**.

100   **Waste of Woods in Wychwood**

The Abbot of Eynsham's wood at Charlbury was made waste of old. Therefore in mercy.

The same Abbot's wood towards Spelsbury was made waste of old but is re-growing with underwood.

James le Blund's wood of Fawler was made waste of old.

The wood of Asterleigh around Lallingho was made waste of old and anew by the Lady Joan de Saucey. Therefore the wood *is to be taken*. And afterwards she fined for 2 marks to have her wood back, by sureties of Ralph Gamel of Asterleigh and William de Riston, clerk.

The wood of Wlokesham [error for Bloxham] was made waste of old and anew etc. In the keeping of lord John Gyrray. Therefore *it is to be taken*.

The wood of Glympton was made waste of old but is re-growing with underwood. In the keeping of lord Humphrey de Watton.

William le Moyne's wood of Shipton was made waste of old.

The wood of Witney is in [a state of] old waste.

Bladon wood is in [a state of] old waste, but is re-growing with underwood.

The wood of Wlokesham [Bloxham] towards Stonesfield was newly wasted.

Walter de Gray's wood was made waste of old .

The wood of the Prior of the Hospital towards Stanton was newly wasted.

The wood of W. Anketel and the wood of Geoffrey son of Nicholas de Wyccheford were newly made waste by these [men]. Therefore, etc.

[There are some illegible lines of writing at the bottom of this membrane, and an additional piece of parchment has been sewn onto it to create the present outer cover of the roll. This also bears some illegible words]

Pleas of the Forest in Oxfordshire one month after Easter Day in the 56th year of the reign of King Henry son of King John [22 May 1272] **before Roger de Clifford, Matthew de Colombars, Nicholas of Romsey and Reginald of Oakley, Justices appointed to hear and decide the same pleas.**

1   *Charter of the Abbot of Locus Sancti Edwardi* [Netley Abbey]
Henry by the grace of God King of England, Lord of Ireland and Duke of Aquitaine, to all his bailiffs and faithful subjects to whom the present letters shall have come, greetings. Let it be known that we have granted to our beloved in Christ, the Abbot of locus Sancti Edwardi, who has gone overseas on business for his church, that brother William of North Leigh, monk, and brother Felix de Selferton, lay brother, whom the same Abbot appointed in his place in our presence, are acknowledged as attorneys of the same Abbot to win or lose in all pleas or suits instituted by or against himself in whatsoever courts. And that the aforesaid William and Felix or either of them can appoint an attorney or attorneys to win or lose in place of the same Abbot in all the aforesaid pleas and suits, or remove the attorneys or attorney and substitute other attorneys or attorney in his place in the before-mentioned [suits] as often as seems to be expedient. And therefore we order you to receive the aforesaid William and Felix or either of them if both cannot be present, and the attorney or attorneys whom either or both of them may wish to depute or substitute in place of the Abbot himself, without obstruction in this. In testimony of this we have caused these our letters to be made patent for the term of the duration [of the Abbot's absence] unless meanwhile he returns from the said parts. Myself being witness, at Clarendon the fifth day of December in the 56th year of our reign [1271].

2   *Charter of the Abbot of Eynsham*[1]
Henry King of England and Duke of Normandy and Aquitaine and Count of Anjou to the Justices and sheriffs and ministers and foresters and regarders of the forests in Oxfordshire, greetings. Let it be known that we have granted to the Abbot and monks of Eynsham that they may assart and have in perpetual alms all the land which is between the Bladen and the stony way, and be quit of assart and not numbered among the assarts. These being witness, Manser Basset [Bisset] steward and Henry de Oylli constable at Woodstock.

---

[1]   This charter is also recorded in *Eynsham Cart. i,* 54, where it is dated to 1159x63. The Bladen is the river now known as the Evenlode, and the stony way must be in Charlbury, since at that date Eynsham Abbey did not hold Fawler. *V.C.H. Oxfordshire, x,* 138.

3   *Charter of the Templars*
The Lord King who now is granted to the brothers Knights of the Temple of
Solomon throughout England that all the lands and assarts belonging to them
and their men, already made with proper assent and to be made in the future,
should be quit in perpetuity of waste and regard and view of the forest and of
all other services. Further he granted to the same brothers that they could assart
and cultivate in all their woods which they have at present within the bounds of
the forest, without licence from him or his heirs and their bailiffs. So that they
would not be molested in anything by the same Lord King or his heirs or his
bailiffs in perpetuity. And the same Lord King willed that they and their men
should be quit in perpetuity of the expedition of their dogs, and the same
brothers and their successors should have all amercements of their men in
perpetuity, and that the same brothers should not be impleaded except before
the Lord King himself or his chief Justices.

4   *Charter of Bogo de Clare*
Henry by the grace of God King of England. Let it be known that by our special
grace we have pardoned our dearly beloved Bogo de Clare, Dean of Stafford,
and his men for all offences, wrongs and transgressions done by them in
whatsoever of our forests throughout England up to the present day. Wishing
and granting for ourselves and our heirs that the aforesaid Bogo and his men
aforesaid should be quit of the aforesaid offences, wrongs and transgressions in
the aforesaid forest. And therefore we order that the said Bogo and his men
should not be troubled or oppressed in anything against our aforesaid
concession. In testimony of this we have made our letters patent. Myself being
witness, at Westminster 26th day of May in the 56th year of our reign [1272]

5   *Charter of the Abbot of Bruern*
Let it be known to all men that John Abbot of Bruern made a fine with the Lord
King who now is for fifty marks, for all transgressions for which he was
prosecuted before Robert Passelewe, Geoffrey de Langley and their fellows,
Justices in eyre for the forest pleas in the County of Oxford, regarding waste
made in the demesne wood by the same Abbot of Bruern within the forest of
Wychwood etc.[2]

---

[2]   In *Cal. Pat. 1232-1247, 472,* it is recorded that on 20th January 1246, the Abbot of Bruern was
fined 500 marks by Robert Passelewe and Geoffrey de Langley when they held Pleas of the Forest in
Oxfordshire. This entry presumably records the final payment of a long-standing debt.

6   *Charter of Hugh de Plescy*

King John granted and confirmed by his charter to Thomas Basset, who is dead, and his heirs, to whose right and inheritance Hugh de Plescy succeeded, that they should have by inheritance in perpetuity warren in the manors of Kidlington and Wytteford. And that the said Thomas and his heirs should have their dogs throughout the whole land of the said Lord King Henry [sic] to hunt wolves, hares and cats. Wherefore he wishes etc. that they should have the aforesaid liberty without any vexation, complaint, hindrance or accusation in perpetuity as aforesaid.

7   *Charter of the Abbot of Osney*[3]

Henry the King who now is granted and confirmed by his charter to the Abbot and Convent of Osney, for himself and his heirs in perpetuity, that he and his successors, from their woods within the bounds of the forest in the Counties of Oxford and Buckingham, could take and carry away their estovers without complaint or hindrance, freely and without view and delivery or danger of the foresters and verderers or other bailiffs of the same Lord King, provided that they did not thereby make waste or destruction or assart. But that if they should make waste or destruction thereby, by selling or in another way, they would be punished for this according to the assize of his forest; saving to the same Abbot and convent their enclosed parks and groves of Forest Hill in Stow with the liberty and freedom which they used to have in them. Wherefore he wished and firmly ordered [this]

8   *Charter of the lord Osbert Giffard*

Henry by the grace of God King of England etc. To all to who the present letters will come, greetings. Let it be known that we have pardoned our well-beloved and faithful Osbert Giffard and all others of his household and company all offences and transgressions which they made by reason of the non-observance of the provision or statute of Oxford,[4] as is said, concerning which a disturbance formerly arose in our reign, and also all actions brought against the same petitioners by reason of the aforesaid offences and transgressions up to the present day. And moreover we have remised them of all rancour and odium which we conceived for them for the aforesaid reason, up to the aforesaid day, promising them with good faith that we will willingly keep them immune from injury from anyone complaining or about to complain about them by reason of the offences and transgressions made by them at the

---

3   This charter is also recorded in *Cartulary of Oseney Abbey,* ed H.E. Salter, Oxfordshire Historical Society *iv,* 41. "Stow" is Stowood. Osney Abbey's enclosed grove called Horsmoor in Forest Hill is recorded in 1279: *Rot. Hund. ii,* 717.

4   Also recorded in *Cal. Pat. 1266-1272,* 279. Osbert Giffard, having fought for Simon de Montfort at the battle of Lewes, changed sides, was pardoned by the king, and made "keeper of the peace in Oxford and the surrounding parts" in the later stages of the rebellion: *Cal. Pat. 1258-1266,* 670.

time of the aforesaid dispute, and we have caused our letters patent to be made separately for everyone whomsoever of his household and company, in the aforesaid form, since the said Osbert petitioned us through his letters patent and brought those being of his household and company at the aforesaid time to testify that they would be true and faithful to us and our heirs in future. In witness of this testimony we have made these our letters patent. Myself being witness at Westminster 10th day of March in the fifty-second year of our reign [1268].

9 *Charter of Alexander de Aundeville*[5]
Henry the king who now is granted to Alexander de Aundeville that for the whole period of his life he should have this liberty, namely that with his own dogs he could hunt hares, wolves, badgers and cats throughout all the forests of himself the Lord King in the County of Oxford whenever he wished, except the forbidden month. And take them freely and carry them away where he wished without molestation and hindrance to him and his heirs by the Justices, verderers, foresters and all his other bailiffs and ministers of the forest. Provided that he does not, by reason of this grant, take any of his great beasts nor hunt in his warrens nor in the warrens of others. In testimony etc. Given at Woodstock, the 11th day of August in the fifty-first year of the reign of the same Lord King [1267].

10 *Charter of the Abbot of Abingdon*[6]
Henry the King who now is granted to the Abbot of Abingdon and the Monks serving God there and their successors in perpetuity, for himself and his heirs, that the Abbot and monks could enclose with a ditch and hedge twentysix and a half acres from which they gave the crop of wood to the same Lord King for the building of the walls of his town of Oxford,[7] which acres they caused to be assarted previously in their wood of Shawe with the permission of the Lord King; they could enclose [them] with a ditch and hedge, and could cultivate those acres without hindrance, provided that the beasts of the chase could enter and leave freely. And that those acres should be quit in perpetuity of waste made in them up to the time of the making of this his present charter. Wherefore he wished etc.

---

[5] Also recorded in *Cal. Pat. 1266-1272*, 97. Alexander de Aundeville was lord of Pudlicote: *Rot. Hund. ii*, 731.
[6] This grant, with others, is also recorded in *Cal. Chart. R.* I, 121, and in *Two Cartularies of Abingdon Abbey*, ed. Gabrielle Lambrick and C F Slade, vol. 2, Oxfordshire Historical Society 33 (1991), 280.
[7] Osbert Giffard was ordered to "repair the ... defects of the wall ... of the town [of Oxford]" on 27 April 1266: *Cal. Pat. 1258-66*, 663.

m. 1 dorse]

11 *Charter of Walter Archbishop of York*
Henry the king who now is granted to Walter, Archbishop of York, Primate of England, and his heirs or assigns and their heirs, that his own wood of Cogges, which the same Archbishop has within the Forest of Wychwood and which he bought from Joan Arsic and Thomas de Hyde and Alexandra his wife, should be, in perpetuity, [free] of regard and view of the foresters and verderers and all their bailiffs and ministers, and that they [the archbishop and his heirs] should cause the wood to be kept by their own forester. So that in respect of that wood they are not answerable to any forester or verderer of himself the Lord King nor to their bailiffs or ministers, except only to his chief Justices of the forest and their heirs. And that henceforth no forester nor bailiff nor minister of the same forest by reason of the said forest should come to the house of himself, the Archbishop, or of his heirs or assigns or their heirs, or of his men or to any of their lands for lodging there or food except by their own goodwill. He, the Lord King, wished and granted for himself and his heirs to the same Archbishop that he and his heirs or assigns and their heirs and his men should be quit of all waste made in the same wood up to the day of the making of this charter. Wherefore he wished etc. Given by the hand of the said Lord King at Winchester the 28th day of April in the 26th year of his reign [1242]

12 *Charter of the Prior of St. Frideswide*[8]
Henry the king who now is gave and granted to the Prior and canons of Saint Frideswide his wood of Gery, contained within the following bounds, namely, that wood which lies between Panshill towards the east and Arngrove towards the east [sic] and the wood of John de Fresney towards the south and the wood of the lepers of the Hospital of Saint Bartholomew outside Oxford towards the north. To be held etc. of the said Lord King by the same Prior and Canons and their successors in free pure and perpetual alms. Furthermore the same King granted to the same Prior and Canons that the said wood should be quit of waste in perpetuity, and that they could take their estovers in that wood without hindrance. Wherefore he wished etc.

[8] This grant is also recorded in the *Cartulary of the Monastery of St. Frideswide,* ed. S. R. Wigram, Oxf. Hist. Soc. XXXI, *I*, 52, No. 50 and in *Cal. Chart. R. 1226-1257,* 113, where it is dated 6 February 1229/30. In both Gery was said to be between Panshill on the east and Arngrove on the west (in Bernwood Forest).

m. 2]

Pleas of the Forest in the County of Oxford one month after Easter in the fifty-sixth year in the reign of Henry son of King John before Roger de Clifford, Matthew de Colombars and Nicholas of Romsey, appointed to hear and determine those pleas.

13   Names of those who presented themselves on the first day

Richard son of Thomas of Piddington
Michael Fromund of the same
Henry de Preston of Chadlington
William clerk of the same
Richard Terry of the same
Richard le Colyere of Ditchley
Hugh le Colyere of the same
Adam le Fox of the same
Ralph of Chilson
John atte Wode of Stonesfield
Walter Mundelgume of Hailey
William Valance of the same
William atte Mershe of Stonesfield

14   Those excused [because] of death

Geoffrey at Well of Chilson by Ralph son of Geoffrey of the same
William Tocy by John Long of Combe
Humphrey reeve of Combe by John Gode of the same
Robert atte hethe of the same by Robert his son of the same
William Edune of the same by Reginald of Hanborough
Alan Edune of the same by John Edune of the same
Robert atte Stokke of the same by Reginald atte Stokke of the same
Osbert Botte of the same by Peter le Chaunceler of the same
William le May of the same by John le May of the same
Robert Aldun of Stonesfield by Walter son of Emma of the same
William Wastepayn of Wheatley by Simon Boylon of the same
John Terry of Combe by Thomas West of the same
Hugh le Scwak of Brill by William Bynne of the same
William de Bray by Richard of Boriens
Geoffrey Cobbler of Wilcote by William Alayn of Combe
Robert Frayn of Combe by Thomas dame Alys of the same
William Joye of Stonesfield by Thomas atte Grene
William Edward of Enstone by John son of William of the same
Robert Russel of Taynton by Matthew reeve of the same
Walter atte Boxe by Ralph of Ditchley

15   Of Vert in Wychwood

[In the document the following is written in two columns.]

[Column 1]

From William le Freman of Ascott for vert in demesne	2s.
From Roger attehulle of Radford for a surety	2s.
From William atte Welle of Enstone for the same	2s.
From Nicholas son of Alexander of Leafield for the same	2s.
From Walter son of Robert of Ramsden for the same	2s.
From Robert de Beningho of [North] Leigh for vert in demesne	2s.
From Walter Yngeleys of North Leigh for a surety	2s.
From Hugh de Beningho for vert in demesne	2s.
From John le Freman of Ascott for vert in demesne	4s.
(From William de Oylly of Walcot for the same	12d.)
From William le Kreps of the same for a surety	2s.
From William Goddot of Leafield for the same	12d.
From Walter of Hanborough <of Ramsden > in Hailey for vert	4s.
From Alexander son of Roger of the same for a surety	½ mark
From William son of Robert Coy of the same for the same	2s.
From Richard son of Roger of Ramsden for vert	4s.
From Walter Colling senior of Ascott for a surety	12d.
From Richard Utlawe of Walcot for vert	2s.
From Walter Roger of Shorthampton for the same	2s.
From Hugh le Carboner of Ditchley for vert	elsewhere
From William Harold of Finstock for attachment as a charcoal burner	2s.
From Walter in Angulo of the same for a surety and for vert	4s.
From Henry Wylot of the same for the same	2s.
From John Crabbe of Wilcote for a surety	12d.
From Adam Wymark of Shipton for vert in demesne	½ mark
From Richard Gunnild of the same for a surety	2s.
From William Tril of Ascott for vert	2s.
From Richard son of Roger of Ramsden for the same	4s.
From Walter de Wytenhull of la Leye [North Leigh] for a surety	2s.
From Robert Tryl of Leafield for vert	12d.
From Richard of Hanborough in Ramsden for the same	4s.
From Walter of Hanborough in the same for the same	2s.
From William Cubbel of Walcot for vert in demesne	2s.
From Henry Devereus of the same for the same	2s.
From Humphrey Baker of Woodstock for vert	[blank]
From William Saleman of Leafield for the same	5s.
From Geoffrey Saleman (of the same) for the same	2s.
From Ralph (Terry) of Slape for vert	2s.

From William Doylly of Walcot for the same	elsewhere
From William atte Hurne in Wilcote for a surety	40d.
From Nicholas Alex' atte Feld [Leafield] for vert	elsewhere
From Robert Bole in Leafield for a surety	12d.
From Richard Calkayn of Ascott for vert	12d.
From Reginald Harold of Wilcote for a surety	2s.
From Stephen Coy of the same for a surety	½ mark
From John of Boriens for vert outside [demesne]	2s.
From John Loveny of Bladon for the same	2s.
From Walter Bothe of the same for the same	2s.
From Roger Harold of North Leigh for the same *elsewhere*	12d.
From Walter Wal of the same for a surety	4s.
From Walter Waryn of Shorthampton for vert	12d.
From Nigel le Tornor	dead
From John le Poter of Ascott for vert	12d.
From Richard Paynel of Fawler for the same	2s.
From John Poue of Charlbury for a surety	2s.
From Elias le Peleter of the same for the same	2s.
From Geoffrey of Woodstock in Shorthampton for vert	2s.
From Walter of Walcot for a surety	12d.
From Robert of Brailes in Charlbury for the same	12d.
From Richard son of Walter of Shorthampton for the same	12d.
From William Trobbel of Charlbury for the same	2s.
From Stephen Aluerd of Stonesfield for the same	2s.
From Robert of Witney in Charlbury for the same	2s.
From Robert Aldon of Stonesfield for the same	2s.
From Ralph Lorens of Leafield for a surety	2s.
From Geoffrey Daunvers of Fawler for the same	2s.
From Robert atte Wode of Stonesfield for the same	2s.
From Adam Smith of Wilcote for a surety	12d.
From John Harold of Finstock for vert	½ mark
From Walter Dodde of Fawler for the same	2s.
From Thomas son of Walter of Stonesfield for a surety	2s.
From Robert le Kyng of Finstock for the same	2s.
From Philip of Felelegh[9] for a surety	12d.
From Robert Copping of North Leigh for vert	12d.
From Nicholas son of Hugh of the same for a surety	12d.
From Nicholas Burgeys of Leafield for the same	2s.
From Simon Fyge of the same for the same	12d.
From Ralph Miller of Fawler for the same	12d.
From Stephen Coker of the same for the same	2s.

[9] Felelegh (Phelleley) was the site of a small monastic settlement or hermitage in Bloxham Wood. *V.C.H. Oxfordshire, ix,* 79.

[Column 2]

From Thomas le Charpenter of Stonesfield for a surety and for vert	2s.
From Robert le Frere of the same for the same	12d.
From John Forthriht of Leafield for vert	12d.
From Richard Cosin of the same for a surety	12d.
From Nicholas son of Geoffrey of the same for the same	12d.
From Simon Hod of Leafield for the same	12d.
From Walter of Walcot in Charlbury for vert	12d.
From Geoffrey Sturthup of the same for the same	2s.
From Henry Bole of the same for the same	2s.
From John Thedone of Wilcote for the same	40d.
From Richard Gest of Ascott for the same	12d.
From John Dawe of Stonesfield for the same	2s.
From William Sprot of Combe for the same	12d.
From Robert de la Hethe of the same for the same	elsewhere
From Thomas West of the same for the same	½ mark
From Thomas Aleyn of Combe for the same	2s.
From Hugh Wood of the same for the same	12d.
From Robert Sewadd of the same for the same	40d.
From John de Saucey of the same for the same	2s.
(From John Herberd of the same for the same	12d.)
From John Miller of the same for the same	[erased, ?2s.]
From William Ferbras of the same for a surety	4s.
From Walter Emme of Stonesfield for vert	12d.
From Robert son of John of Combe for the same	2s.
From John Sewad of the same for the same	12d.
From William attestreme of the same for the same	r
From Robert le Lung of the same for the same	12d.
From Robert Norman of the same for the same	2s.
From Richard Hokedol of Stonesfield for the same	12d.
From Robert <Fabro> le Frere of the same for the same	12d.
From Robert son of William atte Hethe of the same for the same	12d.
From Thomas son of Alice West of the same for the same	12d.
From Reginald Est of the same for the same	2s.
From Alan Edone of the same for the same	dead
From Nicholas son of Matilda of the same for the same	12d.
From Robert atteWythege of the same for the same	12d.
From John le Frere of Stonesfield for the same	2s.
From John le Wriste of the same for the same	12d.
From William Sprot of Combe for the same	2s.
From John le Clerk of the same for a surety	12d.
From Robert Creps of the same for the same	2s.

From Alan Edyeth of the same for the same	12d.
From Walter atte Hethe of the same for the same	12d.
From Richard son of Matilda of Stonesfield for the same	12d.
From William son of Alan of Combe for the same	12d.
From William le Lung of Stonesfield for the same	2s.
From William le Frere of the same for the same	[illegible]
From Geoffrey Joye of the same for a surety	12d.
From John Slodde of Combe for vert	12d.
From Robert attestreme of the same for the same	12d.
From John son of John Waleraund of Stonesfield for a surety	2s.
From Nicholas son of Hugh of Stonesfield for vert	12d.
From Alan West of Combe for the same	12d.
From Robert Est of the same for the same	12d.
From William son of Nicholas of Stonesfield for the same	40d.
From Richard Alayn of Combe for the same	[illegible]
From John Galeway of the same for the same	12d.
From Alan Galeway of the same for the same	[illegible]
From Ralph of Chadlington of the same for the same	12d.
From Robert Fesaunt of the same for the same	[illegible]
From John Wythod of the same for the same	40d.
From Reginald of Stockey of Combe for the same	[illegible]
From Walter son of John Waleraund of Stonesfield for the same	[illegible]
From Stephen Alured of the same for the same	elsewhere
From John Emme of the same for the same	12d.
From Robert atte Boxe of Combe for the same	12d.
From Thomas son of Alan West of the same for the same	2s.
From Stephen son of Nicholas of Stonesfield for the same	12d.
From Reginald Baldon of Combe for the same	12d.
From Andrew of Stonesfield for the same	2s.
From Simon son of Robert le Lung of the same for the same	12d.
From Robert Cok of Combe for the same	elsewhere
From Richerus of Stonesfield for the same	elsewhere
From Richard Sweyn of Finstock for the same	2s.
From Robert Gode of Combe for the same	12d.
From Thomas atte Grene of Stonesfield for the same	elsewhere

m. 2 dorse]

16   [Column 1]

From Peter le Chaunceler of Combe for the same	2s.
From Robert Margarete of the same for the same	[blank]
From Thomas Creps of the same for the same	40d.
From John le Mey of the same for the same	12d.
From John Wulnaf of the same for the same	12d.
From John Alayn of Combe for the same	12d.
From William underWode of Leafield for the same	½ mark
From Geoffrey le Lepare of the same for the same	4s.
From Roger Tryl of the same for the same.	2s.
From William attebroke of Fulbrook for the same	½ mark
From Kimme Clement of the same for the same	½ mark
From Gilbert le Tylkere of the same for the same	½ mark
From Henry Miller of the same for the same	40d.
From William Orpede of Leafield for the same	12d.
From Richard le Poter of the same for the same	12d.
From Nicholas le Poter of the same for the same	12d.
From Walter Durolf of <Ascott> Baunton' for the same	12d.
From Isaac son of Geoffrey of Chilson for the same	12d.
From Walter Lefgyve of Shipton for the same	40d.
From Robert Curteys of Stonesfield for the same	12d.
From John Upehulle of Combe for the same	40d.
From Reginald of Hardeberwe [sic, Hanborough] of the same for the same	2s.
From John clerk of the same for the same	dead
From William Kyn of Fulbrook for the same	40d.
From John Lovel of Combe for the same	12d.
From Thomas Lovel of the same for the same	12d.
From John at the Mill of the same for the same	elsewhere
From John le Akerman of the same for the same	elsewhere
From Walter le Chaunceler of the same for the same	12d.
From William Aldon of the same for the same	12d.
From William Creps of the same for the same	12d.
From Simon of Slape for the same	2s.
From Geoffrey de Radeweye of the same for the same	poor
From Roger of Slape for the same	12d.
From William le Lepere of the same for the same	12d.
From Robert Martin of Boriens for the same	2s.
From John Brid of the same for the same	12d.
From William son of Hugh of Glympton for the same	elsewhere
From John Mauncel of the same for the same	12d.
From Richard Bouquer of the same for the same	12d.

From Gilbert le Moner of the same for the same	12d.
From William Jordan of the same for the same	12d.
From Thomas Tragyn of the same for the same	12d.
From Roger Tragyn of the same for the same	12d.
From John son of Henry of Boriens in the same for the same	2s.
From John a bovetune in Glympton for the same	2s.
From Alan de Dene in Kiddington for the same	2s.
From Hugh Smith of the same for the same	12d.
From Roger Gold of the same for the same	12d.
From Fray Punchard of the same for the same	2s.
From Robert Chop of the same for the same	2s.
From Ralph aboveton of the same for the same	12d.
From William Upehulle of Wootton for the same	2s.
From Thomas le Capiere of the same for the same	2s.
From Robert Lovesone of the same for the same	12d.
From Richard le Mey of the same for the same	12d.
From John Holeweye of the same for the same	12d.
From Thomas Trut of the same for the same	12d.
From John le Capyere of the same for the same	2s.
From John Tuf of the same for the same	12d.
From Nicholas Cut of the same for the same	12d.
From Hugh Budde of the same for the same	[margin only] *dead*
From John le Rowere of the same for the same	2s.
From William Kemel of the same for the same	2s.
From William Vigerus of the same for the same	12d.
From Edith widow of the same for the same	[erased, 12d.]
From William of Ludwell of the same for the same	2s.
From William Londen of the same for the same	12d.
From Roger Russel of the same for the same	12d.
From William Prat of the same for the same	40d.
From Isabella of Hensington for the same	[blank]
From Stephen Malebisse of the same for the same	12d.
From Walter Lewy of the same for the same	12d.
From Walter Thurkyl of the same for the same	2s.
From Adam Lovesone of the same for the same	12d.
From Geoffrey Brun of the same for the same	[blank]
From Alice Edwaker of Combe for the same	elsewhere
From Juliana Slodde of the same for the same	[blank]
From Adam Wymark of Shipton for the same	½ mark
From Nicholas atte Wythege of the same for the same	½ mark
From William son of Roger Creps of Combe for the same	12d.
From Lovekin of Hanborough (of North Leigh) for the same	2s.

From Walter le Mershe of North Leigh for the same	2s.
From Hugh Dyrray of the same for the same	2s.
From Thomas Godefray of the same for the same	2s.
From Walter Yngelays of the same for the same	4s.
From Lovekin son of the same of the same for the same	2s.
From Robert Jones of the same for the same	2s.
From Giles le Walays of Hailey for the same	12d.
From Walter de Panyton' of the same for the same	12d.
From John de Wolleshulle in Ramsden for the same	elsewhere
From Henry, servant of the same John, for the same	elsewhere
From John Gek of the same for the same	12d.
From William son of Roger of Ramsden for the same	2s.
From Walter of Hanborough in Ramsden for the same	12d.
From Richard of Denlegh in Hailey for the same	12d.
From William brother of the same Richard of the same for the same	12d.
From William le Iofne of Hailey for the same	2s.
From John Lovekin of <the same> Cherdesle[10] for the same	12d.
From Ralph le Cir of Ramsden for the same	12d.
From Adam de la Chaumbre of the same for the same	12d.
From John Hirdman of the same for the same	12d.
From John Manyman of the same for the same	12d.
From Richard son of Geoffrey of Poffley for the same	2s.
From Jordan at Well of Witney for the same	4s.
From Richard of Hailey, servant of the same, for the same	12d.
From Richard son of William of Ramsden	12d.

[Column 2]

From Walter de Wytenhulle of North Leigh for the same	12d.
From Reginald Harold of the same for the same	2s.
From Walter Waryn of Shorthampton for the same	12d.
From Stephen Doberal of Witney for the same	2s.
From Roger Ballard of the same for the same	12d.
From John Ballard of the same for the same	4s.
From Henry le Gyn of Hailey for the same	2s.
From Robert of Cherdeslegh' of the same for the same	2s.
From Richard de Wythrode of the same for the same	½ mark
From Richard Sirecock of Crawley for the same	12d.
From Richard Hilde of Hailey for the same	dead
From Richard le Carpenter of the same for the same	12d.

[10] Cherdesle was possibly a hamlet in the northern half of Witney manor although its location is not known. Denlegh (above) and Poffley (below) were other hamlets there, which have survived as Delly End and Poffley End.

From Richard le Wodeward of the same for the same	2s.
From John de Lusingrave of the same for the same	12d.
From Geoffrey of Poffley of the same for the same	12d.
From William Such of the same for the same	2s.
From Walter Hilde of the same for the same	12d.
From Walter Edone of the same for the same	12d.
From Richard Ruter of the same for the same	12d.
From Richard Malyn of the same for the same	12d.
From Richard Costowe of the same for the same	2s.
From Walter atte Mershe of North Leigh for the same	2s.
From John atte Mershe of the same for the same	2s.
From Lovekyn Bagard of the same for the same	2s.
From John in the Wolde of the same for the same	2s.
From William de Wytenhulle of the same for the same	2s.
From Walter le Bulke of the same for the same	12d.
From Walter in the Wolde of the same for the same	2s.
From Richard Aylward of the same for the same	12d.
From Jordan Notbein of the same for the same	40d.
(From John le Lokere of the same for the same	4s.
From William Carpenter of the same for the same	2s.
From John Cole of the same for the same	4s.
From William le May of the same for the same	½ mark
From Hugh Aunfray of the same for the same	2s.
From Alexander son of Roger of Ramsden for the same	4s.
From William Faukener of the same for the same	12d.
From Robert de Hardepenne of the same for the same	½ mark
From Robert Osbern of the same for the same	½ mark
From Richard de Wytenhulle of the same for the same	12d.
From John de Wytenhulle of the same for the same	2s.
From William Terry of Combe for the same	[blank]
From William Bisshop of the same for the same	12d.
From Robert Cok of the same for the same	elsewhere

17 It was presented and found by all the ministers of the forest that John le Wyte of Ditchley, Hugh son of Nicholas of the same, John Harold of Finstock, Humphrey son of Ralph in Ramsden (2s.), Gilbert Cross of the same (12d.), Richard of Hanborough in Ramsden are habitual wrongdoers to the vert, as much in the demesne woods of the Lord King as in the woods of others in the forest, both by day and by night. They are also charcoal burners in the same, without warrant; who came and being convicted regarding this are in prison.

m. 3]
Pleas of the Venison of the Forest of Wychwood

18   It was presented and found by Thomas of Langley, Chief Forester of the forest of Wychwood and by Henry of Ditchley and John de Legh, sons and heirs of Ralph of Ditchley and Peter de Legh, formerly verderers in the said forest, who presented the rolls of their deceased fathers, and also by John of Fifield (1 mark), Stephen de la More (1 mark), Walter of Sarsden (1 mark) and Nicholas Gardener (1 mark), now verderers in the same forest, that Henry of Kidlington, Walter Mundelgome of Hailey, William Valence of the same, John Attewode of Stonesfield, Adam le Fox of Ditchley, Robert son of Robert atte Hethe of Combe, Adam of Hanborough, Henry of Hanborough his brother, Simon de Dissinton [and] Hugh son of Nicholas le Carboner of Ditchley are habitual evildoers to the Lord King's venison in the aforesaid Forest. And the aforesaid Walter, William, Adam le Fox, [Adam] of Hanborough and Hugh came and were committed to prison. And the aforesaid Henry of Kidlington and Simon de Dissinton were not found therefore they are to be exacted etc.. And the aforesaid Henry did not come nor does he have [anything] by which he can be attached, but he is said to be in Scotland, therefore he is not outlawed, but he was bailed by William of St. Owen, William of Hanborough, Stephen of Walcot, Thomas le Boteler of Wilcote and the aforesaid Adam brother of the same Henry; who bailed to have him before the Justices wherever they were in Eyre fifteen days after Michaelmas [13th October], or before the Chief Justices wherever the Lord King's parliament was then, if the Justices were not in Eyre, to satisfy etc.. And the aforesaid Robert atte Hethe did not come nor was he attached. Therefore the Sheriff is instructed that he should make him come from day to day. Afterwards the aforesaid John atte Wode came and was committed to prison. And the aforesaid Henry of Hanborough came and was committed to prison.

19   It was presented by the same etc. that William son of Hugh of Glympton is a frequent evildoer to the venison in the aforesaid Forest, who was taken elsewhere and handed over on bail, by the order of the Lord King, to the lord Nicholas of Yattendon,[11] Walter de Crokesford in Kidlington, William of Boriens, Richard of Boriens, John Boveton of Glympton, John Aleyn of the same, Richard le Pipere of the same, Thomas Cok of the same, Roger atte Dene of the same, Roger son of Hugh of the same, and Ralph Carter of the same, who did not have him on the first day, therefore they themselves are *in mercy*. Afterwards the said William son of Hugh came and was committed to *prison*.

---

[11] Lord of the manor of Glympton in right of his marriage to Aline, widow of Henry of Bath who had bought the manor. *V.C.H. Oxfordshire ix,* 123.

Furthermore the vills of Wootton, Blokesle,[12] Nether Kiddington and Asterleigh did not come fully to the inquisitions made regarding the accomplices of the same William, therefore they are *in mercy*.

20 It was presented by the same and found that Walter de Bekeford, a servant and member of the household of Ralph, woodward of the Abbot of Winchcombe for his wood of La Boxe, used to carry a bow and arrows both in the aforesaid wood and elsewhere in the Forest, (under the aforesaid woodward) against the assize of the forest since he had not been sworn; and that the same Walter hunted a stag in the aforesaid Forest, namely in the Lord King's wood of Bloxham, on Saturday next after the feast of the Purification of the Blessed Mary in the 49th year [7 February 1265], which afterwards was found dead and putrid by the Lord King's huntsmen. The aforesaid Walter, when he knew that he had been indicted for the aforesaid offence by the inquisition made regarding it by the vills of Wootton, Glympton, and Kiddington, absconded and now is excused by reason of his death.

21 The vills of Asthall, Fulbrook, Swinbrook and Widford, Charlbury, Spelsbury, Fifield and Taynton did not come fully when summoned to certain inquisitions regarding wrongdoers in the Forest, therefore *in mercy*.

22 John le Capiere of Wootton and Ralph of Slape did not have before the Justices Geoffrey of Slape, for whom they were sureties. Therefore *in mercy*.

23 It was presented etc. that Henry of Preston of Chadlington and William clerk of the same are evildoers to the venison in the aforesaid Forest, and that the same Henry and William were taken in the Abbot of Eynsham's wood above Charlbury and imprisoned for that reason until they were freed by writ of the Justices of the forest. And now they came and being convicted of this were committed to *prison*.

24 It was presented etc, that Richard Terry of Chadlington, who was the woodward of Walter de Pridinton for his wood of Chadlington, is an evildoer to the Lord King's deer in the aforesaid forest with certain devices which are called trappes; who was captured with these devices in the aforesaid wood of which he was woodward, acting wrongly at that time as aforesaid. He was led to the prison at Langley[13] (and detained there) until he was handed over on bail, by writ of the Lord King. Now he came and being convicted of this was

---

[12] This is presumably a name for that part of the hamlet of Ditchley which was in Bloxham Wood.
[13] Home, by this date, of the hereditary Forester of Wychwood.

committed to *prison*. And the aforesaid wood was taken into the Lord King's hand. *Let the wood be taken.*

25   It was presented etc. that Hugh le Carboner of Ditchley and Richard le Carboner of the same are habitual evildoers to the Lord King's deer in the aforesaid forest with various devices; who were taken and imprisoned until they were freed on bail by the Lord King's writ; and now they came and were committed to *prison*.

26   It was presented etc. that William atte Mershe of Stonesfield is an evil-doer to the Lord King's venison in the aforesaid Forest. Who came and was committed to *prison* .

27   It was presented etc. that Richard Cok of Stonesfield, Henry of Charlbury, Philip son of Richard le Bedel of the same, [and] Thomas Pylet of Langley are habitual evildoers to the venison in the aforesaid Forest and were frequently received, with the venison which they caught, at the house of Robert of Ware, parson of the Church of Kiddington, and at the house of Robert vicar of the church of Cassington and at the house of Robert vicar of the parish church of Eynsham and at the house of Master Bartholomew, parson of the church of Charlbury, who knew of the evil deeds of these men, and supported them with rewards which they gave them. And the aforesaid Richard came and was committed to *prison*. And the aforesaid Philip fled and cannot be found, therefore he is *to be exacted* etc. And the Bishop of Lincoln is *commanded* to cause the said clerics, who are beneficed in his diocese, to come on Thursday in the octave of Ascension [9 June 1272]. And the sheriff is *instructed* to make the aforesaid Thomas and Henry come from day to day. And since the same Thomas was a forester in the aforesaid forest at the time when he was an evildoer as aforesaid, therefore Richard de Pomeray of [Brize] Norton[14] and Simon Truant of Shipton, his sureties that he would faithfully serve the Lord King, are *in mercy*. Afterwards Henry of Charlbury came and was committed to *prison*. And the aforesaid Master Bartholomew came and was committed to *prison*. And the aforesaid Thomas Pilet came and was committed to *prison*.

28   It was presented that John of Slape, Nicholas brother of the lord John of St. Valery and Ralph son of Roger the parson of the church of Widford are evildoers to the venison of the Lord King in the aforesaid Forest. And they did not come, nor were they attached. And the aforesaid Ralph was not found therefore he is to be exacted etc. And the sheriff was instructed to distrain the aforesaid John of St. Valery so that he has the aforesaid Nicholas his brother

---

[14]   Richard de Pomeray is recorded as holding a tenure in Brize Norton in 1279: *Rot. Hund. ii*, 693.

from day to day, since he is of his family and household and used to be received at his house at Fulbrook, John however not knowing about his wrongdoing. And the sheriff was instructed to make the aforesaid John (of Slape) come from day to day. Afterwards the said John of Slape came and was committed to *prison*. And Ralph came and was committed to prison.

m. 3 dorse]

29   It was presented by the same and found that Alexander Daundeville, Thomas Chendut and William le Chaumberlayn his squires, Andrew his huntsman and Haykin (of Chilson), who at some time was his woodward for his wood belonging to his manor of Pudlicote, are habitual evildoers to the venison in the aforesaid forest with dogs and greyhounds, bows and arrows. And Nicholas of Langley, Thomas son of Thomas de la Thurne [and] Robert of Chilson son of the aforesaid Haykin are likewise wrongdoers with them. And the aforesaid William and Nicholas came and were committed to *prison*. And the aforesaid Alexander *has a day*, namely the Sunday next after the feast of the Ascension of the Lord [5 June 1272], to answer regarding the said offence and to have before the Justices all others who are of his household and his men. And the aforesaid Haykin was Woodward of the aforesaid wood and sworn to the Lord King regarding his venison at the time when he was an offender both in the same wood and elsewhere in the forest as aforesaid, therefore the same *wood is to be taken* into the hands of the Lord King. And the aforesaid Thomas de la Thurne came and was committed to *prison*. Afterwards the aforesaid Alexander and Thomas Chenduyt came and were committed to prison.

30   It was presented etc. that John le Eyr of Leafield, John de Wolseshulle, Robert the son of the former vicar of Ascott and Philip at the Mill of Pudlicote are evildoers to the venison in the aforesaid Forest. The aforesaid John and Philip came and were committed to *prison*. And the aforesaid Robert was not attached nor was he found. Therefore he is to be exacted etc.. And the aforesaid John de Wolseshulle did not come therefore the sheriff was instructed to make him come from day to day.

31   It was presented by the same and found that Crespus le Noreys, woodward of the Bishop of Winchester for his wood belonging to his Manor of Witney, is a frequent evildoer to the venison both in that wood and elsewhere in the Forest with certain other persons of the same Bishop's liberty, for whose names enquiry is to be made more fully, and the leader of many malefactors in the same Forest in their wrongdoing. And the aforesaid Crispus came and was committed to prison.

32 It was presented etc. that Robert le Ireys of Spelsbury, Richard Payn of Swinbrook, William le Lung of Stonesfield, Richerus atteGrene of the same, John le Wyte of Ditchley, William le Wyte of the same, Hugh in the Wolde of North Leigh, and William his son are evildoers to the venison in the aforesaid Forest. And that the aforesaid (Robert) is the leader of more wrongdoers in the same forest. And the aforesaid Richard Payn and John le Wyte came and were committed to *prison*. It was found also that Thomas Attegrene of Stonesfield is likewise an evildoer to the venison, who came and was committed to *prison*. And William le Lung came and was committed to *prison*. And the aforesaid Richerus came and was committed to *prison*.

33 It was presented etc. that Simon son of Simon [word erased] parson of Great Tew is a harbourer of the aforesaid John le Wyte, an evildoer to the venison, and his supporter in wrongdoing and his accomplice in his crimes, giving him wheat and other rewards for the venison which he brings him from the forest; who did not come nor was he attached. Therefore the Bishop of Lincoln is *commanded* to make him come on Thursday in the octave of the Ascension of the Lord [9 Jun 1272].

34 It was presented that James Beauchamp (parson of the church of Chadlington) with certain others for whose names inquiry is to be made took a doe in the aforesaid forest at Little Dustfield[15] on Sunday next after the feast of the Assumption of the blessed Mary in the 55th year [16 August 1271]. Who did not come, nor was he attached. Therefore the Bishop of Lincoln is *commanded* to make him come (on Thursday) in the octave of the Ascension of the Lord [9 June 1272].

35 It was presented etc. that John, Abbot of Eynsham, and two of his monks whose names are not known, William of London, John le Porter and Henry of Woodeaton, squires of the same Abbot, while travelling through the aforesaid forest in the week next before Lent in the 54th year [February 1270], took a doe in the same, namely at Stockey, and carried it away to Eynsham.

36 It was presented etc. that Hugh de Wolseshulle, Benedict de Wolseshulle and Richard Trubbel of Leafield are habitual evildoers to the venison in the aforesaid forest. And the aforesaid Richard came and being convicted of this was committed to *prison*. And the aforesaid Benedict and Hugh did not come nor were they attached. Therefore the sheriff was *instructed* to make them come from day to day. And the aforesaid Richard was indicted elsewhere of this sort of offence and enrolled in the rolls of the verderers and foresters [a whole line is erased and crossed through at this point] and John of Wootton, sons and heirs of the dead verderers in whose rolls the aforesaid

---

[15] Dustfield is in Charlbury. See p. 189, **196**.

Richard was enrolled, made no mention of him in the rolls which they presented in the name of their fathers but concealed this. Therefore *judgement* is to be given against them. Afterwards it was declared that the aforesaid Benedict is dead and was not attached therefore nothing from him. Afterwards the aforesaid Hugh de Wolseshulle came and was committed to *prison*.

37 It was presented that men and household members of Matilda, Countess of Gloucester, for whose names enquiry is to be made, coming into the aforesaid forest at times in the 54th year, took four does in the same, and two does in the 55th year, without licence, and carried the venison away to the house of the same Countess at Shipton; who knowingly received them, with the aforesaid venison. It was also found that when the same Countess came to that place her men and servants were accustomed to enter the aforesaid forest with dogs and greyhounds, bows and arrows and to take venison at will, and to be received in the house of the aforesaid Countess, she herself knowing [about this]. It was also found that Richard, former reeve of Shipton, is the leader of the same wrongdoers in the forest, teaching them which places the Lord King's deer frequent the most, and how they will be able to catch them most quickly. And Laurence of St. Andrew and Hugh de Elylond are among the aforesaid wrongdoers.

m. 4]

Still of the venison of Wychwood

38 It was presented by the same and found that Hugh de Plescy, who has liberty by a charter of the Lord King to hunt hares, wolves and cats in the aforesaid forest, took a buck in the same, in Pinsley Wood on Wednesday next before the Nativity of the Lord in the 55th year [24 December 1270], and a doe in Lent, without warrant.[16] And that the same Hugh and his men while hunting with dogs by reason of the aforesaid liberty were accustomed to do harm to the Lord King regarding his deer in the same Forest. Afterwards the aforesaid Hugh came and was committed to prison [this sentence is written in a different ink].

39 It was presented and found etc. that John Giffard de Bremmesfeld, coming into the aforesaid forest at times and staying there, took thirteen deer since the last pleas, without warrant.

40 Osbert Giffard likewise took eight bucks and does and a hind without warrant.

[16] His charter, **9** on p. 54, did not allow him to hunt venison. Pinsley Wood is in Hanborough.

41   Nicholas Syfrewast likewise took four bucks and does without warrant.

42   Similarly Giles de Argentym [and] Humphrey de Boun who is dead took 24 deer there. And the aforesaid Giles did not come nor was he attached. Therefore the Sheriff of Hereford was *instructed* to make him come in the Octave of the ascension of the Lord [9 June]

43   Miles de Boun took a doe there without warrant. And he did not come nor was he attached, and it is not known where it would be possible to distrain [him], therefore e*nquiry* is to be made where he has lands by which etc.

44   Robert de Vere, earl of Oxford, took four deer in the aforesaid Forest without warrant; he did not come and he was not attached. Therefore he is to go *before the king*.

45   Nicholas, Bishop of Winchester,[17] took eight deer in the aforesaid forest without Warrant. And he did not come and was not attached. Therefore he is to go *before the king*.

46   Gilbert, earl of Gloucester, at his coming, took twelve deer in the aforesaid forest without warrant. *before the king* [marginal note only]

47   It was presented etc. that Reginald (£10), parson of the church of Churchill, is a harbourer of evildoers to the venison of the Lord King in the aforesaid Forest.

[m. 4 dorse is blank]

m. 5]

Regard of the Forest of Wychwood

48   Regard of the Forest of Wychwood presented by John le Myre de Saunford (dead), Reginald de Waucham (½ mark), William William [sic] de Colunce (½ mark), William of Cornwell (½ mark), Robert Toky of Milton (½ mark), Robert Warner of Shipton (½ mark), John le Despencer of Chilson (½ mark), Alexander de la Thurne (½ mark), John le Rus of Taynton (½ mark), William atte Hulle of Swinbrook (½ mark), Henry of Ditchley (½ mark), and Walter of Preston (½ mark), regarders, who say:

---

17   Nicholas of Ely, Bishop of Winchester 1268-1280: *D.N.B. 17,* 345.

New Assarts

49   Richard Cok of Stonesfield,[18] William atte Mershe of the same, Stephen Alured of the same, Andrew atte Wode of the same, William Chichele of the same, Richard son of Hugh of the same, William le Lung of the same, Walter Waleraund of the same, Thomas de la Grene of the same, Geoffrey Joye of the same, Nicholas son of Hugh of the same, William le Tornur of Woodstock, William le Moner of Stonesfield, Walter son of Emma of the same [and] John Dawe of the same made a new assart at Stonesfield of four acres from the demesne wood of the Lord King without warrant, and hold it, therefore they are *in mercy* and the land is *to be taken*. And that place was made waste of old and again anew by the vill of Stonesfield and by other wrongdoers in those parts so that the crop [of wood] was of little value when it was assarted. Also the same assart was sown once with wheat and twice with oats, for which all the aforesaid men should answer. Also the *fencing* around the same assart is *to be taken down*. And it is sown   8s.

New Assarts

50   Nicholas Cat of Stonesfield, William atte Mershe of the same [and] John le Frere of the same assarted newly in the same place and hold half an acre of the Lord King's wood, without warrant, therefore they are in *mercy* and the land is *to be taken*. And that place was waste as [described] previously. And the aforesaid Nicholas built a certain *house* (to the damage of the Forest) on half of the aforesaid assart, which is *to be taken down*, and the other half which the aforesaid William and John hold [sentence not completed]. And it was sown once with wheat and three times with oats for which they should answer with   7½d.

51   Walter Waleraund of Stonesfield, John Waleraund of the same and Robert of Hordley assarted newly in the same place and hold half an acre of the demesne of the Lord King, without warrant. Therefore they are in *mercy* and the land *is to be taken*; and that place was made waste as previously [described] and sown once with wheat and three times with oats, for which they should answer with   15d.

52   William Chichelye and Andrew of Stonesfield assarted newly in the same place and hold one rood of the same demesne (and enclosed it with a ditch and hedge) without warrant. Therefore they are *in mercy* and the land *is to be taken*. *The fencing is to be levelled* [marginal note only]. And the land was sown once with wheat and four times with summer corn, for which they should answer with   10d.

---

[18]   Many of the names in this entry and those following are also found in the records of assarts in Stonesfield in *Rot. Hund. ii,* 48 and 873.

53 William atte Mershe of the same assarted newly in the same place and holds, of the same demesne, half an acre of land without warrant. Therefore etc. In *mercy, to be taken* [marginal note only]. And it was sown twice with summer corn for which he should answer with   6d.

54 Walter Waleraund assarted newly in the same place and holds three roods of land of the same demesne without warrant therefore etc. *Mercy, to be taken* [marginal note]. And it was sown twice with summer corn, for which he should answer with   9d.

55 Robert son of William Nicholas of the same assarted newly in the same place and holds a third part of one rood in the same demesne without warrant. Therefore, etc. *Mercy, to be taken* [marginal note] And it was sown twice with summer corn for which he should answer for   1d.

56 [This paragraph is written in a different ink]
And because it was testified that all the aforesaid assarts were arrented, and that the bailiff (of the manor) of Woodstock answers for their rent to the Lord King's exchequer, therefore nothing from these. It was also testified that all old assarts in the demesne of the Lord King in the aforesaid forest are arrented in the same way; therefore let there be no mention of them.

57 Richard Cok of the same assarted newly in the same place and holds half an acre of the Abbot of Eynsham's wood. Therefore in mercy, the land is to be taken, and it was sown once with winter wheat and three times with oats 15d.

[The last sentence is written in a different ink, as also are the following entries.]

58 Emma Joye of Finstock assarted newly and holds one and a half acres in the chase of Gatewell,[19] from the said Abbot's wood. Therefore etc. And it was sown as above   3s.9d.

59 Stephen Wylot of the same assarted newly and holds at Finstock two and a half acres of the said Abbot's wood. Therefore etc. And it was sown once with wheat and six times with summer corn   10s.

60 Henry Wylot of the same assarted newly and holds one acre of the same Abbot's wood. Therefore, etc. And it was sown once with wheat and six times with summer corn   4s.

---

[19] Gatewell or Gadding Well was in Finstock: *V.C.H. Oxfordshire x*, 133.

61 Gilbert of Finstock assarted newly and holds one acre of the same wood. Therefore, etc. And it was sown once with wheat and six times with summer corn 4s.

62 Richard Sweyn of the same assarted newly and holds in the same place half an acre of the same wood.Therefore, etc. And it was sown as above   2s.

63 Walter in Angulo in Finstock assarted newly and holds one rood of the same fee. Therefore, etc. And it was sown as above   12d.

64 Martin Aunfray of North Leigh assarted newly and holds 1 acre of the same fee. Therefore, etc. And it was sown as above   4s.

65 Robert de Beningho in North Leigh assarted newly and holds 1 acre of the same fee. Therefore, etc. And it was sown as above.   4s.

66 John Sprot of Finstock and Joel his brother assarted newly and hold one and a half acres of the same fee. Therefore, etc. And it was sown in the same way 6s.

67 Jordan at Well of North Leigh assarted newly and holds an acre of the same fee. Therefore, etc. And it was sown as above   4s.

68 Hugh of Wilcote, clerk, assarted newly in the same place and holds a acre of the same fee. Therefore, etc. And it was sown as above   4s.

69 William de Angulo and John Le Lokere of North Leigh assarted newly and hold one and a half acres of the same fee. Therefore, etc. And it was sown as above   6s.

70 John Miller of Finstock assarted newly and holds 1 rood of the same fee. Therefore, etc. And it was sown as above   12d.

71 Hugh le Blund of Ramsden assarted newly and holds two acres at Lurteden of the aforesaid Abbot's fee. Therefore, etc. And it was sown once with winter wheat and three times with summer corn   5s.

72 Walter of Ramsden, Henry Wylot, Julian Harold, Robert Cotel [and] John Joye of Finstock assarted newly in the same place and hold 1 acre of the same Abbot's fee. Therefore, etc. And it was sown three times with summer corn   18d.

73   Philip of Pudlicote assarted newly and holds at Fawler half an acre of the same Abbot's fee. Therefore, etc. And it was sown three times with oats

10d. [9d.]

74   The same Philip, Richard at Water of Fawler, Richard Poue of the same, Roger Hering of the same, John Dod of the same, Oliver of the same, Godfrey Daunvers, Adam de Broxham, Robert Daunvers, William Aldon, Walter Dod of Fawler, Godric of the same, Stephen Alisaundre of the same, Denise widow of the cobbler, Nicholas Cobbler, Richard Paynel and Philip Daunvers assarted newly above Fawler and hold two acres of the aforesaid Abbot's fee. Therefore, etc. And it was sown three times with summer corn

3s.

75   Richard Poue of the same assarted newly in the same place half an acre of the same Abbot's fee. Therefore, etc. And it was sown as above   [blank]

76   Alexander, Abbot of Eynsham, who is dead assarted newly in the same place 1 acre of his own fee. John, the present Abbot, holds [it].[20] Therefore, etc. And it was sown once with winter wheat and four times with summer corn   3s.

77   John Capel of Fawler assarted newly at Baywell one rood and holds it, of the fee of the same Abbot. Therefore, etc. And it was sown once with oats

<¾d. > 1½d.

78   Philip of Pudlicote assarted newly (above Fawler) and holds three acres of the same Abbot's fee. Therefore, etc. And it was sown once with oats

18d.

79   Nicholas of Langley[21] assarted newly at Finstock and holds four acres of the same Abbot's fee. Therefore, etc. And (two acres) were sown once with winter wheat and once with oats, and the other two once with oats   4s.

80   Robert Cotel of Finstock assarted newly and holds, in the same place, 1 rood of the same fee. Therefore, etc. And it was sown once with summer corn   1½d.

---

[20] Alexander of Brackley was Abbot of Eynsham from 1264 to 1268. He was succeeded by John of Oxford, 1268-81: *Eynsham Cart. I*, xxii.
[21] Nicholas of Langley already held seven acres of land in Finstock, by grant from the Abbot of Eynsham: *Eynsham Cart. I*, 283.

81 John Dod assarted newly at Grendon beneath Bradeleye and holds three roods of the same fee. Therefore, etc. And it was sown three times with oats 13½d.

82 John baker of Charlbury assarted newly and holds above Fawler 1 acre of the same fee. Therefore, etc. And it was sown three times with oats 18d.

m. 5 dorse]

Still of the Regard of Wychwood

83 John of London assarted newly and holds 1 acre and 1 rood of the Lord King's demesne wood which is called Burleigh belonging to the Manor of Bladon,[22] without warrant. Therefore *in mercy* and let the land *be taken*; and it was sown [sentence not completed]. *Let it be arrented* [marginal note only]

84 Humphrey le Gerisshe assarted newly and holds of the Lord King's soil in the heath of Hanborough half an acre, without warrant. Therefore *in mercy,* let the land be *taken. Let it be arrented* [marginal note only].

85 Robert le Eyr, bailiff of Woodstock,[23] occupied newly and holds a certain place in the Lord King's demesne of Combe which contains three perches in length and one perch in width, in order to enlarge his court in the same place, without warrant. Therefore etc. *mercy* [marginal note only], let the land *be taken.*

86 William de la Stokke assarted newly in the same place and holds half an acre of the Lord King's demesne without warrant, Therefore let the land *be taken. Mercy* [marginal note]

87   **Of Old Assarts**

From Roger Doylly for two acres of old assart at Ascott, sown four times with oats   4s.
From Cecilia who was the wife of John le Fox for half an acre and half a rood of old assart at Enstone sown as above   15d.

---

[22] John of London, a royal clerk, held the manor of Bladon for life from 1265 to 1306: *V.C.H. Oxfordshire xii,* 21. This grant is recorded in *Rot. Hund. ii,* 46, where it is stated that the wood of Burleigh and the meadow of Burgham were granted to him at the same time, but as part of the manor of Hanborough (which was within the Forest), not of Bladon (which was outside). This presumably explains why Burleigh Wood and Burgham are recorded with Hanborough in the Survey of Wychwood Forest made almost 350 years later; see p. 203, **315** and **316.**

[23] Robert le Eyr is recorded as Bailiff of Woodstock from 1264 to 1291: *Cal. Lib. R. v 1260-67,* 154 *Cal. Close 1288-1296,* 172.

From Thomas of Williamscot for one rood at Asterleigh sown twice with
    winter wheat and twice with summer corn   9d.
From Alexander Daundeville for one and a half acres at Pudlicote sown four
    times with summer corn   4s.
From John son of the reeve of Charlbury for half a rood sown once with wheat
    and three times with oats   3¾d.
From John Danvers of Fawler for one acre at Fawler sown in the same way
                        2s.6d.
From Richard Aylward for one rood in the same place sown in the same way
                        6½d.
From Adam Short, Agnes Dod, Alice Sprot, Edward Kyng, Peter le
    Pechere and Hugh Newman for three acres at Finstock, sown in the
    same way   7s.
From Richard Sweyn for half an acre in the same place sown in the same
    way   15d.
From Walter Aylward and Emma who was the wife of John Leky for 1
    rood in the same place sown in the same way   7½d.
From Adam Short, Elias Sweyn and Henry Wylot for 1 and a half acres
    sown in the same way   3s.9d.
From Philip Miller for one and a half acres at Fawler sown as above   3s.9d.
(From Walter of Ramsden for 1 rood in the same place sown in the same way
                        7½d.)
From Stephen Wylot for three and a half acres in Finstock sown as above
                        8s.9d.
From Emma Joye for four acres in the same place sown in the same way
                        10s.
From William le Kyng for half an acre in the same place sown as above
                        15d.
From Emma Leky for half an acre sown as above   15d.
From Walter de Angulo for 1 and a half acres in the same place sown
    as above   3s.9d.
From Richard of Swindon in Wilcote for 1 acre at Wilcote sown as above
                        2s.6d.
From John Sprot for one rood in the same place sown as above   7½d.
From Philip Miller of Fawler for 2 acres at Mereden sown as above   5s.
From John le Pestur of Charlbury for one rood at Smale Wayes Ende
    sown as above   7½d.
From Philip Miller of Fawler for 2 and a half acres at Lefriches Haleweye
    sown as above   7s.6d.
From Richard of Swinden for two acres at Fawler sown as above   5s.

From Walter of Ramsden for three perches in Finstock sown as above
                                                                      22½d.
From Walter de Angulo for two and a half acres in the same place sown
    as above   7s.6d.
From Emma Joye for 4 acres in the same place, sown in the same way
                                                                      10s.
From Stephen Wylot for 5 acres at Gatewell Chace sown as above   12s.6d.
From Henry Wylot for half an acre at Finstock sown as above   15d.
From William Harold for half an acre at Gatewell Chace sown as above
                                                                      15d.
From the Abbot of Eynsham for 3 and a half roods at Charlbury, sown as
    above   10½d.
From William de Angulo of North Leigh for 3 and a half acres and one
    rood at Finstock, sown as above   8s.1½d.
From John Sprot and Joel Sprot for one acre at Ordweygrave[24] sown as
    above   2s.6d.
From the Abbot of Eynsham for two acres at Phelleley[25] sown as above   5s.

88   Henry de Burghulle,[26] Justice of the Lord King, Justice of the Forest this
side of Trent in the place of Roger de Clifford senior while the same Roger
was in the parts of Ireland on business for the Lord Edward son of the King,
when passing through the Forest of Wychwood found a certain assart in the
wood of Hulwerk belonging to the Manor of Shipton which Matilda Countess
of Gloucester holds in dower;[27] and the same assart contained 120 acres and
more by estimation, and was made on the instructions of the aforesaid
Countess who committed parcels of the assarted wood to Richard of Hanborough in Ramsden, Adam de Camera in the same, John le Ieofne in Hailey,
John de Wolseshulle in Ramsden, Jordan at Well [in] Hailey, William de
Merlawe then a servant at Shipton, William Letice of Ascott and William
Mirable of Ramsden, to be assarted; who caused them to be assarted by Giles
le Walays then a servant of the aforesaid Richard of Hanborough, Walter de
Pavinton, John Hyrdman, John of Cherdesle, Richard son of Geoffrey of
Poffley, Henry son of John Miller, Richard son of Roger le Wy[illegible],

---

[24]   Ordweygrove was in Finstock, near Tapwell. It is recorded in *Eynsham Cart. ii*, 29 under "Fawler",
although almost all of the fields named with it are actually in Finstock.
[25]   The hermitage at Phelleley had been granted to Eynsham Abbey by Henry I: *V.C.H. Oxfordshire ix,*
79 and *Eynsham Cart. I*, 52-53.
[26]   Henry de Burghulle was appointed as Justice of the Forest south of Trent, during the absence from
England of Roger de Clifford, on 5th February 1270: *Cal. Pat. 1266-1272*, 405.
[27]   Matilda (de Lacy) was the widow of Richard de Clare, earl of Gloucester, who died in 1262:
Complete Peerage 5, 700. This assart was in Ramsden, which was a member of Shipton manor.

Richard son of Richard of Hailey, Richard son of William of the same, Richard de Denele, William his brother, William Susanne of Ramsden, William Syward, Richard le Ieofne, Richard de Costowe, Richard le Roter, William of North Leigh, Ralph of Ramsden and John le Gek of the same. And all these were attached by the aforesaid Justice and now they have come and in respect of this call the aforesaid Countess as warrantor. And Roger de Merlawe, steward of the same Countess, came in her place and conceded that the Countess herself instructed that the aforesaid assart should be made as aforesaid, and that she was well able to do this since, although it is acknowledged that the aforesaid wood is in the King's Forest, yet it is without the regard; so that the aforesaid Countess may take of the aforesaid wood whatever she wishes and cut down and carry away at will as those who held the aforesaid [wood] before her were accustomed to do. But whereas, according to the assize of the forest, those who have woods within the King's forest and outside the regard, in which however the King's [deer] ought to be safe and have peace, may take from the same woods as much as is needed for their own use, namely for the upkeep of the manors to which the same woods belong, without view and delivery of the King's foresters, [this is] provided however that those woods are not destroyed wholly or in part so that the King's deer lose their haunt and refuge in that place. And the aforesaid place so assarted in which the King's deer used to take refuge is entirely cleared, as aforesaid, therefore [sentence not completed]

m. 6]

Still of [blank]

89 Stephen, Prior of Deerhurst, brought a complaint before the Justices that Nicholas Ored of Sulbrok [sic, Fulbrook] (½ mark), Robert Clement of the same (½ mark), Gilbert le Tynkere of the same (elsewhere), Aunfredus reeve of the same (½ mark), Kynne de Brok of the same (elsewhere), William le Rodere of the same (2s.), Robert Dyonise of the same (½ mark), Walter attebroke of the same (2s.), William Calsweyn of the same (2s.), Nicholas Wythelard of the same (2s.), William atte broke of the same (elsewhere) Richard Bolle of the same (12d.), William le Macon (2s.), Richard Wythelard of the same (2s.), Gilbert Grete of the same (12d.), Ralph Bolle of the same (12d.) Richard Coketad of the same (2s.) and Robert of Poreshulle in Swinbrook (40d.), men of John of St. Valery of whom certain ones are members of the same John's household and others his tenants in Fulbrook, entering the aforesaid Prior's wood belonging to his Manor of Taynton[28] within the aforesaid forest on many

---

[28] The manor of Taynton had been granted by Edward the Confessor to the Abbey of St. Denis in Paris, to which the priory of Deerhurst also belonged: Margaret Gelling, *The Early Charters of the Thames Valley*, 142-4.

occasions, made great destruction in the same wood against the will of the same Prior, namely of thirty-two or more oaks in different places and of a great quantity of underwood; and they would not allow themselves to be attached, but assaulted the same Prior's woodward when he came to attach them and treated him violently against the peace etc. And regarding this he requested the Lord King that they should make amends. Moreover the aforesaid wood is within the aforesaid forest of the Lord King and within the regard, and because of this no vert of any kind can or ought to be taken in the same wood without view or delivery by the Lord King's sworn foresters, and this for the reasonable upkeep of the same Prior's aforesaid manor to which the same wood belongs; and more-over, besides the loss of the aforesaid oaks and underwood which he sustained because of the said waste, the Prior himself could be charged by the Lord King according to the assize of the Forest. And the foresters, verderers and regarders when questioned about this testified that the aforesaid Nicholas Ored and the others previously named made the aforesaid waste of the aforesaid thirty-two or more oaks and of the aforesaid underwood in the aforesaid Prior's wood against the will of the prior himself as previously said. And that Thomas Fuke, woodward of the aforesaid John of St. Valery, knew of this and supported the evildoers and defended them against the aforesaid Prior and against his Wood-ward of the aforesaid wood, so that they were not attached as previously said. Who came and being convicted of this was committed to prison. And the afore-said Robert Clement, Gilbert le Tynkere, Aunfredus, Kynne, William le Rodere, Robert Dyonise, Walter attebroke, William Calsweyn and Richard Coketad came and confessed that they had done the aforesaid deed, and in respect thereof called John of St. Valery as warrantor, for whose work they had felled the aforesaid oaks and underwood; and they produced certain tallies with which the number of the aforesaid oaks was counted to witness that they felled the same oaks on the instructions of Stephen, servant of the aforesaid John their lord at Fulbrook, and of the aforesaid Thomas his woodward, as previously said; which [oaks] were applied to the use of the same lord at Fulbrook. And they requested a day, namely the Wednesday next after the feast of the Ascension of the Lord [8 June], to have their aforesaid lord to act as warrantor for this, and it was given to them by a safe surety. And the other wrongdoers did not come therefore the sheriff was instructed to cause them to come from day to day. And the aforesaid John of St. Valery came on the aforesaid day and said that neither by his knowledge nor his wish were the aforesaid oaks or underwood felled in the aforesaid prior's aforesaid wood, but truly he said that he commanded his aforesaid bailiff and men that they should take, in his own wood belonging to his Manor of Fulbrook, certain oaks to repair their houses in that place and a certain amount of underwood to maintain their hedges, by view and delivery of the Lord King's sworn foresters; wherefore if the aforesaid oaks and underwood were felled by his aforesaid men within the aforesaid Prior's wood he entirely disavowed their act; And if they were felled in his wood belonging to the aforesaid manor of Fulbrook he vouched for their deed, as long as it was done by view and delivery of the Lord King's foresters as previously said. And because it was found that the aforesaid oaks and underwood were felled by Nicholas Ored and the others named above in the aforesaid wood of the aforesaid Prior, to the harm of the Lord King's forest as previously said, therefore it was decided that the aforesaid wrongdoers are in the Lord King's mercy, and amends ought to be made to the aforesaid Prior. It was also found that Nicholas le Lung of Fulbrook (2s.) [and] Robert le Tinkere junior (12d.) of the same were present at the aforesaid transgressions and offences as the others previously mentioned were, therefore they are in *mercy*.

Of wastes in demesne

90   It was presented and found that much destruction occurred in the aforesaid forest in this fashion; in the villages of Combe, Stonesfield and Wootton are 80 of the Lord King's tenants every one of whom has a cart with which he enters both the Demesne woods of the Lord King and the woods of the lords the Abbot of Eynsham, Amaury of St. Amand[29] and others having woods in the forest, and takes away wood both from the high wood and the underwood, and he takes wood for fencing with which to enclose his corn, and when the same corn is carried away he is accustomed to take that fencing to Oxford or to other markets around, for sale, together with other wood which he takes in the aforesaid woods both by day and night, either himself or through his servants. So that, reckoning according to more or less, each one of them has every week two cartloads of wood at least from the aforesaid forest, to its great destruction. Therefore the number of cartloads of wood taken from the forest per year by the aforesaid 80 carts, each one of them to go twice a week as previously said: 8528

Besides there are in the same villages countless cottagers continually going into the aforesaid woods and taking away an infinite number of bundles of branches and underwood to the great destruction of the forest.

Besides there are in the village of North Leigh twenty-three tenants of the Abbot of Netley every one of whom has a cart continually going into the aforesaid forest, namely both the demesne woods of the Lord King and the woods of others, and taking away wood as previously said. And the sum of cartloads so removed every year: 2392

There are also in the same village many cottagers continually going into the aforesaid woods and taking away an infinite number of bundles of branches and underwood to the great destruction of the forest.

---

[29]   The Abbot of Eynsham's woods referred to here were presumably those in Charlbury and Fawler, while that of Amaury of St. Amand was his part of Bloxham Wood, in the northern part of Stonesfield parish.

There are also as many or more tenants of the Bishop of Winchester in his Manor of Witney every one of whom has a cart continually going into the aforesaid forest, namely both in the Lord King's demesne woods and in the woods of others, and carrying away firewood as previously said. And the sum of cartloads of wood so taken is 2392.

There are also in the same Manor with its members countless cottagers continually going into the aforesaid woods and carrying away an infinite amount of branches and underwood to the great destruction of the forest.

Besides there are in the villages of Shipton and Ramsden 20 or more tenants of the Countess of Gloucester's fee every one of whom has a cart continually going into the aforesaid forest, namely both the demesne woods of the Lord King and the woods of others and taking away firewood as aforesaid. And the sum of the cartloads thus taken yearly is 2272.

There are also in the same villages many cottagers going into the aforesaid woods and carrying away an infinite amount of branches and underwood to the great destruction of the forest.

In the villages of Kiddington (1 mark), Glympton (½ mark), Boriens (½ mark), Asterleigh (½ mark), Slape (40d.), Spelsbury (elsewhere), Charlbury (elsewhere), Chadlington (1 mark), Walcot (40d.), Shorthampton (40d.), Chilson (40d.), Ascott (40d.), Taynton (elsewhere), Fulbrook (else-where), Swinbrook (elsewhere), Widford (elsewhere), Asthall (elsewhere), and Minster (½ mark), which are near and around the covert of Wychwood, there are countless customary tenants of whom some with carts, some with horses, and the greater number carrying on their back, remove and carry away infinite cartloads, horseloads and bundles both from the Lord King's demesne woods and from the woods of others, to the great damage of the forest.

m 6. dorse]

Of wastes of woods in Wychwood

91   The wood of Asterleigh which is called Pedersle was wasted of old and again newly by Joan de Falkote[30] who is dead, and partly by Thomas of Williamscot who now holds the same wood. Therefore he is in *mercy* and the wood is *to be taken*. Afterwards the same Thomas came and paid a fine, both for Mercy and to regain his wood, of   20s.

---

[30] Joan de Falkote is presumably Joan de Saucey, see p. 50, **100.**

The wood of Nicholas of Yattendon of Glympton was wasted of old and again newly by the vill of Glympton and other neighbouring vills which were amerced above. The wood is *to be taken*.   ½ mark

The woods of John of St. Valery which are called Westgrave, Losengrave and Estgrave were wasted of old, for which the aforesaid John answers with   ½ mark

The same John's woods which are called Fastgrave, Smalnhok and Farendon[31] were wasted of old for which waste the same John answered with   ½ mark

However the aforesaid John's woods were in the hands of Gilbert earl of Gloucester in the time of war and the same John in the earl's prison; and it was in that time that the same woods were destroyed both of high wood and of underwood.

The wood which is called Prestgrave belonging to the prebends in Shipton and Swinbrook were [sic] wasted of old by Master Simon de Miggeham, Chancellor of Salisbury, holder of the aforesaid prebend in Swinbrook, and William de Brinton, holder of the aforesaid prebend in Shipton;[32] who hold the aforesaid wood [and] ought to answer for   ½ mark

The wood of Widford was taken into the Lord King's hand at another time and still remains.

The Lord King's wood which is called Cornbury is in defence for the whole year so that no one has common in that place, and if animals are found there once or twice they should be sent back for a sure surety; and if a third time they should be appraised for the Lord King's service. And Thomas of Langley Chief Forester answers for no attachments of this type nor the value of animals found in the aforesaid wood although many animals were often grazing in that place. Indeed Henry de Burghull, appointed by the Lord King as Justice of the Forest this side of Trent in the place of Roger de Clifford senior formerly the Justice of the aforesaid Forest while the same Roger was in the parts of Ireland on business for the Lord Edward son of the King, on passing through the aforesaid wood of Cornbury once with certain verderers and regarders of the Forest of

---

[31] The woods in these two paragraphs belonged to Fulbrook manor, which John of St. Valery held, and in the nineteenth century they still formed detached (or almost detached) portions of that parish. West Grove and Lousie Grove were near Asthall Leigh, Fawsgrove near Pain's Farm, and Smallhook and Faringdon in what is now the northern part of Swinbrook parish. East Grove had been assarted (see p. 103, fn. 1).

[32] Priestgrove survives, in Ascott-under-Wychwood. Simon de Micham was Chancellor of Salisbury, from 1272 to 1287: Diana E. Greenway, ed. *John le Neve, Fasti Ecclesiae Anglicanae 1066-1300 IV* 19. William de Brimpton was presented to the living of Shipton-under-Wychwood in 1268: F. N. Davis, ed. *Rotuli Ricardi Gravesende*, Canterbury & York Society XXXI, 220.

Wychwood found that wood of Cornbury and other demesne woods of the
Lord King in the same Forest wasted of old and again newly both of oaks
everywhere and branches and underwood, through the bad keeping of the
forest under the aforesaid Thomas as is clearly shown elsewhere under wastes
of woods. He also found the aforesaid wood of Cornbury everywhere grazed
by cattle and dug up by pigs. Therefore *to judgement* for the aforesaid Thomas
and his under-foresters, and it remains to be investigated regarding the value of
the pannage and herbage of the same woods for each year and which of the
same received the profit.

92   **Agistment of the forest of Wychwood**

Robert Fromund, heir of Ralph clerk of Shipton, and Robert of Broadstone,
heir of Robert of Broadstone, answer for the agistment of the aforesaid forest
from the time of their fathers, agisters of the aforesaid forest, namely
    From the 47th year [1263-4]   38s.
    From the 48th, 49th and 50th years [1264-6]   nothing for lack of mast

Also Nicholas of Fulbrook and Ralph of Radford (now) agisters of the same
Forest answer, namely
    From the 51st year [1267]   4s.2d.
    From the 52nd, 53rd, 54th and 55th years [1268-71]
                                    nothing for lack of mast

And the aforesaid agisters, questioned about the Lord King's pannage in
Cornbury, in which no one has common, say that they [answer for] nothing
from it because Thomas of Langley, the Forester, did not allow them to
interfere in any way with the agistment of the aforesaid wood. [And the
aforesaid] Thomas did not answer for the pannage of the said wood, therefore
to judgement with him. And it remains to enquire about the value [of the
pannage]; the aforesaid agisters are also ordered to concern themselves about
the aforesaid agistment when [it ought] to be agisted so that they would be able
to answer to the Lord King.

m 7.]
93   **Of vert of Shotover and Stowood**

From John Ernaud of Horspath for vert	12d.
From John de Scaccario <of> in Begbroke for a surety	elsewhere
From Peter Aylwynne in Horspath for the same	2s.
From Richard le Prest of Marston for vert in the forbidden month	12d.
From Walter Paron of the same for a surety	4s.
From Thomas Hardekyn of the same for the same	4s.

From Robert Hoddy of Holton for vert in the forbidden month	12d.
From William Smart of the same for the same	12d.
From Thomas le Gardener of the same for a surety	2s.
<From Richard le Fraunk>	

94 *elsewhere*

From Eustace Spileman of the same for the value of two of his pigs seized within the covert of the forest in the forbidden month (*2s.*). The same Eustace did not have the aforesaid price, therefore he and Richard le Seriaunt of Holton, his surety that he would have it, are *in mercy*.

From Sybil Daunz of Horspath for the value of one pig seized as previously *12d.* The same Sybil did not have that price therefore she and Alan of Horspath (12d.) and Ernaldus (elsewhere) of the same, her sureties that she would have etc. *in mercy*.

From Peter Aylwyne of the same for the value of one pig seized as previously, 12d.

From William le Careter of the same for the value of one pig seized as previously 12d. And because he did not have that price therefore etc. *in mercy*.

From the same William and Ernaldus of Horspath 2s. for which they were sureties for two pigs of Gunnilda Cachero, seized as above.

From Ernaldus of Horspath and Hugh of the same 12d. for which they were sureties, for the value of one pig which belonged to Richard Chaplain, seized as above.

Of venison in Shotover

95 It was presented and found by William Golye, who at some time since the last Pleas of the Forest in this County held the bailiwick of Shotover by grant of the Lord King, and by Philip le Moynne and William Bastard (½ mark), verderers of the same forest, that William huntsman and John le Barber, men of John earl of Warwick who is dead, took a hind in the forest of Stowood on Saturday next after the feast of the Circumcision of the Lord in the 48th year [5 January 1264].

96 It was presented etc. that Reginald de Grey, Reginald son of Peter, Amary of St. Albans, Roger de Molis (20 marks), Geoffrey de Nevile and Ralph de Crumwelle (15 marks) took one stag in the aforesaid forest on Monday next after the feast of All Saints in the aforesaid year [5 November 1263] and a buck and four does in the forest of Shotover without warrant.

Still of the venison of Shotover in the time of Philip Mymekan

97 It was presented by Philip Mymekan, Forester in fee of the aforesaid forest,[33] and by the aforesaid verderers, that Osbert Giffard, Richard le Engleys his huntsman and Hugh de Plescy took two bucks in the aforesaid forest of Shotover on Monday next after the feast of St. Bartholomew in the 49th year [31 August 1265] without warrant. The aforesaid Osbert and Richard his huntsman took a buck and a doe in the forest of Shotover on Wednesday next after the feast of St. Giles in the aforesaid year [2 September] without warrant, and two bucks on Friday next before the feast of St. Michael in the aforesaid year [25 September]. And two roebucks on Tuesday next before the feast of St. George in the 50th year [20 April 1266]. And a buck on Friday next before the feast of St. Augustine in the same year [21 May]. And a doe and a hind on the vigil of the Ascension of the Lord in the same year [5 May]. And a buck on Monday next before the feast of Pentecost in the same year [10 May], in the same place.

98 Roger de Mortimer [34] took a hind in Shotover on Thursday next after the feast of St. Andrew in the 50th year [3 December 1265] without warrant. *Before the king*

99 Nicholas Cyfrewast, John de la Rose in Ewelme (1 mark) and William de Scalebrok in Little Haseley took a stag in Stowood on Saturday next before Ash Wednesday in the fifty-first year [26 February 1267] without warrant. And they did not come and they were not attached, therefore the sheriff is *instructed* to make them come from day to day. Afterwards the aforesaid John came and was committed to *prison.*

100 Nicholas of Yattendon[35] took a roe-buck in the forest of Stowood in the last week of Lent in the 51st year [April 1267] without warrant. The same Nicholas hunted a stag in the same place on the eve of the Translation of St. Thomas the Martyr in the same year [6 July 1267] without warrant, which [stag] escaped but was weak for a long time and so died. And the same Nicholas came and produced a writ of pardon from the Lord King therefore he is *acquitted* of this.

---

[33] Philip Mymekan inherited the position of keeper of Shotover from his father of the same name, who died in 1249/50. The son, however, did not come of age until 1264 and presumably William Golye (see **95**) held Shotover during his minority: *Cal. Inq. p. m. I, Henry III,* 48 & 178.

[34] Roger de Mortimer, Baron of Wigmore, ?1231-1282: *D.N.B. 39,* 131-4.

[35] At this date Nicholas of Yattendon had replaced Osbert Giffard as keeper of the peace in Oxford and the parts adjacent: *Cal. Pat. 1258-1266,* 603.

101 A certain hind, being hunted, fell dead in the vill of Holton within the forest on the day after St. Bartholomew in the fifty-first year [25 August 1267], which same hind had been hunted by certain unknown evildoers who were then in the forest, about whom an inquisition was held by the foresters, verderers and by the vills of Holton, Wheatley, Forest Hill and Stanton [St. John], by whom nothing could be ascertained. Therefore further enquiry is to be made. And because the aforesaid vills did not come fully etc. therefore *in mercy*.

102 It is presented etc. that Ralph of Essex, formerly hayward and woodward of Ralph Basset deceased at Elsfield, hunted a certain stag in the wood of Sydele which is within the forest of Stowood[36] on Dies carniprivii in the fifty-second year [22 February 1268], and a certain other stag in the same place on Tuesday next after the feast of the exaltation of the Holy Cross in the same year [18 September 1268], which after it was hunted fled into the liberty and was captured there. And the same Ralph did not come and was not attached because he was not found. Therefore he is *to be exacted* etc. And the vills of Woodeaton, Beckley, Noke and Headington did not come fully etc. therefore *in mercy*.

103 It was presented that Walter de Merton[37] took a roe-buck in Stowood, and he had a charter from the Lord King whereby for the whole of his life he had this liberty, that when he passed through the Lord King's forests he could take one or two deer in each. Therefore he is quit of this capture.

104 It was presented by the same etc. that Bogo de Clare[38] took two hinds in the forest of Stowood on Friday next after the feast of Epiphany in the 50th year [8 January 1266] without warrant. And that Adam, huntsman of the same Bogo, took a hind in the same place on Sunday next before Carniprivium in the same year [8 February] without warrant. And the aforesaid Bogo took a roe-buck in the same place in the last week of Lent in the same year [March 1266] without warrant. And the aforesaid Bogo produced letters patent from the Lord King by which he pardoned him and his men all offences and transgressions made by them in whatsoever of the Lord King's forests until the 26th day of May in the fifty-sixth year of the reign of the Lord King [1272]. Therefore the aforesaid Bogo and his huntsman are quit of these offences.

---

[36] There were two woods called Sydele in Shotover and Stowood, one of them being Elsfield's wood: *Rot. Hund. ii*, 720.

[37] Presumably Walter de Merton, Bishop of Rochester and Chancellor of England 1261-64: *D.N.B.* 27, 297-299.

[38] See Bogo de Clare's charter p. 57, **4**. His presence in Oxfordshire is explained by the fact that, in addition to his deanery of Stafford, he held the church of St. Peter-in-the-East, Oxford, with those of St. Cross and Wolvercote, and the manor of Holywell: *Rot. Hund. ii*, 805.

m. 7 dorse]

Still of Venison in Shotover

105 Nicholas Cyfrewast had the Lord King's writ so that he could have two bucks in the aforesaid forest by his gift; and beyond those two he took a doe without warrant. An order referring to him was given above [**99**].

106 John le Halte (½ mark) of Forest Hill, having been attached because he was an accomplice of evildoers to the venison in the aforesaid forest and sold the venison which those malefactors caught there to certain unknown men at Oxford, came and being convicted of these things was committed to *prison*.

107 Osbert Giffard hunted the Lord King's deer with his dogs in the forest of Shotover on the day after St. Andrew's day in the 50th year [1 December 1265] without warrant, but it could not be ascertained that he took any venison on that day.

108 Stephen (½ mark) son of Roger le Despencer of Elsfield was arrested with a certain mastiff within the covert of the Forest of Stowood in the forbidden month; he came but is not suspected of any offence against the venison. However because he entered the aforesaid covert with the aforesaid mastiff in the forbidden month as aforesaid, against the assize of the forest, therefore he is in *mercy*. His sureties, Walter Wychindon of Elsfield and Hugh of Stowood.

109 It was presented that Thomas de Sancto Vigore, at the time when he was sheriff of Oxford, namely in the 53rd and 54th years [1268-1270], used to send Robert Beneyt and certain others of his household whose names are not known into the forest of Shotover both by day and by night to do harm to the Lord King's deer. And they did not come and were not attached. Therefore the sheriff is ordered to make the said Thomas come in the octave of the holy Trinity [26 June 1272], so that he has the aforesaid Robert.

110 It was presented that Hugh de Plescy who holds the manor of Headington and Philip Mymekan [sentence not completed]

111 Of vert in Shotover and Stowood in the time of Philip Mymekan

From Thomas le Lung of Wheatley for vert in demesne by night	2s.
Simon Prat of Wheatley and Thomas Prat of the same sureties	
From William Badde of Old Barton[39] for vert in demesne in the forbidden month	[blank]
From Robert Aynolf of the same for a surety	12d.
From William son of William Richardes of the same for the same sureties for payment John Godefray of Forest Hill and William father of the same William	2s.
From John servant of Eustace Spileman of Holton, arrested in the forbidden month because he carried arms made of iron against the assize	[blank]
From Roger le Seriaunt of Holton for a surety	*elsewhere*
From Ralph son of Juliana of Old Barton for vert in demesne	12d.
From Richard Cocy of Old Barton for the same by night	2s.
From Richard Aylrich of the same for a surety	*elsewhere*
From William le Lorekere of Horspath for the same	12d.
From Hugh of Horspath for the same	4s.
From Godfrey of Nether Horspath for the same	4s.
From William son of Roger of Over Horspath	12d.
From Godfrey Baseley of Nether Horspath for the same	4s.
From Richard Harm of the same for the same	4s.

112 Eustace Spileman of Holton was attached because of his sheep [which were] grazing in the demesne of the Lord King within the covert in the forbidden month. And the second time he should have been attached for the same and did not allow himself to be attached, but refused bail and sureties to the foresters, and rescued his sheep; who came and being convicted of this was committed to *prison*; and fined for his offences ½ mark

113 Certain great lords, being in the muster with the Lord King at Oxford before he began his journey towards the town of Northampton to take it from his enemies,[40] took for their fire fifty-six oaks or pollards in the Forest of Shotover.

114 From Hugh atte Wode of Holton for vert both in the Lord King's wood and in the Abbot of Abingdon's wood 12d.

---

[39] In Headington: *V.C.H. Oxfordshire v*, 158.

[40] The king was at Oxford, with his followers, for about a month before marching to Northampton in April 1264: *V.C.H. Oxfordshire iv*, 14.

From Robert Scrobin of the same for the same   12d.
From Henry Keft of the same for the same   12d.
From John le Rede of the same for the same   12d.

[The next paragraph is in another hand]
Pleas of the Forest in the County of Oxford from Easter day [illegible] month
in the 56th year in the reign of King Henry son of King John before R. de
Clifford, M. de Columbar, N. of Romsey and R. de [illegible] Justices to hear
and determine the same pleas [illegible word]
    Wychwood Shotover Stowood Bernwood

m. 8]

Regard of Shotover and Stowood

115 Regard of Shotover and Stowood presented by William of Combe (½
mark), William of the Mill (½ mark), John Ewstach (½ mark), Henry Mace (½
mark), John Payn of Garsington (½ mark), William son of Roger of Baldon (½
mark), Henry de la Grave (½ mark), Robert de Louches (½ mark), Nicholas
Algar de Newham (½ mark), Hugh de Hauvile of Garsington (½ mark) Richard
of Sandford (½ mark), regarders [Marginal note *Memorandum for the servant.*]

116 Richard King of Germany who is dead[41] caused one rood to be assarted
newly at Horton from his own wood without warrant. Edmund his son holds
the land, *let it be taken.* And it was sown once with wheat and once with
summer corn, for which Edmund answers.   4½d.

117 Edmund, son of the aforesaid King, holds eleven acres of assart which his
same father caused to be assarted from the demesne wood of the Lord King of
England in Stowood, and no warrant was shown for this; and they were sown,
since the last eyre, three times with winter wheat and three times with oats. To
be impleaded   49s.6d.
    The same Edmund holds fourteen acres of old assart which his aforesaid
father caused to be assarted from his own soil between the wood of Noke and
the vill of Beckley, and it belongs to the vill of Beckley and was sown as
previously   63s.
    The same Edmund holds 8 acres of old assart which his aforesaid father
caused to be assarted from his own wood which was called Bradele.

---

[41] The king's brother Richard, earl of Cornwall, was elected as King of Germany in 1257, and died in
April 1272. Beckley (which included Horton) had been granted to him in 1227: *D.N.B. 48,* 170,
V.C.H. Oxfordshire v, 61.

The same Edmund holds half an acre of old assart which his aforesaid father caused to be assarted from his wood at Horton, and he showed no warrant for this, and it was sewn as previously. 2s.3d.

118 John of St. John holds 11 acres of old assart which John his grand-father, who is dead, assarted from his wood of Stanton without warrant, and it was sown as previously, for which he answers. 49s.6d.

The same John holds two acres of old assart at Dupeden and 24 in Pipere Hangre which his aforesaid grandfather assarted etc. without warrant. And it was sown as previously 107s.

119 Emma who was the wife of Roger de la Vente holds one acre of old assart at Horton[42] which Herbert de la Vente assarted without warrant. And it was sewn as previously, for which she answers. 4s.6d.

120 The Prioress of Littlemore holds three roods of old assart which Matthew de Bixethrop, who is dead, assarted without warrant.[43]

121 The Abbot of Eynsham holds at Woodeaton half an acre of old assart which the Abbot his predecessor assarted without warrant, and it was sown as previously, for which he answers.

122 Robert le Parker of Beckley holds, at Noke, two acres of old assart which a certain parson of Beckley assarted without warrant. And it was sown as previously.

123 Roger de Amaury holds at Woodperry five acres of old assart which Robert de Amaury, who is dead, assarted without warrant. And it was sown as previously.

124 Alan de Plogenet holds at Piddington three acres and one rood of old assart which the tenants of the aforesaid manor of Piddington, which is the Lord King's demesne, assarted from the same demesne without warrant.[44] And they were sown as previously.

---

[42] A place name Vent Field is found in Horton (see map of Beckley in *V.C.H. Oxfordshire v,* 65).

[43] This assart was presumably at Minchincourt Farm in Stanton St. John, which was held by Littlemore Priory. Matthew de Bixethrop held land there (and in Forest Hill) *circa* 1220, although, according to *V.C.H. Oxfordshire v,* 130, his hide in Stanton St. John passed not to Littlemore but to Studley Priory.

[44] Piddington was a royal manor until 1270 when the king gave it to Alan de Plogenet in exchange for lands elsewhere: *Cal. Pat. 1266-1272,* 408; *Rot. Hund. ii,* 30 .

125 The Prior of Bicester holds one acre of old assart at Arncott which a certain Abbot of Missenden[45] assarted without warrant. And it was sown as previously.

126 Margery de Clifford holds at Lillingstone 9 and a half acres of old assart which Hugh de St. Martin,[46] who is dead, assarted of his own soil without warrant. And it was sown as previously for which she answers.

127 John of Olney holds in the same place 14 acres of old assart which Walter his father, who is dead, assarted without warrant.[47] And they were sown as previously.

128 Elyas of Hertford holds in the same place 12 acres of old assart which William le Avener assarted from the wood which belonged to Thomas le Barber without warrant, for which he was amerced elsewhere. And it was sown as previously, for which the same Elyas answers.

129 The Abbot of Osney holds at Sandhills two and a half acres which a certain predecessor of his, who is dead, assarted;[48] and the aforesaid Abbot showed letters of the Lord King in these words, Henry by the grace of God King of England etc.. To all etc. greetings. Let it be known that we have given to the Abbot and Convent of Osney 14 acres of assart and two and a half acres of assart in the County of Oxford with the crop which is on the same assarts, which had been taken into our hand, free in perpetuity of all rents just as they held them previously, so that the assarts will be within our forest with our licence. In [testimony] of this etc. The King being witness, the 15th day of August in the 30th year [1246] etc. Therefore the said Abbot is quit of the aforesaid assart.

130 Michael, parson of the church of Beckley, holds at Beckley eighteen acres of old assart which a certain predecessor of his, who is dead, assarted within the forest and out of the regard, without warrant; and they were sown three times with wheat and three times with oats.

---

[45] Bicester Priory purchased Lower Arncott from Missenden Abbey in 1232: *V.C.H. Oxfordshire v,* 19.

[46] Hugh de St. Martin was overlord of Lillingstone Lovell in 1235, but his son Peter had alienated the overlordship by 1247. The Cliffords were their tenants. *V.C.H. Buckinghamshire iv,* 192.

[47] Walter of Olney and Thomas le Barbur (see **128**) each held a wood and an assart in Lillingstone in 1254: *Rot. Hund. ii,* 44.

[48] This assart was presumably in the two carucates in Forest Hill which had been given to Osney Abbey by Hugh of Tew before 1160: *Osney Cart. 1,* 6.

131 Hugh de Plescy holds one acre of old assart at Muswell which a certain Abbot of Missenden[49] assarted without warrant, and it was sown as previously, for which the same Hugh answers.

132 Edmund of Almain holds two and a half acres of purpresture at Horton which a certain King of Germany his father occupied, from his own soil in the same place, and no warrant was shown for this.

133 The wood of John de Scaccario which is called Akermel[50] was made waste of old and again newly of oaks by the same, therefore he is in mercy and the wood is to be taken.

134 Edmund of Almain's wood at Holton, which is called Chelle, was wasted of old and again newly of oaks by the same.

135 The wood of Elsfield is newly wasted everywhere by felling and sales which Philip Basset, who is dead, made in the same, and which Roger Bygod (Earl Marshall) who now holds the same wood similarly made in the same without warrant.[51] And the aforesaid Philip did not permit, nor does the aforesaid earl permit, any wrongdoers in the aforesaid wood, which is within the forest and in regard, to be attached, and they do not allow any forester to interfere in any way in the said wood. And it was testified [that] the place used to be a great haunt of deer and their best refuge. The wood is to be taken. And regarding the aforesaid earl, before the king.

[From this point the edge of the membrane is torn and words are lost in increasing numbers]

136 [The wood] of Stanton which is called Sydele, and which John of St. John now holds, was wasted of old and again [newly by Emma] of St. John who is dead; the wood to be taken.
    [The wood of the same] John in the same place which is called Hornle was wasted of old by the same Emma without warrant; the wood is to be taken.

137 [The wood of Sampson Fo]lliot at Noke was wasted of old and again newly by Gilbert de Clare, earl of Gloucester, and by [... who] held the same wood during the time when the aforesaid Sampson was in prison at Dover, and who [felled] 60 oaks and underwood at will. And it was testified that the same

---

[49] Muswell was in Piddington. Once a hermitage, it was given to Missenden Abbey by Joan of Piddington in 1152, and sold by the Abbey to John de Plescy in 1236x40: *Boarstall Cartulary,* 100, 105 No. 303.
[50] John de Scaccario held land in Over Horspath with a wood called Akermel in 1279. This was the Musard fee there, and presumably the wood is that recorded on p. 45, **57**: *Rot. Hund. ii,* 716-7.
[51] Elsfield had been held by Philip Basset until his death in 1271, when it was inherited by his daughter Aline, wife of Roger Bygod: *Cal. Inq. I Henry III,* 272 No. 807.

Sampson [did not show any warrant]. Therefore he answered for the old waste
by pleading in the King's court.   ½ mark

138 [...] of Perry   ½ mark
    [...] and Henry Foliot for old waste of woods
        which they hold, together, in Thomley   ½ [mark]
    [...] Hasley   ½ mark
    [...] was wasted of old, [he?] has a charter and
                                  therefore is quit
    [...] Piddington   ½ mark
    [...] of old and anew by James Audley[52] without [warrant]
    [...] the same Prior answers for old waste and for
        new waste by pleading at the King's Court
    [... Lilling]stone   ½ mark
    [...] Boycott   ½ mark
    [...]   ½ mark

m. 8 dorse]

Oxon
[The rest of the membrane is blank]

m. 9]

139   **Amercements for defaults**

From Martin de Gay for a default for his tenement in Taynton   100s.
From Brian de Braunton for the same   20s.
   He has a writ from the King
From Jordan le Forester in Lyneham for the same   40s.
From Roger de Oylly in Ascott for the same   £10
From Matilda Countess of Gloucester for the same   [blank]
   Before the king
From John de Lusingrave in Hailey for the same   40d.
From the vill of Hailey for the same   1 mark
From the vill of Crawley for the same   10s.
From Margery de Clifford in Lillingstone for the same   [blank]
From Isabella de Grey[53] for the same   [blank]

---

[52] James Audley held Stratton (Audley) and half of Wretchwick, which was his wife's inheritance, but neither of these manors had woodland. This entry may refer to the wood belonging to Bicester, recorded later (**151**).

[53] Isabella was the widow of Walter de Grey, who was the nephew of Walter, Archbishop of York, and his successor as lord of Cogges. She is recorded as holding Cogges in dower in 1279: *V.C.H. Oxfordshire xii*, 59.

From John Bacun of Eynsham for the same	4s.
From John Bacon junior of the same for the same	2s.
From Henry Avenel of the same for the same	12d.
From Richard le Mey of Wootton for the same	½ mark
From Master Simon de Miggeham for the same	£10
From Robert de la Chaumbre for his land in Swinbrook for the same	½ mark
From the Prior of the Hospital of St. John Jerusalem for the same	20 marks
From William de Brynton parson of the church of Shipton for the same	20s.
From Roger Bygod, earl of Norfolk, for the same	*before the king*
From William le Speycer of Oxford for the same	[blank]
From Sampson Foliot for the same	100s.
From Peter clerk of Ledhale for the same	2s.
From Edmund son of the king of Germany for the same	[blank] *before the king*
From Henry de Camera of Beckley for the same	½ mark
From Alan Plugenet for the same	[blank]
From Thomas Goldhine of Arncott for the same	1 mark
From William le Chamberleyn of Stanton for the same	4s.
From Roger le Seriaunt of Holton for the same	½ mark
From John Hosel of Lillingstone for the same	[blank]
From John Dolneye [of Olney] for the same	[blank]
From Richard Ace (of the same) for the same	[blank]
From John brother of the parson of the same for the same	[blank]
From William le Avener for the same	[blank]
From the vill of Great Lillingstone for the same	[blank]
From the vill of Boycott for the same	[blank]
From Philip le Marshal of Noke for the same	[blank]
From William Gardener in Cogges for the same	20s.
From the vill of Asthall because it did not come	1 mark
From the vill of Fulbrook for the same	1 mark
From the vill of Swinbrook for the same	10s.
From the vill of Widford for the same	½ mark
From the vill of Charlbury with its members	2 marks
From the vill of Spelsbury for the same	40s.
From the vill of Fifield for the same	½ mark
From the vill of Taynton for the same	1 mark
From the vill of Holton for the same	1 mark
From the vill of Wheatley for the same	1 mark
From the vill of Stanton [St. John] for the same	20s.
From the vill of Woodeaton for the same	4s.

From the vill of Beckley for the same	1 mark
From the vill of Noke for the same	½ mark
From the vill of Headington for the same with its members	20s.

[m. 9 dorse is blank]
m. 10]

Of vert in the Forest of Bernwood in the County of Oxford

140

From Stephen Ladde of Boarstall for vert	12d.
From William Pud of the same for a surety and for vert	12d.
From Roger Mollepayne of the same for the same	12d.
From William in the Hale of Oakley for the same	12d.
From Thomas at Well of Garsington for vert	2s.
From Henry Wolfrich of Thomley for a surety	2s.
From Robert Gery of the same for the same	2s.
From Hugh Fosterling of Forest Hill for vert	12d.
From Nicholas Fifgod of Boarstall for a surety and for vert	12d.
From Robert Cullecuppe of Dodershulle for a surety	12d.
From Walter le Wyse of Oakley for the same	12d.
From Eustace Spileman of Holton for vert	elsewhere
From Thomas son of Hugh of Waterperry for a surety	12d.
From Robert le Noreys of Thomley for vert	12d.
From Simon Leurych of Ledhale for the same	12d.
From Thomas Leurych of the same for the same	12d.
From Robert Tripel of the same for the same	12d.
From John Cobbe of the same for the same	12d.
From Richard Smith of Ludgershall for vert	20 marks
From William Colebyle of Ledhale	12d.
From Robert Colebile of the same for the same	12d.
From Simon le Brazor of the same for the same	2s.
From Thomas of Claydon in Piddington for vert	2s.
From John Martin of Piddington for a surety	12d.
From Walter atte Hegge of the same for the same	12d.
From Simon le Carboner of Arncott for vert	12d.
From Robert Pesewombe of Thomley for a surety	12d.
From Gilbert Forsterling of Arncott for vert	12d.
From Hamo of Arncott for a surety	12d.

In the County of Buckingham

141 Roger de Mullepayn (elsewhere) of Oakley was attached within the covert of the Forest in the forbidden month by [the officer] who inspected the forest, against the assize; and now he did not come therefore he and his sureties, namely Richard le Notte of Worminghall (12d.) and Richard le Tynkere of Oakley (12d.), are *in mercy*.

142 Adam Forsterling of Arncott was attached in the same fashion, and he did not come therefore he and his sureties, namely Stephen le Fern of Arncott (2s.) and Hamo le Forester of the same are *in mercy*.

143 A certain oak was felled at night after the feast of St. Michael in the 48th year [29 September 1264] in the Lord King's wood of Panshill, which has pursuit for seven leagues around outside the bounds of the wood; perceiving which, John FitzNigel, Chief Forester, taking the verderers with him, followed the tracks of the cart in which the aforesaid oak had been carried away as far as the house of Robert Miller (½ mark) at Merton, which is only one league distant from the aforesaid wood, where the same John and the verderers found the stolen oak under a certain stack of straw. The said Robert did not allow himself to be attached by the aforesaid John because he was outside the bounds of the forest, and now he did not come. Therefore the sheriff is ordered to make him come from day to day.

Of the venison of the Forest of Bernwood

[The edge of the membrane is very stained and some words are illegible.]
144 It was presented and found by John FitzNigel, Chief Forester of Bernwood in the County of Oxford and by Nicholas Brun who at one time was a verderer in the same forest, and by John Morel of Addingrove and William le Venur of West... [and John] Brok of Marston who now are verderers in the same, that Michael Fromund de Wynton' and Richard son of Thomas of Piddington [entering] the same forest on the eve of the Translation of St. Thomas the martyr in the 47th year [6 July 1263] to do harm to the Lord King's venison, [illegible words] bucks without warrant. Who came on the first day and were released on bail, namely for the aforesaid Richard by Richard le Chapm[an of] [illegible] *(2s.)*, Hugh Grey of the same *(2s.)*, and William of Claydon *(2s.)*, in the same. And for the aforesaid Michael [by] William of Headington *(2s.)* in Piddington, Adam RakeMawe (2s.), [illegible] Roger le Ioefne (2s.) of the same who bound themselves to have them from day to day to answer etc. And now they have not come [therefore *in mercy*] and the sheriff is *ordered* to distrain them to have them from day to day.

And the vills of Piddington (*1 mark*), Arncott [illegible] [and Forest] Hill (*½ mark)* were summoned to hold an inquisition on the aforesaid offence and they did not come fully according to the assize of the Forest. Afterwards the aforesaid Michael and Richard came and were committed to *prison*. And the aforesaid Michael fined for ½ mark by sureties of Richard le Chap[man] of [illegible] [and Hugh] le Grey of the same; and Richard fined for ½ mark by sureties of William of Claydon, Adam Rakemawe and Roger le Iofne [of the same].

145 It was presented that when John le Naper, the Lord King's huntsman, hunted in the aforesaid forest and took [a buck for] the Lord King's use with his greyhounds on the eve of St. Bartholomew in the 50th year [23 August 1266], Richard Gypcien, servant of Agnes [illegible words] of Agnes le Cuppild of Horton, came to the place where the aforesaid buck was felled and they drove off the aforesaid greyhounds and took [it] away, no-one knows where, therefore enquiry is still to be made regarding this. And the aforesaid Richard and John withdrew themselves and did not come at this time and were not found therefore etc. *To be exacted* [marginal note only]. The chattels of the aforesaid Richard were valued at [illegible words, marginal note *20s.*] ...goin, Renaud of Merlake and John de la Hyde in the same answer for this. And that the same Hugh (*2s.*) and John (*2s.*) [illegible words] ... le Spyndlere suspected of the said offence and they did not have him, therefore in mercy. Afterwards the same [illegible] submitted himself to the verdict of the foresters and verderers who say that he is not guilty, therefore acquitted. Richard Gypcien [came] and was committed to *prison* and fined for 2 marks so that the aforesaid 20s. is reckoned in the same by the [sureties] of William Gypcien of Blackthorn and Walter Martin of the same.

m. 10 dorse]

Still of the Venison of the Forest of Bernwood
in the County of Oxford

146 Osbert Giffard took a buck and a doe in the aforesaid forest on Monday next after the feast of the Assumption of the blessed Mary in the 49th year [17 August 1265] and two does on Thursday next before the feast of the Exaltation of the Holy Cross in the same year [10 September 1265] and three does on Thursday in the week of Pentecost in the 50th year [20 May 1265] without warrant.

147 James Audley took two bucks of the second year in the aforesaid forest on Monday next before Ash Wednesday in the 50th year [8 February 1266] without warrant, and he is in Ireland in the Lord King's service, therefore [action] regarding this is adjourned.

148 It was presented etc. that Nicholas Syfrewast, who has a certain charter which says that he may hunt hares, wolves and cats in the Lord King's forests in the County of Oxford provided that he does not take any of his great beasts,[54] used to course with his dogs in the aforesaid forest and do harm to the Lord King regarding his deer, by reason of the liberty contained in the aforesaid charter; but he also took a doe there on St. Michael's day in the 50th year [29 September 1266] and a doe in the octave of St. Michael in the 51st year [6 October 1267] without warrant. The same Nicholas did not come therefore the sheriff was instructed about him as is shown elsewhere. And because he was convicted of many offences committed by him in various forests in the aforesaid County by reason of his aforesaid liberty, therefore to judgement regarding the same liberty. It was also found that John de la Rose took part in the aforesaid offences and he did not come and was not attached. Therefore the sheriff is ordered to make him come as is shown elsewhere. Regarding the aforesaid John it is shown elsewhere in the forest of Shotover.

149 Roger de Clifford senior, then Justice of the Forest,[55] gave Hugh de Plescy a doe in the aforesaid forest, who came to capture it himself on Thursday next after the feast of St. Michael in the 51st year [6 October 1267], and let slip his hounds at a certain herd of deer; which caught a certain doe and a fawn, and it was declared that the same fawn was taken against the will of the aforesaid Hugh and that immediately after it was caught he took it to the foresters who were with him. They however refused to receive it, therefore adjourned regarding this.

150 John Giffard the younger took a buck in the aforesaid Forest in the vigil of St. Michael in the 52nd year [28th September 1268] without warrant, and he did not come nor was he attached; therefore the sheriff is ordered to make him come from day to day.

151 It was presented etc. that James Audley, at the time when he had the Manor of Bicester in his hand, caused destruction to be made both in the Prior of Bicester's wood in Arncott and in the wood which now is Henry de Lacy's belonging to his manor of Bicester, which woods are within the forest and in regard, namely of oaks everywhere and of branches of thorn and underwood, by Nicholas then a servant of the same James at Stratton [Audley], Matthew reeve of the same, Simon Carbonarius of Arncott, Hugh his son and Richard then Carter of the same James; and that Hugh de la Sale of Stratton, Matthew le Stilkere of the same, Godwin of Finmere in the same, Gilbert le Best in the same and Elias son of Golda in the same similarly caused great destruction in

---

54 Nicholas Syfrewast was appointed Sheriff of Oxford in August 1266. On October 11th of the same year he was granted a licence to hunt hares etc. in that county and others: *Cal. Pat. 1258-1266,* 633, 646.
55 Roger de Clifford was appointed as Justice of the Forest South of Trent on August 8 1265: *Cal. Pat. 1258-1266,* 435.

the aforesaid woods and took away from that place wood timber and charcoal as far as the adjacent vills to sell, a great injury to the aforesaid Prior and Henry and a great detriment to the Lord King's Forest; and they did not want to cease this [damage] because of the forester's prohibition, nor allow themselves in any way to [be subject to] the Justices. And the aforesaid Matthew, Hugh, Godwyn, Gilbert, Elias and Simon came and were committed to prison. Regarding the aforesaid James, since he is in the Lord Edward's service in Ireland, and regarding the others aforesaid who are of his following and household, adjourned, excepting the aforesaid Hugh son of Simon for whom his father promised to answer and give satisfaction.

Special Inquisition, 1302

[In the transcripts of this and other inquisitions the groups of foresters, regarders, etc. on the jury have been separated for clarity.]

Edward by the grace of God King of England, Lord of Ireland and Duke of Aquitaine, to his beloved and faithful Hugh Le Despencer, Justice of his forest this side of Trent, greetings. Our sworn men of the manor of Combe, which is ancient demesne of our crown, have shown us that whereas they ought to have, and they and their predecessors as tenants of the same manor were accustomed to have from time immemorial until now, common of pasture in sixty acres of our woods which are within the bounds of our forest of Wychwood, and free entrance and egress to a certain ... horsepond [*waerum*] in the same wood to water their animals of all kinds in that place, a certain Edmund of Woodstock has newly assarted the aforesaid wood[1] and reduced it to cultivation, and enclosed the land thus reduced to cultivation and the aforesaid pond with a ditch, so that our men cannot have their common of pasture in that place or water their animals at the aforesaid pond (as they and their aforesaid predecessors were accustomed to have and to water in times past), a serious injury and manifest impoverishment to them, our men. And [illegible] we wish, through you, to ascertain more fully whether the aforesaid Edmund assarted the aforesaid wood and reduced it to cultivation and enclosed the land thus reduced to cultivation and the aforesaid pond by a grant or by a lease made to him in our name or not; and if by a grant or lease of this kind, then by which men or man that grant or lease was made to him and by what right and in what way; and also whether our aforesaid men ought and were accustomed to have common of pasture in that place and to water their animals at the aforesaid pond, as previously said, or not. We command you to enquire diligently about the foregoing matters to be more fully ascertained, by oath of the foresters, verderers and other bailiffs and ministers of our aforesaid forest as well as those good and law-worthy men of your bailiwick through whom the truth may best be known. And to [send] the [finding of the] inquisition thus separately and openly made to us under your seal and the seals of those by whom it was made, so that we have it in 40 days from Easter next wherever we may then be in England. Myself being witness, at [illegible] 21st day of February in the thirtieth year of our reign [1302].

---

[1] In *V.C.H. Oxfordshire xii*, 85 this assart is located near Combe Weir, but there would have been no need of a Special Inquisition if it was in Combe manor. Combe tenants had rights of common in the woodland of other manors, and this assart is more probably the Old Woodstock Sarte recorded later (p. 192, **234**), which was in Wootton.

Inquisition taken at Oxford near Combe in the Forest of Wychwood before Hugh Le Despenser, Justice of the Forest this side of Trent, on Thursday next after the feast of Saint Cuthbert the Bishop in the thirtieth year of the reign of King Edward [22 March 1302] by the King's writ, by the oath of

John of Langley, keeper of the aforesaid forest,

Thomas Ulgar and other foresters of the same forest,

John de la Sale, John Le Mire and Reginald of Lyneham verderers of the same forest, the regarders and all other ministers of the aforesaid forest,

Walter de Whythull, Walter Bounde, Hugh of Barton, Adam de Hombre, John Wering, Robert le Clerc, John of Lodwell, Walter le Welshe, Richard Le Harpour, Richard le Younge, John atte Betcheie and Thomas atte Betcheie, free and law-worthy jurors.

Whether Edmund of Woodstock assarted and reduced to cultivation sixty acres of the Lord King's wood in the aforesaid Forest and enclosed the land thus reduced to cultivation and a certain pond being in the wood by grant or lease made to him in the name of the Lord King or not; and if by a grant or lease of this sort then by which man or men that grant or lease was made to him and by what right and in what way; and also whether or not the men of the Lord King's manor of Combe, which is ancient demesne of the crown, ought and were accustomed to have common of pasture in the same sixty acres and to water their animals at the aforesaid pond.

Who say on their oath that Edmund of Woodstock, by grant and demise and lease from the lord William Trussel,[2] appointed to assess wastes and assarts in the Lord King's forests this side of Trent, assarted forty acres in the Lord King's wood, of the same Lord King's soil, within the bounds of the same forest, of the roots of the thorns with a quarter of a thousand trees which were growing in that place, and reduced it to cultivation for a certain rent paid annually to the Lord King's exchequer and by fine paid to the Lord King for entrance.

They also say that Edmund did not enclose the aforesaid pond or cause any hindrance [illegible words] the Lord King's men of Combe could water all manner of animals at will, and have free ingress and egress to the said pond.

They also say that the aforesaid men of Combe were accustomed to common in the aforesaid pasture just as others of the country did before the arrentation, and they still common after the crop on the said assart has been gathered, [in the same way] as the said Edmund and others of the country, as well as the said men of Combe, ought to common in their assarts which they recently took and arrented from the Lord King in the said wood. In witness of these things the

---

[2]   William Trussel, John de Crokesle and Richard de Lughteburgh were appointed "to arrent the King's wastes, whether of his own soil or the soil of others ... in the King's parks, forests and woods this side of Trent" on 15th April 1298: *Cal. Pat. 1292-1301*, 344.

aforesaid jurors of this inquisition affixed their seals, the day, place and year written above.

C47/11/6 (8) [1307?]

[The document consists of two parchment membranes, the first of which is in a bad state of preservation and half illegible. It is a writ from the King to John of Langley, Forester of Wychwood, regarding an assart of 69½ acres 1½ roods, measured by the twenty-foot perch, made from the wastes of the forest, which had been arrented to Robert Peverel by Walter of Gloucester,[1] to be enclosed with a low hedge and a little ditch, reduced to cultivation, and held by the same Robert and his heirs in perpetuity, by payment of seventeen shillings and ... pence to the sheriff, without danger from the king or his justices, foresters, verderers or other officers. Robert had brought a complaint before the king that he was being prevented from using the assart. John of Langley's reply is on the second membrane]

m 2.]
The tenure disputed in this brief was formerly in the hands of Geoffrey lord of Widford, and the said Geoffrey wasted the growth of the said woods so that the said wood was taken into the Lord King's hand because of waste. And in the Lord King's hand the said wood was kept by the foresters so that oaks and other underwood grew and there was better refuge and feed for all the game in that part. And if the said land should be assarted the Lord King's chase in the aforesaid forest would decrease greatly.

Moreover if the said land was enclosed or reduced to cultivation the earl of Gloucester, the earl of Warwick, Edmund de Mauley, John Lovel, Edmund of Cornwall[2] and many other magnates and the whole community of the aforesaid forest and others commoning in the said forest would be hindered henceforth in entrance and egress for their [animals?] to the great damage of their right of common.

---

[1]   This land, described as "69½ acres 1½ roods in the Forest of Whicchewode in an assart in the wood of Whitele" was granted to Robert Peverel on 5 June 1307: *Cal. Pat. 1303-1307,* 518. Whitele was one of four woods belonging to Fulbrook manor which are recorded in the 1298 Perambulation of Wychwood as having been taken into the king's hand for waste in the reign of Henry III: J. Y. Akerman, *"A View of the Ancient Limits of the Forest of Wychwood"*, *Archaeologia 37*, 427. The other three woods were Losnegrove, Westgrove and Purveance, and presumably Purveance and Whitele made up the "Eastgrove" which was recorded for Fulbrook in 1272: (see p. 82)
[2]   Lords of the manors of Shipton, Spelsbury and part of Chadlington, Ascott, Minster Lovell and Asthall respectively: *Feudal Aids iv,* 161-2, 164.

Moreover the said land was attached to the manor of Fulbrook and neither Robert Peverel nor other of his predecessors had entrance to the aforesaid land unless by usurpation.

Moreover since my bailiwick renders seven pounds every year[3], which comes from divers amercements and attachments and [illegible] belonging to the farm of my bailiwick, if the said land is enclosed and reduced to cultivation [this will be] to my disinheritance and a grave injury to my office.

And if my bailiwick should come into the Lord King's custody this will be to the disadvantage of the Lord King.

[3]   This sum is recorded in the Pipe Rolls as the *census* (annual payment) for the Forest of 'Cornbury', from 1156 onwards.

[The volume in which the following records are found is entitled Wastes in Divers Forests Tem Ed I]

p. 27   Oxon. Wychwood

The same Walter and William[1] in the month of May in the 33rd year of the reign of King Edward son of Henry [1305] rented and recorded the number of acres of the wastes written below, namely

1   *33rd Year* [1305], *of other soil*
To William le Blunt of Fawler, at the time of the perambulation newly revoked[2] 36 acres by the 20 foot perch of his own soil in a certain place which is called Stockey, which waste had been taken into the Lord King's hand for old waste before the perambulation; rendering for it 6d. [?s.] a year at Michaelmas to the Lord King's Exchequer by the hand of the Sheriff of Oxfordshire for the time being, namely 2d. per acre, the first term of payment beginning at Michaelmas in the 33rd year of the aforesaid Lord King Edward. The said waste to be held by the same William and his heirs of the Lord King and his heirs, enclosed with a little ditch and a low hedge according to the assize of the forest, and reduced to cultivation.

[A note relating to the following two entries has been written in the right hand margin] *by the perch as above for* [payment] *handed to the Sheriff at Michaelmas as above provided that as above*

2   *34th year* [1306], *of the King's soil*
And to Stephen le Botiller 17 and a half acres by the 20 foot perch of the King's soil at Bradeley near Akeman Street,[3] rendering for it 3s.4½d. a year as above, namely 3d. per acre, the first payment beginning at Michaelmas in the 34th year of the aforesaid King Edward. To be held by the same Robert [sic] and his heirs as above provided that it is lawful[ly enclosed] as above.

---

[1]   Presumably these men are Walter of Gloucester and William Harden who were appointed to arrent wastes on 4th September 1303: *Cal. Pat. 1301-1307*, 156.
[2]   Two identical Perambulations of Wychwood were made in 1298 and 1300, by which large areas were disafforested. All such perambulations were nullified by a Papal Bull of 1305 and the Forest Ordinance of 1306, although, apparently, reinstated in 1327: Young, Charles R., *The Royal Forests of England*, 140-1. But see also p. xi.
[3]   Location unknown. Robert Butler held Wilcote, through which Akeman Street ran, but there was no "King's soil" there: *V.C.H. Oxfordshire xii*, 299.

3 *35th year* [1307]

And to Robert Peverel 69½ acres 1½ roods in a certain assart in the wood of Whytele,[4] rendering per year as above 17s.5¾d., namely 3d. per acre, the first term of payment beginning at Michaelmas in the 35th year of the aforesaid King Edward.

Transcript of the rolls of arrentation made in the Forest of Wychwood by J. [sic] Trussel and J. Crokesle[5]

4 *26th year* [1298] *of the King's soil*

The same W. and J. arrented the waste written below in the month of November in the 26th year of the aforesaid King Edward, to wit to the Lord King's Sokemen of his manor of Combe 162½ acres 1 rood by the 20 foot perch of the Lord Edward's soil in a certain assart at Combe,[6] namely

to John Walter of Bladon	4 acres	
to Reginald Est	1 acre	1 rood
to Matthew Kinne	2½ acres	
to Peter of Ditchley	1 acre	1 rood
to Hugh Kynne	1 acre	1 rood
to William Jacob	2½ acres	
to John Smith	1 acre	1 rood
to Robert reeve	1 acre	1 rood
to Andrew parson	10 acres	
to William Jacob	1 acre and [blank]	
to Reginald Est	2 acres	
to John Dundy	1½ acres	
to Reginald Fesant	1½ acres	
to William Smith	1 acre	
to John Smith	2 acres	
to Robert reeve	3 acres	
to William Jacob	2 acres	1 rood
to John Kynne	3 acres	
to Adam Folioth	2½ acres	
to John Turry	2 acres	
to Reginald Fesaunt	2 acres	
to John Alein	9 acres	
to Robert Millon'	1½ acres	
to Andrew parson	10 acres	
to Margery atte Stocke	4 acres	

---

4 This is the assart referred to in the previous document.

5 *recte* William Trussel. See p. 102, fn 2.

6 These assarts are also recorded in the following document, pp. 116-7.

to John le Turnour	1 acre	
to William Wolnaf	1 acre	
to John Aleyn	6 acres	
to Reginald Fesaunt	4 acres	
to John de Radeleghe	2 acres	
to John le Turnour	1 acre	
to John Aleyn	5 acres	1 rood
to Robert Baldon	1 acre	1 rood
to John Shepherd of Wootton	5 acres	
to Reginald miller	2½ acres	
to Robert fisher and John atte Stocke	2½ acres	
to John Aleyn	5 acres	
to John de Radeleye	5 acres	
to John Turnour	2½ acres	
to Reginald miller	2½ acres	
to William Wolnaft	1 rood	
to John Godhynne	4 acres	
to Richard fisher	2½ acres	
to Agnes Norman	2½ acres	1 rood
to Matilda Roson	2½ acres	1 rood
to William Wolnaft	2½ acres	1 rood
to Hugh Kynne	2½ acres	1 rood
to William Aliz	2½ acres	1 rood
to William Galeweye	2½ acres	1 rood
to Robert of Hanborough	2 acres	1 rood
to William Sauett	2½ acres	
to Thomas atte Hull	1 acre	1 rood
to Robert of Hanborough	2 acres	2 roods
to Hugh son of John Aleyn	4 acres	
to John atte Stoki	4 acres	
to Roger atte Stoki [figure almost erased]	2 acres	
to Nicholas Faucis	3 acres	

rendering 40s.8¼d. a year namely each one for the part appertaining to them, and for each 3d. per acre, every person's payment to begin at Michaelmas in the 26th year of the aforesaid King Edward [1298]. To be held by them of the Lord King and his heirs for the rent aforesaid in the fore-going, so that it will be lawful for them to enclose the aforesaid waste with a little ditch and a low hedge according to the assize of the forest, and reduce it to cultivation.

5 To William de Dysces	16 acres	
to Roger le potag'	2 acres	
to John Cuggel	1 acre	

to William Salamon   1 acre and
to Andrew Saleman   1 acre
by the 20 foot perch, in a certain place at Leafield in la Holewehokes quarter,
paying for it as above 7s., namely each one for the part appertaining to them,
and for each 4d. per acre.[7] To be held by them on the aforesaid terms.

6   And to John of Langley 41½ acres by the aforesaid perch in a certain place
at Langley and Northgrove, rendering for it as above 10s. 4½d., namely 4d. per
acre.

30th year [1302]
7   And to the same John at Michaelmas in the 30th year 17½ acres between
Cutteshacch and Forkedich, and 15 acres between Leafield and Lovebury[8],
rendering per year as above 8s.1½d., namely 4d. per acre, the term of payment
to begin at Michaelmas in the 31st year. To be held on the aforesaid terms.

**Transcript of the rolls of wastes and usurpations without warrant in the
time of Roger Lestrange, Justice of the Forest,[9] but it is not known in what
year.**

8   John of Langley usurped to himself and appropriated from the King's
soil in the same Forest in divers places the wastes written below [illegible
words]
    Between Quernhale and Northgrove ½ acre 2 roods 20 perches, and between
Pouwodelegh and Northgrove 6 acres 20 perches, and between Stymele and
the King's wood 2 acres 1 rood 10 perches, and between Bradelegh and
Naterigge 3 roods 20 perches, and between the new sheepfold and Naterigge
16½ perches and under the Lord King's park at Cornbury 1 acre 1 rood, to
enlarge his meadow, and opposite Robert Dobbe's wood at Langley 1 rood 24
perches.

26th year [1298]
9   And William de Lysors usurped and appropriated in the aforesaid 26th
year of the aforesaid King Edward 2 acres of the Lord King's soil in
Holewokes quarter and it is worth 3d. a year in rent.

---

[7]   Also recorded in *E32/138*, p. 119 **188-192**.
[8]   The first of these assarts was in Langley, the other in Leafield.
[9]   Roger Lestrange became Justice of the Forest south of Trent on 21st October 1283 and was still
Justice in April 1296 when he was appointed to arrent wastes. However, by February 1297 Hugh le
Despencer had succeeded him as Justice: *Cals. Pat. 1281-1292*, 84, *1292-1301*, 187 and 238.

30th year [1302]

10   And John of Langley usurped as above at Michaelmas in the 30th year of the aforesaid King Edward 8½ acres 1 rood 18 perches of the King's soil, namely 1 acre 16 perches between Empteshacch and Folkedeok and 2 acres 2 roods 2 perches at Donecrondles.

35th year [1307] *other soil*

11   Also the aforesaid William on Sunday in Easter in the 35th year of the aforesaid King Edward [26 March 1307] arrented to the Abbot and Convent of Winchcombe 22 acres of waste of their own soil, namely 20 acres between the earl of Warwick's wood and the demesne land of the manor of Asterleigh, and 2 acres between the King's wood and the wood of the aforesaid Abbot,[10] at a rent of 11d. a year as above, to be first paid by them at Michaelmas in the 35th year. To be held by the same Abbot and Convent and their successors of the King and his heirs as above.

Other soil

12   And to the same Abbot 93 acres 1 rood of waste, namely 78 acres and 30 perches between the northern headland of the 20 acres arrented to the same abbot as is shown above and the fields of the men of the vill of Enstone, and 14½ acres 10 perches between the messuage and croft of Agnes of Bloxham of Ditchley and the aforesaid Abbot's wood on both sides of Grim's Ditch; paying 3s.10¾d. per year as above, and for entry ½d.

Of the King's soil

13   And to John de Ulwork of Leafield 2 acres of the King's soil at Studley,[11] paying 7d. per year for it as above, and for entry 4 pence.

14   And to John of Langley 1½ roods and 18 perches, namely 25 perches next to the same John's place at Cleyput, and 1 rood 12 perches opposite Robert Dobbe's wood next to the place of John himself.[12] Paying as above 2d.

---

[10]   This assart and the following were in the south-eastern part of Winchcombe's manor of Enstone, and they effectively cleared the area between Enstone's existing arable fields and the hamlet of Ditchley. The earl of Warwick's wood was in Spelsbury. The licences for these assarts are recorded in *Landbuc sive Registrum Monasterium Beatae Virginis Mariae et Sancti Cenhelmi de Winchelcumba*, ed. D Royce, *ii*, 25 and *iv*, 125.

[11]   Studley was at the eastern end of Leafield. See p. 193, **324**.

[12]   At Langley; Robert Dobbe was there in 1327 when he was assessed 4s. for tax. At the same date the assessment of Thomas of Langley, son of John of Langley, was 5s.6d. and that of Joan of Langley, John's widow, 6s.8d: E137/161/9.

Assarts in Wychwood, 1337

Bartholomew de Burgherssh, Keeper of the Lord King's Forest this side of Trent, to Thomas of Langley, keeper of the Forest of Wychwood, or to him who holds his place in the same, greetings. Since in the regard of the regarders of the aforesaid Forest at the last perambulation it was presented in the account

1   that William le Blund assarted newly at Finstock two and a half acres of land in the same

2   and that Robert carter of Charlbury assarted newly in the same place five acres of land in the same

3   and that Richard of Cornbury assarted newly in the same place four acres of land in the same

4   and that William Chamberlein assarted newly in the same place [illegible] acres of land in the same

5   and that Robert Swayn assarted newly in the same place one rood

6   and that Robert le Frere of Fawler assarted newly in the same place at Grenedich five acres of land in the same

7   and that Henry Dichele assarted newly in the same place ten acres of land in the same

8   and that Henry Smith of Cote assarted newly in the same place half an acre and one rood of land in the same

9   and that William son of Stephen Wylot assarted newly in the same place half an acre of land in the same

10   and that Henry Wylot assarted newly in the same place half an acre of land in the same

11   and that John at Well and Gilbert son of Robert Jeol assarted newly in the same place half an acre and one perch of land in the same

12   and that Thomas Tril and John son of Walter of Ramsden assarted newly in the same place half an acre and one perch in the same

13   and that Walter son of Walter of Ramsden and John Joye assarted newly in the same place half an acre and half a perch of land in the same

14   and that Reginald and Gilbert Jeol assarted newly in the same place one acre and one rood of land in the same

15   and that Thomas son of Walter in the Hyrne assarted newly in the same place [no acreage given]

16   and that Hugh le White assarted newly in the same place one and a half acre in the same

17   and that Henry Hickeman and Henry son of Gilbert assarted newly in the same place one acre and one rood of land in the same

18   and that Nicholas son of Nicholas of Langley and Margery daughter of August' assarted newly in the same place one acre and one rood of land in the same

19   and that William son of Walter in the Hyrne assarted newly in the same place one rood of land in the same

20   and that William of Hempton assarted newly in Ordweywoode one and a half acres of land in the same

21   and that Richard de Coumlya assarted newly in Asthall three roods of land in the same

22   and that Agnes who was the wife of Bedelh', Robert of Witney and John Smith of Charlbury assarted newly at Charlbury one acre and a half of land in the same

23   and that Roger of Langley and Henry of Tilgarsley assarted newly in the same place two acres of land in the same

24   and that William Berald and Roger Carpenter and Gregory son of John assarted newly in the same place half an acre and one rood of land in the same

25   and that Henry of Woodstock assarted newly in the same place half an acre and half a rood of land in the same

26   and that William of Cornbury assarted newly in the same place two acres of land in the same

27   and that John of Brailes and Gilbert in le Slade assarted newly in the same place one acre of land in the same

28   and that Robert Swayn assarted newly in the same place two acres of land in the same

29   and that Reginald Stirthup and Richard Bubby assarted newly in the same place one acre of land in the same

30   and that Geoffrey Gerbot and John Pone assarted newly in the same place two acres of land in the same

31   and that John atte Wode and Henry Neuman assarted newly in the same place one acre of land in the same

32   and that Robert Gilbert and Simon his brother assarted newly in the same place half an acre of land in the same

33   and that John of Piddington assarted newly in the same place one acre of land in the same

34   and that John Gerbod assarted newly in the same place half an acre of land in the same

35   and that William of Fulwell assarted newly in the same place half an acre of land in the same

36   and that William Toky assarted newly in the same place two acres of land in the same

37   and that Robert son of Richard of Cote assarted newly in the same place half an acre of land in the same

38   and that Geoffrey Clement and John Ailward assarted newly in the same place two acres of land in the same

39   and that Robert Pone assarted newly in the wood of Lardesleye one acre and one and a half roods of land in the same

40   and that Richard Bubby William Gerbod and William le Stondare assarted newly one and a half acres of land in the same

41   and that Roger of Langley assarted newly in the same place one and a half acres and one and a half roods of land in the same

42   and that William shepherd and John Smith assarted newly in the same place one acre and one rood of land in the same

43   and that William atte Diche and Alice Durdaum assarted newly in the same place half an acre and half a rood of land in the same

44   and that Henry Bedell assarted newly in the same place half an acre and half a rood of land in the same

45   and that Robert Carpenter assarted newly in the same place one acre and one rood of land in the same

46   and that Richard atte hulle assarted newly in the same place half an acre of land in the same

47   and that Henry Bedell and William Chamberleyn assarted newly in the same place two acres and a half of land in the same

48   and that Geoffrey assarted newly in the same place one and a half acres of land in the same

49   and that John of Brailes assarted newly in the same place half an acre and half a rood of land in the same

50   and that John de North assarted newly in the same place one and a half acres and one rood of land in the same

51   and that Walter shepherd assarted newly in the same place one and a half acres and one rood of land in the same

52   and that Richard in le Slade and John Gladlich assarted newly in the same place one acre and one rood of land in the same

53   and that Matilda in le Slade assarted newly in the same place one rood of land in the same

54   and that Robert Pone assarted newly in the same place one acre and one rood of land in the same

55   and that John Joye assarted newly in the same place [illegible] acr' and half a rood of land in the same

56   and that Thomas le Venour assarted newly in the same place five acres of land in the same

57   and that William Ulger assarted newly in the same place one and a half acres and half a rood of land in the same

58   and that William le Valer of Ramsden assarted newly in the same place half an acre of land in the same

59   and that Gilbert of Langley and Peter le Gigour assarted newly in the same place five acres of land in the same

60   and that Thomas son of Oliver assarted newly in the same place one rood of land in the same

61   and that Agnes Danvers assarted newly in the same place one rood of land in the same

62   and that Richard of Cornbury assarted newly in the same place ten acres of land in the same

63   and that Peter Wylot and William in le Hyrne assarted newly in the same place half an acre and half a rood of land in the same

64   and that William of Ramsden, Gilbert Cross and John de Swindene assarted newly in the same place one acre of land in the same

65   and the Gilbert Jeol and John Joye assarted newly in the same place half an acre of land in the same

66   and that John Tillyng and William Wilot assarted newly in the same place one acre of land in the same

67   and that Henry Willot and Gilbert of Finstock assarted newly in the same place one acre and one rood of land in the same

68   and that Walter of Ramsden and Geoffrey of Leafield assarted newly in the same place one acre and half a rood of land in the same

69   and that Lovekyn Wal assarted newly in the same place half an acre and half a rood of land in the same

70   and that John Richard de Swynden assarted newly in the same place one acre and half a rood of land in the same

71   and that Richard Coket assarted newly in the same place half an acre of land in the same

72   and that Thomas de Colby assarted newly in the same place half an acre of land in the same

73   and that Thomas at Well assarted newly in the same place half an acre and half a rood of land in the same

74   and that Thomas Petty [illegible word] of Wilcote assarted newly in the same place two and a half acres of land in the same

75   and that Richard Wilot assarted newly in the same place half an acre and half a rood of land in the same

76   and that Gilbert de Langeton assarted newly in the same place one and a half rood of land in the same

77   and that Walter de Witherhall assarted newly in the same place one acre of land in the same

78   and that Robert Benyngho and Gilbert de Langeton assarted newly in the same place half an acre of land in the same

79   and that Walter Boucher assarted newly in the same place half an acre of land in the same

80   and that Robert Leyng assarted newly in the same place one rood of land in the same

81   and that Hugh le Wyte assarted newly in the same place two acres of land in the same

82   and that Richard in le Slade assarted newly in the same place half an [illegible] of land in the same

83   and that Gilbert in le Slade and John of Brailes assarted newly in the same place half an acre of land in the same

84   and that William le Chamberleyn assarted newly in the same place three roods of land in the same

85   and that Roger Sturthup assarted newly in the same place half an acre and half a rood of land in the same

86   and that Robert carter assarted newly in the same place half an acre and half a rood of land in the same

87   and that Robert Galewaye and William atte Diche assarted newly in the same place half an acre of land in the same

88   and that William Gerbod and John Pone assarted newly in the same place half an acre of land in the same

89   and that Peter le Gigour assarted newly in the same place one acre one rood of land in the same

90   and that Robert le Heyre, Robert le Mareschal of Tackley assarted newly in the same place seven acres of land in the same

91   and that Nicholas Ithel assarted newly in the same place half an acre of land in the same

92   and that Philip Basset of Kirtlington assarted newly at Grenedich twenty acres of land in the same

93   and that William Chamberleyn assarted newly at Makerelshawe[1] four acres of land in the same

94   and that John of Brailes and John in le Slade assarted newly in the same place half an acre of land in the same

95   and that Robert Sweyn and John atte Wode assarted newly in the same place two acres of land in the same

96   and that John Pone and John Smith, John Hert and Roger of Langley, John Geffrey, John of Brailes [and] Gilbert in le Slade assarted newly in the same place three acres of land in the same

97   and that William Gerbod and William de Stondare assarted newly in the same place half an acre of land in the same

98   and that Thomas atte Grene assarted newly in the same place at Stonesfield of the Abbot of Eynsham's fee[2] one acre and one rood of land in the same

99   and that John le Chauncel' assarted newly in the same place half an acre of land in the same

---

[1]   Makerelshawe survived as a field name, Mackerelshire, in Charlbury: PRO IR29/27/30, IR30/27/30.

[2]   The Abbot of Eynsham held no land in Stonesfield manor, and this assart was presumably in Fawler but at its boundary with Stonesfield..

100 and that Richard [illegible] assarted newly in the same place half an acre and one rood of land in the same

101 and that Richard of Stonesfield assarted newly in the same place one acre and one rood of land in the same

102 and that Nicholas Cat assarted newly in the same place one acre and half a rood of land in the same

103 and that Walter Walerand and John Inge assarted newly in the same place three acres and half a rood of land in the same

104 and that Robert Pomeray assarted newly in the same place seven acres of land in the same

105 and that John Sampson assarted newly in the same place one acre and half a rood of land in the same

106 and that William Dame Emma assarted newly in the same place two acres of land in the same

107 and that Richard son of Walter of Ramsden and Richard de Wenden assarted newly in the same place one acre of land in the same

108 and that Robert Curteis assarted newly in the same place two acres and one rood of land in the same

109 and that Robert Gladlich assarted newly in the same place half an acre and one rood of land in the same

110 and that John Gerbode assarted newly at Fawler of the Abbot of Eynsham's fee one and a half roods of land in the same

111 and that Richard atte Waye and Maurice his son and Henry Oliver and William Horsman assarted newly in the same place one acre of land in the same

112 and that William Horsman assarted newly in the same place one acre of land in the same

113 and that Peter le Gigour assarted newly in the same place one rood of land in the same

114 and that William le Blount assarted newly in the same place one acre and three roods of land in the same

115 and that Robert Pone assarted newly in the same place half an acre of land in the same

116 and that Richard Cross and William Fiden assarted newly in the same place half an acre of land in the same

117 and that William shepherd and Henry Neuman assarted newly in the same place half an acre of land in the same

118 and that John Wy...tor of Ditchley assarted newly in the same place one rood of land in the same

119 and that William Chauncel' Robert Chancel' and John Fairbere assarted newly in the same place one and a half acres of land in the same

120 and that John at Well assarted newly in the same place one rood of land in the same

121 and that Agnes of Finstock assarted newly at Finstock five acres of land in the same

122 and that Hugh Clerk of Finstock assarted newly in the same place three acres of land in the same

123 and that Thomas Yolger assarted newly in the same place two acres and a half of land in the same

124 and that Henry Gilbert assarted newly in the same place three acres of land in the same

125 and that John Wilot assarted newly in the same place three acres of land in the same

126 and that William Walters assarted newly in the same place one acre of land in the same

127 and that Henry de Denleye assarted newly in the same place one acre of land in the same

128 and that John son of Walter of Ramsden assarted newly in the same place one acre of land in the same

129 and that Thomas and William sons of Walter in le Hyrne assarted newly in the same place one acre in the same

130 and that Nicholas le White assarted newly in the same place one acre and one rood of land in the same

131 and that Ralph Schakelok assarted newly in the same place one acre of land in the same

132 and that John Pone assarted newly in the same place two acres of land in the same

133 and that Gilbert Cross assarted newly in the same place one acre of land in the same

134 and that Gilbert Howes assarted newly in the same place one acre of land in the same

135 and that Thomas Tril assarted newly in the same place one acre of land in the same which John at Well now holds[3]

136 and that Henry Wilot assarted newly in the same place one acre of land in the same

137 and that Agnes of Finstock assarted newly in the same place one acre of land in the same which Nicholas son of Nicholas of Langley now holds

138 and that Henry Hikeman assarted newly in the same place one acre of land in the same which Alice who was the wife of the said Henry now holds

139 and that Richard Wilot assarted newly in the same place one acre of land in the same

---

[3] From this point on the entries refer to old assarts, most of them being those at Combe listed on pp. 106-7, although they are in reverse order and in some cases the assart had changed hands or been divided.

140 and that Nicholas Faukes of Combe now holds an assart at Combe containing three acres of land in the same

141 and that William atte Stokke holds a certain assart in the same place containing two acres of land

142 and that John atte Stokke holds a certain assart in the same place containing four acres of land in the same

143 and that Hugh son of John holds a certain assart in the same place containing two acres of land in the same

144 and that John son of John Aleyn holds a certain assart in the same place containing two acres of land in the same

145 and that Robert of Hanborough holds in the same place a certain assart containing two acres one rood of land in the same

146 and that Thomas son of Nicholas Rose holds in the same place a certain assart containing one rood of land

147 and that William Sewat holds in the same place a certain assart containing one acre

148 and that Robert Mille holds in the same place a certain assart containing three acres and one rood of land in the same

149 and that John son of Reginald of Hanborough and Isabell his sister hold in the same place a certain assart containing two acres of land and one rood of land in the same

150 and that William Galeway holds in the same place a certain assart containing two and a half acres and one rood of land in the same

151 and that William and Thomas West hold in the same place a certain assart containing two [acres] and a half and one rood of land in the same

152 and that John Gode holds in the same place a certain assart containing two acres and one rood of land

153 and that William Wolnath holds in the same place a certain assart containing four and a half [acres] and one rood of land in the same

154 and that John Wolnath holds in the same place a certain assart containing two and a half acres and one rood in the same

155 and that Hugh son of William Crisp and Agnes Hert hold in the same place a certain assart containing two and a half acres one rood of land in the same

156 and that John Godhyne holds in the same place a certain assart containing four acres of land in the same

157 and that Reginald Miller holds in the same place a certain assart containing five acres of land in the same

158 and that John le Tornour holds in the same place a certain assart containing [illegible] acres and a half of land in the same

159 and that John de Radleye holds in the same place a certain assart containing seven acres of land in the same

160 and that William son of John Al[eyn] holds in the same place a certain assart containing two and a half acres in the same

161 and that Robert son of John Aleyn holds a certain assart in the same place containing two and a half acres of land in the same

162 and that Richard Fisher holds a certain assart in the same place containing two and a half acres in the same

163 and that Robert fisher and Illona his sister hold a certain assart in the same place containing two and a half acres of land in the same

164 and that John Capplinus holds a certain assart in the same place containing five acres of land in the same

165 and that Robert Baldon holds a certain assart in the same place containing one acre and one rood of land in the same

166 and that John Aleyn holds a certain assart in the same place containing half an acre of land in the same

167 and that Reginald Feraur holds a certain assart in the same place containing three and a half acres of land in the same

168 and that John son of William holds a certain assart in the same place containing one acre of land in the same

169 and that William and Edmund sons of [blank] de Folyot hold in the same place a certain assart containing one acre in the same

170 and that Matthew of Hanborough holds in the same place a certain assart containing three acres of land in the same

171 and that John and Hugh sons of William Kynne hold in the same place a certain assart containing two acres of land in the same

172 and that William Jacob' holds a certain assart in the same place containing three and a half acres of land in the same

173 and that Alice and Agnes daughters of [illegible] hold a certain assart in the same place containing two acres and one rood of land in the same

174 and that Robert West holds in the same place a certain assart containing four acres and one rood of land in the same

175 and that John smith holds in the same place a certain assart containing three [acres] and one rood of land in the same

176 and that William son of Emma and John Smith hold in the same place a certain assart containing one rood of land in the same

177 and that John Londy holds in the same place a certain assart containing one and a half acres of land in the same

178 and that Reginald [illegible] holds in the same place a certain assart containing three acres and one rood of land in the same

179 and that Cristina Gode and Simon Gode hold in the same place a certain assart containing twenty acres of land in the same

180 and that Reginald atte Stokke holds in the same place a certain assart containing four acres of land in the same

181 and that Hugh son of William Kynne holds in the same place a certain assart containing one acre and one rood of land in the same

182 and that Peter of Bladon holds in the same place a certain assart containing one acre and one rood in the same

183 and that Peter son of William miller holds in the same place a certain assart containing one rood of land in the same

184 and that John Walters holds in the same place a certain assart containing four acres of land in the same

185 and that Martin son of Richard le Bounder holds in the same place a certain assart containing four acres of land in the same

186 and that John of Langley[4] holds in the same place a certain assart at North[grove] in Langele Mill Weye and Sheper[y]dingh containing thirtyfour acres of land in the same

187 and that William le Hert of Leafield and Emma his wife hold in the same place a certain assart containing sixteen acres of land in the same

188 and that Roger le Portar of Leafield holds in the same place a certain assart containing one acre of land in the same.

189 and that John Cuggel of Leafield holds in the same place a certain assart containing one acre of land in the same

190 and that William Saleman holds in the same place a certain assart containing one acre of land in the same

191 and that Robert [illegible] holds in the same place a certain assart containing one acre of land in the same

which assarts made without warrant and occupied by the aforesaid Robert carter of Charlbury and William le Blount and others beforenamed were enclosed with a ditch and a high wooden fence against the assize of the Forest to the damage of the Lord King and the destruction of his beasts in the same forest. On the Lord King's behalf I command you [illegible words] to take all the aforesaid assarts into the Lord King's hand [illegible] cause to be kept so that neither they nor others [illegible] by them gain anything from the newly won land [illegible] from the Lord King or us thereof [illegible] so that they answer for the value of the revenue arising therefrom. And what is done regarding the aforementioned is to be sent to me or to our deputy on Wednesday next after the feast of St. John at the Latin Gate next at Witney [7 May] to make every question clear. And in no way ignore this and have this letter in the same place.

Given at London on the 16th day of April in the eleventh year of the reign of King Edward the third after the conquest [1337].

---

4   John of Langley, Forester of Wychwood, died in 1324, and in 1337 this assart should have been held by his son Thomas: *Cal. Inq. p. m 6,* No 590.

Purprestures in Wychwood, 1337

[The membrane is heavily stained and parts are illegible]

Bartholomew de Burgherssh, keeper of the Lord King's forest this side of Trent, to Thomas of Langley, keeper of the forest of Wychwood or [whoever is] taking his place in the same, greetings. Whereas in the regard [made] by the regarders of the aforesaid forest at the last forest perambulation it was presented and accounted

1   that Adam le Folour purprestured at Spelsbury one and a half roods of land in the same which Reginald de Stocwell now holds

2   and that Roger of Fulwell purprestured at Fulwell half an acre and one rood of land which William of Fulwell now holds

3   and that Ralph of Cleveley, Adam of Cleveley, William Aboveton and Andrew of Cleveley purprestured in [illegible] of Over Enstone towards Wodefeld four perches of land in length and one perch in breadth in the same

4   and that Robert le Blake and William Aylward purprestured in the same place one and a half acres of land in the same

5   and that William clerk of Combe purprestured at Combe half a rood of land in the same which Adam clerk now holds in the same

6   and that Robert Turry purprestured in the same place half a rood of land which William Turry now holds in the same

7   and that John Turry purprestured in the same place three perches of land in length which John Emme now holds

8   and that Hugh Terry made a certain purpresture in the same place on which he built a certain curtilage which Roger Miller now holds in the same

9   and that Hugh of Radford made a purpresture there of four perches of land which the same Hugh now holds in the same

10   and that Oskere Bisshope [and] Walter de Leya made a certain purpresture in the same place on which they built two curtilages which Wymarc and Walter Ferebras now hold in the same

11   and that Robert Loddere and Robert Long made a purpresture in the same place of six perches of land which William Wodeward and John Shepherd now hold in the same

12   and that Robert de Wydia and Alan Edward made a purpresture in the same place of six perches of land which John de Wydia and William Kynnes now hold in the same

---

[1]   Although this document is dated 1337, the purprestures named in it are not of that date, nor all of the same date. **57**, for example, must date from before 1268 and **56** from before 1272. The purprestures at Combe are found in three different places, **5-37**, **64-70**, and **92-101**, and presumably were made (or first recorded) at three different dates.

13 and that Alan Edward purprestured and holds six perches of land at the same place in the same

14 and that Walter de Leya made a purpresture in the same place of half a perch of land in the same

15 and that Walter atte Streme made a purpresture in the same place of nine perches of land in the same

16 and that Henry Sprot made a purpresture in the same place of three perches of land.in the same which Alice who was the wife of Robert Hered [le Eyr] of Woodstock now holds in the same

17 and that Robert Norman made a purpresture in the same place of one rood which John Whiath now holds in the same

18 and that William Wolnath now holds in the same and purprestured in the same place two perches of land in the same

19 and that Robert atte Stocke made a purpresture in the same place of two roods of land in length and one rood in breadth which Roger atte Stocke now holds

20 and that Herbert reeve made a purpresture in the same place of four perches of land in length and two in breadth which John of London now holds

21 and that William Ferebras made a purpresture in the same place twelve feet in length and four perches in breadth which John of London now holds in the same.

22 and that William May made a purpresture in the same place of a quarter of a rood in length and one rood in breadth which Richard fisher now holds in the same

23 and that Roger son of John made a purpresture in the same place of four roods in length and one rood in breadth of land which Robert de Creston now holds in the same

24 and that Robert de Hethe made a purpresture in the same place of six perches of land in length and one perch in breadth in the same

25 and that Hugh de la Dey made a purpresture in the same place of one acre one rood in the same

26 and that Robert Turry made a purpresture in the same place of half an acre of land which William Creps now holds

27 and that William Herberd and William Wolnath made a purpresture in the same place of one rood of land which John Aleyn now holds in the same

28 and that Henry reeve William Cripps Robert de Stoke Robert Turry Reginald de Strame and John atte Hethe made a purpresture in the same place of one and a half acres of land which R... atte Stocke and Alice wife of Robert le Eyr now hold

29 and that Robert atte Stocke made a purpresture in the same place of one rood and two perches of land which Robert atte Stocke now holds in the same

30 and that Robert Turry and Thomas Alis made a purpresture in the same place of two roods of land which William Turry now holds in the same

31   and that Walter Ferebras [and] Robert atte Hethe made a purpresture in the same place of half an acre of land which Alice who was the wife of Robert le Eyr now holds in the same

32   and that Roger Cripps and Roger Slade made a purpresture in the same place of one rood of land which Alice Cr... and Robert de Ordet now hold in the same

33   and that Henry reeve Roger de la Grene and Robert de Stoke made a purpresture in the same place of an acre of land in the same

34   and that John de Hyett made a purpresture in the same place of three perches of land which Alice who was the wife of Robert le Eyr now holds in the same

35   and that Hugh de Boxe made a purpresture in the same place of four perches of land in length and one perch in breadth in the same which Alice Herd now holds in the same

36   and that John mason Roger Cripps Robert de Stoke William Crips and Roger de Streme Hanfridus carpenter and John Frayn made a purpresture in the same place of one acre and one rood in the same

37   and that Robert le Hey made a purpresture in the same place of three perches in length and one in breadth which Alice his wife now holds in the same

38   and that John Cawe made a purpresture at Stonesfield of the Lord King's fee of three perches of land in length and two perches in breadth in the same

39   and that Geoffrey Turry and Godfrey of Slape made a purpresture at Wootton of the Lord King's fee of three perches of land in the same

40   and that Peter Ponchard, William Josselin, William reeve, Elias Asthard, Fray Punchard, Henry son of Ralph, Henry de la Mare, William Josselyn, Walter Joppe, Gamelyn and Hugh parson made a purpresture at Asterleigh of the fee of Ralph de Saucey of one rood of land in the same

41   and that the lady Letitia de Saucey[2] made a purpresture in the same place of one rood of land which Isabell de Camville now holds in the same

42   and that Roger [illegible] made a purpresture of eight perches of land in the same

43   and that John clerk made a purpresture at North Leigh of the monk's fee, of one and a half acres of land in the same

44   and that Alice de Holeweye made a purpresture in the same place of one and a half roods in the same

45   and that William Curtais made a purpresture in the same place of one acre of land in the same

---

[2]   This purpresture must pre-date 1279, when the de Sauceys had been succeeded as lords of Asterleigh by Richard of Williamscot: *Rot. Hund. ii, 734.*

46   and that Richard Smith made a purpresture in the same place of half an acre of the same

47   and that Thomas Goddefrid made a purpresture in the same place of twenty acres in the same

48   and that Walter in le Hyrne made a purpresture at Charlbury of the Abbot of Eynsham's fee of nine and a half acres in the same

49   and that the Abbot of Eynsham made a purpresture in the same place of sixteen acres of land in the same

50   and that Aileward of Finstock made a purpresture in the same place of one acre of land in the same

51   and that Robert son of Henry Balbuc of Woodstock made a purpresture on the heath of Hanborough of one acre of land which Alice who was his wife now holds in the same

52   and that Humphrey Ligines of Hanborough made a purpresture in the same place of half an acre in the same

53   and that James le Blount made a purpresture at Fawler of three roods of the Abbot of Eynsham's fee which William le Blount now holds in the same

54   and that Peter le Carboner made a purpresture at Tilgarsley of the same Abbot's fee of one acre in the same

55   and that Walter Wynot made a purpresture in the same place of one acre of land in the same

56   and that the lord Richard brother of the Lord King, Reginald of Asthall, Eustace le Oy, Pagan de Mombery, Walter Ariles, Robert le Frere, Eustace de Leya and Hugh Segrym made a purpresture at Asthall of the earl of Cornwall's fee, of thirteen acres of land in the same[3]

57   and that Walter de Grey made a purpresture at Cogges of his own fee of sixteen acres of land which Isabel de Grey now holds in the same[4]

58   and that Richard Herny made a purpresture in the same place of three perches in length and two perches in breadth in the same

59   and that Geoffrey of Abingdon, William le Bull and Richard Bolebac made a purpresture in the same place of two acres in the same

60   and that Ralph of Bledington of Ditchley made a purpresture at Ditchley of one rood of land which Thomas of Ditchley now holds in the same

61   and that Thomas le Boaler of Wilcote made a new purpresture in the vill of Wilcote of one rood of land which Robert of Wilcote now holds in the same

62   and between [illegible place-name] Bloxham wood and the chapel of Fawler are twentyfour acres of waste of the Lord King's soil in the same

63   and Robert of Bledington of Ditchley made a new purpresture at Ditchley of one rood of land in the same

---

[3]   This purpresture must pre-date 1272, the year in which Richard, earl of Cornwall, died.
[4]   Walter de Grey died in 1268. His widow Isabel held Cogges in 1279: *V.C.H. Oxon. xii*, 59.

64   and that John le Causere made a new purpresture at Combe, of the Lord King's fee, of four perches in length and two in breadth in the same

65   and that John Smith of Combe made a new purpresture in the same place of a piece of land on which he built a certain house with a curtilage

66   and that John Clerk made a certain purpresture in the same place on which he built, in the same

67   and that John Goden made a certain curtilage there containing half a perch of land in it on which he built a certain house in the same

68   and that Robert le Eyr made a purpresture in the same place of half a rood of land which his wife now holds in the same

69   and that John Martin of Combe made a purpresture in the same place of half a rood of land in the same

70   and that the same John, Robert atte Hethe, William Bisshop, William his son [and] [illegible] atte Stocke made a new purpresture in the same place of half an acre of land in the same

71   and that Waylin son of William de Wytenhull made a purpresture at North Leigh of the Abbot of Netley's fee of one acre of land in the same

72   and that the Abbot of Netley made a new purpresture in the same place in the vill of North Leigh of two acres of land in the same

73   and that Richard le [tear in membrane] William of North Leigh made a new purpresture in the same place of one rood of land in the same

74   and that William Bilich of North Leigh, Walter Myrabel of the same, Martin [tear] reeve of the same, Roger shepherd of the same, Alice Bouch' of the same, [and] Martin Cross of the same made a new purpresture at Eynsham of the Abbot's fee of one and a half acres, new, on which the said Martin miller built a house in the same

75   and that Walter Pride, Walter le [illegible] and William Herbert made a new purpresture at Finstock of the fee of John de la Wade of one and a half acres of land in the same

76   and that John Whyte reeve of Ditchley made a new purpresture at Ditchley of the Abbot of Winchcombe's fee[5] of one rood of land in the same

77   and that John de Stocwell made a new purpresture in the same place of one rood of land in the same

78   and that Robert atte Deye made a new purpresture in the same place of one acre and three roods of land in the same

79   and that Mackinus le Chauncel [and] Lovekin Jordan made a new purpresture at Stanton of Richard de Harcourt's fee of one and a half acre of land in the same

80   and that William Chauncel', Lovekin Jordan [and] Richard [illegible] purprestured in the same place one and a half [illegible] of land in the same

---

[5]   This purpresture is in that part of Ditchley which lay in Enstone manor. The earlier purpresture there, **62-63**, was presumably in Bloxham Wood.

81 and that Henry le Longe and Walter Dirray made a new purpresture in the same place on one rood of land in the same

82 and that Robert le Blak and Robert Graunger made a new purpresture in the same place of one rood of land in the same

83 and that Alan de la Grene of Stanlake made a new purpresture of one rood of land in the same

84 and that [illegible] de la Hulle made a new purpresture in the same place of one rood of land in the same

85 and that Ralph Schakelok made a new purpresture at Gatewell of the Abbot of Eynsham's fee of one rood of land in the same on which he built

86 and that Richard de Swynden of Finstock made a new purpresture at Finstock of one rood of land in the same on which he built a house and a curtilage

87 and that Thomas Pr[illegible] de Schutelegh made a new purpresture on the Lord King's soil of one perch of land on which he built a house with curtilage in the same

88 and that Pachus of Schutelege made a new purpresture at Finstock of half a rood of land on which he built a house with curtilage in the same

89 and that Walter of Boriens made a new purpresture at Glympton, of Robert de Bray's fee,[6] of one perch of land in the same

90 and that Peter of Boriens made a new purpresture in the same place of one perch of land in the same

91 and that William de Hempton of Wilcote made a new purpresture in the same place of one acre and one rood of land in the same

92 and that Henry Matheu made a new purpresture of the Lord King's fee at Combe of half an acre in the same

93 and that Isabell Wichic made a new purpresture in the same place of half a rood of land in the same

94 and that Thomas London made a new purpresture in the same place of one rood of land in the same

95 and that John Piges made a new purpresture in the same place of one rood of land in the same

96 and that Andrew Howes made a new purpresture in the same place of half an acre of land in the same

97 and that Thomas atte Hull made a new purpresture in the same place of half an acre of land in the same

98 and that Robert Creps made a new purpresture in the same place containing twenty.... feet in length and [illegible]teen in breadth of land in the same

6 Robert de Bray's fee was "The Frith", which probably included part, at least, of Boriens. This purpresture and the next must pre-date 1296, when Robert de Bray sold his land to Thomas de Abberbury: *V.C.H. Oxon. xi*, 124; P.R.O. CP 25(1)/188/12.

99   and that Roger Alayn made a new purpresture in the same place of one rood of land in the same

100   and that John Ward made a new purpresture in the same place of ten feet in breadth in the same

101   and that Roger Aleyn made a new purpresture in the same place of one rood of land in the same

102   and that John Ward made a new purpresture at Stanton, of Roger de Mortimer's fee,[7] of three acres in the same

103   and that the aforesaid John enclosed the wood against the assize

which purprestures, encroached on and cleared by the aforesaid Adam le Folour and Reginald de Stocwell and the others aforesaid in the aforesaid wood, were enclosed with a ditch and high wooden fence against the assize of the forest and without warrant, to the damage of the Lord King and loss to his deer in the same forest; on behalf of the Lord King we order you [illegible words] that all the aforesaid purprestures with the aforesaid wood should be taken into the hand of the Lord King for [illegible words] to be kept safely [illegible] so that neither they nor others [acting] for them [illegible words, should profit from?] the said lands, purprestures or aforesaid wood [illegible] nor in anything from the [illegible] and what is done with regard to the foregoing to be sent to us [or] our deputy on Wednesday next after the feast of St. John at the Latin Gate next [7 May] at Witney, to make all [illegible] clear. And in no way [fail?] to do this. And have this letter in the same place.

   Given at London the 16th day of April in the eleventh year of the reign of King Edward the third after the conquest [1337].

[Endorsed] *12 END Wychewod Forest Oxon ut suppositur*

---

[7]   Roger de Mortimer's manor in Stanton was sold in 1327 to John Wyard: *V.C.H. Oxon. xii*, 277, 279.

[The documents in Class E32/306 are General Inquisitions into the state of the forests of Wychwood or of Shotover and Stowood. They are written on wide parchment membranes and have had seals attached at the bottom, although these have not always survived.]

E32/306/1[1] [1362]

Inquisition held at Charlbury on the Monday next before the feast of the Nativity of the Blessed Mary in the thirty-sixth year of the reign of King Edward the third after the conquest [5 September 1362] before Peter atte Wode, deputy for the keeper of the forest this side of Trent, regarding the state of the forest of Wychwood in the county of Oxford, by oath of

Richard Duffe, deputy for Roger de Elmerugge, keeper of the aforesaid forest,[2]

Geoffrey Bokhurst, Nigel Mereman, Nicholas Wagur, Richard Rykewale, William Squyor [and] William le Ryche, foresters,

Ralph Fretewell and John Carswell verderers,

Eustace Rokayl, Reginald atte Fyfhuyde, John Whytefeld, Roger Radford, Thomas [gap, ?So]ney, William Martyn, Walter Compton, John atte Halle, John Underwode, Richard Smyth, Henry Wappinbury and Walter Taylour, regarders,

Richard atte Bury, Henry Austyn, Henry Tubych, Robert le Webbe, John Edmond, Nicholas Stevenns, Robert le Tailour, William James, John Cosin, John Sompter, John Maynard [and] Nicholas Mainard free tenants within [the forest],

Reginald Wygwold, John le Oyr [Eyr], John atte Brok, John atte Mull, Michael [Nicholas] Raulyn, John Sibbeford, Thomas Batyn, Walter Crook, John le muleward, Thomas Tailour, John Coluns and John Mercer, free tenants outside the bounds of the aforesaid forest

1 Which aforesaid jurors say upon their oaths that William Beauchamp and Thomas le Hunte, together with two unknown servants of the lord John de Nowers for whose name enquiry is to be made, came into the fields of Shipton in the bailiwick of Burford by night on the Saturday next after the feast of St. Lawrence in the 36th year of the aforesaid King [13 August 1362] with six of

---

[1]   This inquisition is also recorded in P.R.O E32/279 m. 7 and E32/283 m 3d. Some names in those documents differ from those found in E32/306/1, and these are added in square brackets.

[2]   An Inquisition of 21 October 1368 stated that Roger de Elmerugge had held the keepership of Wychwood since the death of Thomas of Langley in 1361. The latter died without direct male heirs and some of his sisters' heirs, to whom the keepership was to descend, were under age. De Elmerugge was presumably appointed by the king to take charge of Wychwood until the succession to the keepership was settled, but in 1378 the heirs granted the keepership to him for life: *Cal. Inq. p. m. xii,* 236, No. 249; *Inq. ad quod damnum ii,* 560.

127

the aforesaid lord John de Nowers' greyhounds, to do harm to the Lord King in respect of his venison; but they did not take anything and were arrested at that time in the same place by Nicholas le Forster.

2   They also say that on the Tuesday next before the feast of the Ascension of the Lord in the aforesaid year [24 May 1362] John de Trillow, knight,[3] lord William parson of the church of Wilcote and Thomas Beaufo came with three greyhounds to a certain place called Cogges Wood in the aforesaid forest and there took a buck of the third year.

3   They also say that in the 34th and 35th years of the Lord King [1360-1362] Avice [Alice] le Gray[4] felled 10 acres of underwood in her wood of Cogges Wood without the Lord King's licence and enclosed them at will, to the damage of his forest.

4   They also say that Edmund of Cornwall, knight, caused 60 acres in his wood of Asthall Leigh in the aforesaid forest to be felled and enclosed in a similar fashion.

5   They also say that master Simon of Sudbury, formerly Chancellor of Salisbury,[5] felled and enclosed 10 acres in his wood of Stockley in the aforesaid forest in the aforesaid years.

6   They also say that the Prior of Deerhurst felled and enclosed 20 acres in his wood of Taynton in the aforesaid years.

7   They also say that the earl of Northampton felled and enclosed 10 acres in his wood of Boynhale[6] in the aforesaid years in a similar fashion, to the damage of the forest.

8   They also say that Margaret de Perers in a similar fashion felled and enclosed 20 acres of her wood of Pudlicote.

9   They also say that John Golafre similarly felled and enclosed 12 acres in his wood of Sarsden.

10   They also say that Thomas of Williamscot felled and enclosed 10 acres in his wood of Kiddington in a similar fashion.

11   They also say that John Pipard[7] felled and enclosed 8 acres in his wood [of] Stanton in a similar fashion.

---

[3]   John de Trillow held an estate which lay partly in Finstock and partly in North Leigh.: *V.C.H. Oxfordshire xii,* 221.

[4]   Avice, widow of the 1st Lord Grey, held Cogges in dower: *V.C.H. Oxfordshire xii,* 59.

[5]   Simon of Sudbury was Chancellor of Salisbury from 1356 (possibly 1353) to 1361: *John le Neve, Fasti Ecclesiae Anglicanae 1300-1541,* comp. Joyce M. Horn, 17.

[6]   Boynhale was a wood belonging to Ascott-under-Wychwood. That manor had been granted in 1332 to William de Bohun who was created earl of Northampton in 1337. *Cal. Fine Rolls iv 1327-1337,* 323; *Complete Peerage ix,* 665.

[7]   John Pipard held the small fee in Stanton [Harcourt] which had earlier been held by Henry Pipard (see p. 47, **75**): *V.C.H. Oxfordshire xii,* 276.

12   They also say that Ralph de Ferrers[8] felled and enclosed 10 acres in his wood of Stanton in a similar fashion.

13   They also say that the earl of Warwick felled and enclosed 20 acres in his wood of Spelsbury in a similar fashion.

14   They also say that Roger de Beauchamp felled and enclosed in his wood of Quenewode[9]. [no acreage stated]

15   They also say that Edward de Spencer[10] felled and enclosed 8 acres in his wood of Hullewerk in a similar fashion.

16   They also say that Henry Timmes of Fawler together with other unknown men, regarding whom enquiry is to be made, took an oak valued at 3s.4d. which had been felled for the Lord King's works in the bailiwick of Armele in the aforesaid forest, and they carried it away with a cart and 2 mares, valued at 10s., on the Monday next before the feast of St. Peter in chains in the 35th year of the aforesaid Lord King [26 July 1361].

17   They also say that Thomas of Langley[11] felled and removed from the aforesaid forest 40 oak saplings at various times in the 33rd year of the aforesaid Lord King [1359-1360], to the value of 40s., with which he made a palisade around his garden, which used to be enclosed with hedges, and he built houses in his manor of Langley where no houses were, by colour of his office.

18   They also say that Thomas of Langley, knight, built a grange partly of the Lord King's timber and on the soil of the same Lord King called Whytehevedsplace, which is worth 6d. a year, and he occupied it for ten years without [paying] any rent to the Lord King for it.

19   They also say that the same Thomas built a house and a grange on the Lord King's soil called Smythes tenement, and it is worth 6d. a year; which he occupied for ten years without [paying] any rent to the Lord King for it.

20   They also say that Ricerus Rikwale has a tenement built on the Lord King's soil in Langley which he occupied for 14 years and it is worth 8d. a year, from which Thomas of Langley received the rent for the aforesaid period without [paying] any rent for it to the Lord King.

---

[8]   Ralph de Ferrers was the second husband of Joan, widow of Sir William Harcourt of Stanton Harcourt. She held Stanton until 1369: *V.C.H. Oxfordshire xii,* 275; *Cal. Inq. p. m. xiii,* 60, No. 79.

[9]   Roger de Beauchamp was the holder of the royal manor in Bloxham from 1343 to 1380: *V.C.H. Oxfordshire ix,* 59. The revenue from this manor was often granted to the Queen's use, hence the name Quenewode used for the wood belonging to it.

[10]   Lord of the manor of Shipton by descent from his grandmother Eleanor de Clare, sister and co-heiress of Gilbert, earl of Gloucester: *Complete Peerage iv,* 269, 272-5; *Cal. Inq. p. m. x,* 415, No. 523.

[11]   Forester or Keeper of Wychwood from 1327 to 1361: *Cal. Pat. 1327-30,* 7; and see **25.**

21 They also say that John le Byle has a tenement built on the Lord King's soil in Langley which is worth 4d. a year; and the aforesaid Thomas received the rent for ten years and paid nothing to the Lord King for it.

22 They also say that William Gille has a tenement built on the Lord King's soil in Langley which he occupied for two years, and it is worth 3d. a year, from which the aforesaid received the rent and paid nothing for it to the Lord King.

23 They also say that Crispian Chaney holds a tenement built on the Lord King's soil which he occupied for 13 years, which is worth 6d. a year, from which the aforesaid received the rent and paid nothing for it to the Lord King.

24 They also say that William Wychele holds a tenement built on the Lord King's soil in Langley which he occupied for 10 years, and it is worth 6d a year, from which the aforesaid Thomas received the rent and paid nothing for it to the aforesaid Lord King.

25 They also say that Thomas of Langley died after the feast of St. Michael in the 35th year of the aforesaid Lord King [29 September 1361], after whose death John Giffard married Alice, formerly the wife of the aforesaid Thomas, who holds the manor of Langley and all lands and tenements which belonged to the aforesaid Thomas in the County of Oxford, who [John and Alice] claim to have the rent of all the aforesaid tenements, and they received it to the disinheritance of the Lord King.

26 They also say that Thomas of Langley appropriated 30 perches in length and two perches or more in breadth of the Lord King's soil at Bancroft in the forest, which he occupied for ten years, and it is worth 6d. a year, and the aforesaid John Giffard and Alice his wife now occupy that land.

27 They also say that the said Thomas built a grange and a sheep-fold in his manor of Milton, for which he had a great part of the Lord King's timber, in the 26th year of the Lord King [1352-3]; value of the timber 40s.

28 They also say that the same Thomas in the 18th year of the aforesaid Lord King [1344-5] built a grange and a sheep-fold in his manor of Shorthampton,[12] for which he had a great part of the timber of the Lord King in the aforesaid forest to the value of 40s.

29 They also say that Thomas built a mill called Langley Mill since the twentieth year of the Lord King [1346-7] and after, which is not of the manor of Langley but of the lordship of Shipton,[13] for which he had the Lord King's timber in the aforesaid forest to the value of 40s.

---

[12] Possibly this was on the site of the later Ranger's Lodge.

[13] The Langley family held land and a mill in Shipton as well as their manor in Milton [**27**] and the keepership of Wychwood: *Rot. Hund. ii*, 739.

30 They also say that the same Thomas felled and had 50 oak saplings in Natterugge in the aforesaid forest at times from the 12th year of the Lord King's reign to the 35th [1338-1362], each of them worth 3d.

31 They also say that the same Thomas felled and had 18 larger oak saplings in the same way at Bilstokrudyngg in the aforesaid forest, each of them worth 12d. And they say that John le Free, Walter Pap, John Jakelot, William Comyng and Thomas Perkyn were the fellers of the said oaks and bought their branches from the aforesaid Thomas for 6s. 8d., which money the aforesaid Thomas had; and they say that the aforesaid Thomas has six thousand sklattes [slates], worth 18s. altogether, from the grange of Ewelme, which is the King's grange adjacent to the Chapel of Ewelme[14] which has been in the Lord King's hand since the 20th year of the aforesaid Lord King [1346-7] because the Abbot of Bruern did not make the Lord King's chantry in the aforesaid chapel.

32 And they say that Richard of London had timber from the said grange in the 29th year of the aforesaid Lord King [1355-6], worth 13s. 4d., without the King's licence.

33 They also say that the said Thomas caused a slatepit to be dug in the forest on le churchull worth 6s. 8d.

34 They also say that William Crips felled and had three oak saplings in the bailiwick of Armele in the 33rd year of the aforesaid Lord King [1359-60], worth 6s. 8d.

35 They also say that Thomas of Langley made a clay-pit in the Lord King's soil, for his own use, with damage to the Lord King of 3s. 4d.

In testimony of these things the aforesaid jurors affixed their seals. Given the day year and place written above.

[No surviving seals]

E32/306/2[15]

Inquisition held at Charlbury on the Monday next before the feast of St. Gregory the Pope in the thirty-eighth year of the reign of King Edward the third after the conquest [11 March 1364] before Peter atte Wode, deputy for the keeper of the Lord King's forest this side of Trent, regarding the state of the forest of Wychwood in the county of Oxford by the oath of

Richard London, deputy for Roger de Elmerugge, keeper of the aforesaid forest,

---

[14] Ewelme is New Hill, which is in the surviving remnant of Wychwood. In 1254 it was stated that there were to be two chaplains at the Abbot of Bruern's hermitage there: *Cal. Close R. 1253-4*, 29.

[15] This Inquisition is also recorded in P.R.O E32/269 m. 2d.

Geoffrey Boukhurst, Nicholas Wagur, Nigel Forester, Richard Rikewale, William Squyer, William Riche, Thomas Cok, foresters,

Ralph Fretewelle and John Carswelle, verderers,

Reginald Fyfhyde, Roger Radford, Walter Barton, Walter Compton, John Underwode, Eustace Rokayle, Thomas Soneye, John Sompter, John atte Halle, Reginald Wygwold, Walter Taylour, John Cosyn, regarders,

John Drynkewater, John Cessour, John Coupere, Nicholas Stevenys, Robert Taylour, William Geims, John Sompter, Thomas Deneleye, James Tomelines, Richard atte Bury, Henry atte Halle, John Sompter of Shorthampton, free tenants,

1   Who say that the earl of Warwick felled 12 acres of underwood in his wood called Spelsbury in the 37th year [1363-4].

2   Also that Roger Beauchamp felled and enclosed 6 acres in his wood of Quenewode.

3   Also that the Abbot of Eynsham felled and enclosed in his wood of Charlbury 20 acres.

4   Also that Ralph de Ferrers felled and enclosed in his wood called Pyriho[16] 3 acres.

5   Also that Isabella Gray felled and enclosed in her wood called Cogeswode 8 acres.

6   Also that John Flour[17] felled and enclosed in his wood called Esegare 4 acres.

7   Also that lord Edward Despenser felled and enclosed in his wood called Hullewerk 5 acres.

8   Also that John Golafre felled and enclosed in his wood called Ferthing[18] 4 acres.

9   Also that Thomas de Leye felled and enclosed in his wood called Henngrove[19] 3 acres.

10   Also that Edmund of Cornwall felled and enclosed in his wood called Asthalewode 6 acres.

11   Also that Richard Haward assarted 3 acres of the Prior of Deerhurst's wood in the lordship of Taynton which is called East Hill,[20] and it was enclosed, to the damage of the forest and against the assize of the forest.

[16]   In Stanton Harcourt, see p. 129, **12**.

[17]   A William Flour held a knight's fee in Pudlicote in 1368: *Cal. Close R. 1364-68*, 496.

[18]   "Ferthing" survived as a field name, the Farthings, in Little Langley, see p. 216, **414**.

[19]   Hensgrove was the wood belonging to Swinbrook manor. It survives.

[20]   East Hill is near Pain's Farm, in what was formerly the detached woodland belonging to Taynton.

12   They also say that on the Thursday next before the feast of the Lord's birth in the 37th year [21 December 1363] Adam Chyke and Richard Sheche of Shorthampton caught a doe with ropes.

13   They also say that on the Monday next after the feast of St. Andrew in the aforesaid year [4 December 1363] John Meleward of Swinbrook placed ropes in the close of the Chancellor of Salisbury[21] in the aforesaid forest and in the same place caught a doe which broke the aforesaid ropes and escaped.

14   They also say that on the Thursday next before the feast of the conversion of St. Paul in the above year [18 January 1364] a certain dog caught a fawn in the wood of Asthall, and John de Leye came and hit the said fawn on the head and carried the said fawn away and had it.

15   They also say that the Prior of the Hospital of St. John of Lechlade is bound to find a chaplain to celebrate in the chapel of Lovebury[22] where the Lord King's foresters ought to have masses, because they must move about within the aforesaid forest for the safe keeping of the Lord King's beasts. And the aforesaid Prior refused to find a chaplain in that place, with serious injury to the Lord King and harm to the foresters of his forest.

16   They also say that when Adam Chike and Richard Serche were attached on the Wednesday next after the feast of St. Mathias in the 38th year of the aforesaid Lord King [28 February 1364] for an offence against the venison in the aforesaid forest, [they were] delivered by the Lord King's foresters to William Crips of Walcot, constable in that place, for safe keeping and conducting to the Lord King's prison, [but] the same William let them escape to the great injury to the Lord King and destruction of the aforesaid forest. [Twenty-seven seals remaining]

E32/306/3 [23]

Inquisition held at Charlbury on the Wednesday next after the feast of St. Benedict Abbot in the forty-first year of King Edward the third after the conquest [19 January 1368] before Peter atte Wode, deputy for William of Wykeham, keeper of the Lord King's forest this side of Trent, regarding the state of the forest of Wychwood in the county of Oxford, by oath of

John Merie, deputy for lord Roger de Elmerugge, keeper of the aforesaid forest,

---

[21]   This was Stockley Copse.

[22]   The hermitage of Lovebury was granted to the Hospital of St. John the Baptist, Lechlade, in 1270: *Cal. Charter R..* 139. It was situated in the southern part of Leafield, possibly not on the site of the present Lowbarrow House but at Dawn Cottage, which has medieval features: personal communication, Mrs. S. F. Sutton.

[23]   This inquisition is also recorded in P.R.O. E32/279 m. 14d.

Geoffrey Boukhurst, Nicholas Wagur, Nigel Forester, Richard Rikewale, William Sqwier, Walter Riche and Thomas Cook, foresters,

Ralph Fretewelle and John Carswelle verderers,

Reginald Fyfhyde, Eustace Rokayle, John Cosin, Walter Barton, William [Walter] Martin, Richard Smyth, John Sompter of Leafield, John [James] Lysour, Richard Pachon, Walter Compton, James Morin [Norys] and Henry atte Halle of Fawler, regarders,

William Biles of Ramsden, John Drynkwater, John Wilcockes, William Crips, Henry atte Halle of Chilson, Henry Tobich, Thomas Denele, Robert Saile [Tailor], Thomas Colon, Nicholas Stevenes, William Conyng, John Revesone and William Skachelok, free tenants

1   Which aforesaid jurors say the Ralph de Ferers made a coppice in his wood of Purynho without warrant in the 40th year [1366-7] containing 6 acres.

2   They also say that Thomas of Williamscot made a coppice in his wood of Kiddington in the above year containing 10 acres.

3   They also say that the same Thomas made another coppice in the aforesaid wood without warrant in the 41st year [1367-8], containing 3 acres.

4   They also say that the Abbot of Winchcombe made a coppice in his wood of Boxwode in the 40th year containing 4 acres, without warrant.

5   They also say that Roger de Beauchamp made a coppice in his wood of Quenewode in the 39th year [1365-6] containing 4 acres, without warrant.

6   They also say that the earl of Warwick made a coppice in his wood of Spelsbury in the 39th year without warrant containing 12 acres.

7   They also say that the Abbot of Eynsham made a coppice in his wood of Charlbury without warrant in the 40th year, containing 12 acres.

8   They also say that John Lovel made a coppice in his wood of Minster containing 4 acres in the 40th year, by what warrant they do not know.

9   They also say that on the Wednesday next before the feast of the Assumption of the Blessed Mary in the 40th year [12 August 1366] John Shepherde of Shipton killed a doe in the field of Shipton.

10   They also say that on Thursday in the feast of the apostles Simon and Jude in the 40th year [29 October 1366] John son of John Hawke [Herdewyck] and John Persel killed a doe with their dogs at Echenesfeld[24] (in the same year but the day is not known).

11   They also say that on the Tuesday next before the feast of the Annunciation of the Blessed Mary in the 40th year [24 March 1366] John Liger killed a doe in the bailiwick of Armele with bows and arrows.

12   They also say that on the Friday next before the feast of St. Michael in the 40th year [25 September 1366] a certain servant of the lord Adam de

---

[24]   Echenesfeld was in North Leigh, where the name survived as Edgings Field: *V.C.H. Oxfordshire xii*, 224.

Shareshull, for whose name enquiry is to be made, killed a doe in the field of Lyneham with dogs, the said Adam being ignorant [of this], but the same Adam had the flesh.

13   They also say that John Hancock and Henry Austyn found a doe dead in the field of Chilson and they carried the flesh away, in the 41st year.

14   They also say that the dogs of William Tymes and William Resen killed a doe in the fields of Leafield in the 23rd year [1349-50]

[No seals]

E32/306/4 [25]

Inquisition held at Charlbury on Tuesday in the feast of St. Clement in the 46th year of the reign of King Edward the third after the conquest [23 November 1372] before John de Foxle, keeper of the Lord King's forest this side of Trent, regarding the state of the forest of Wychwood in the County of Oxford by oath of

Nicholas Wagur, deputy for Roger Elmerugge, keeper of the aforesaid forest

Thomas atte More [and] John Carsewell, verderers

Geoffrey Boukhurst, William Squier, Nigel Mereman, Richard Rikewale, William Riche, John Young, John Warewyke and Thomas Cok, foresters

Reginald Fyfhyde, John Cosyn, Henry atte Hall, Richard Snareston, William Geims, Thomas Becheye, Walter Tailour, Philip Colly, John Holewey, James Thomelyns, Thomas Colyns and Eustace Faris, regarders,

John Edmond, John Barnebe, John Sompter, John Lysour, Henry Tobech, Robert Taillour, John Wykyng, Nicholas Stephens, John Clevele, John Whythed, John Revesone and Henry Geims, free tenants within the forest

John Rugon, William Smyth, Richard Shortfrend, John Crips, Richard Whyberd, Andrew Smyth, John Whytefeld, William Martyn, Walter Compton, Richard May, Henry atte Halle [and] William Borgh, free tenants outside the bounds of the forest,

1   Who say on their oath that John Flour felled 50 oak saplings in his wood of Pudlicote in the 45th year [1371-2], without licence.

2   They also say that Roger Cotesford, knight, made a coppice in his wood of Felle[26] in the 45th year without licence, as they believe.

---

[25]   This inquisition is also recorded in P.R.O. E32/271 m. 9d.

[26]   The only known connection between Roger Cotesford and Wychwood is that one of his estates in Bletchingdon was held by an ancient serjeanty variously described as of providing a roast of pork or a spit for roasting the king's dinner when the king hunted in Wychwood/Cornbury: *V.C.H. Oxfordshire vi*, 60. Nowhere else is it recorded that the estate included any wood. The name Felle possibly relates to the hermitage of Phelleley.

3   They also say that Richard Lucy killed a sow from the Lord King's pigs, valued at 2s., in his corn on the feast of St. Peter ad vincula in the 45th year [1 August 1371].

4   They also say that William Picard of Leafield on the Thursday next before the feast of the Epiphany in the 45th year [1 January 1372] killed a doe in the aforesaid forest.

5   They also say that Gilbert Giffard felled 7 acres of underwood in his wood of Boynhale[27] in the 46th year [1372-3].

6   They also say that William Beauchamp, knight,[28] felled 80 oaks in his wood of Spelsbury in the 45th year.

7   They also say that William Crips and Robert Bergh entered the park of Cornbury at dawn on the Sunday next after the feast of St. Bartholomew in the 45th year [31 August 1371] to do harm to the Lord King's venison, but either they took nothing or it is not known, and on leaving the aforesaid park they were caught.

8   They also say that the lady [Amisia] de Grey and John de Grey of Rotherfield, knight, made waste in the wood of Goggeswode, containing 100 acres, in the 43rd, 44th and 45th years [1369-1372].

9   They also say that the Abbot of Eynsham made a coppice in his wood of Charlbury containing 12 acres without licence in the 45th year of the Lord King, against the assize of the forest.

10   They also say that Roger de Beauchamp, knight, felled 20 oaks in his wood of Quenewode without warrant in the 44th year.

[13 seals.]

---

[27]   The manor of Ascott, to which Boynhale belonged, was held by Gilbert Giffard from 1372 until his death in 1374, by grant of its lord Humphrey de Bohun, earl of Hereford and Northampton: *Cal. Inq. p. m. 13,* 146, No. 167.

[28]   William Beauchamp was a younger son of Thomas Beauchamp, earl of Warwick, and the manor of Spelsbury was granted to him for life in 1345: BL Add.MS 28024, Cartulary of the Earls of Warwick, f. 14.

E32/306/5 [29]

Inquisition held at Brill on the Thursday next before the feast of the Nativity of St. John Baptist in the thirty-seventh year of the reign of King Edward the third after the conquest [22 June 1363] before William of Wykeham, keeper of the Lord King's forest this side of Trent, regarding the state of the forest of Shotover and Stowood in the county of Oxford, by oath of

Robert Gamage, deputy of John de Appulby, keeper of the aforesaid forest,[30]

John Thorlton, William Doffeld, Thomas Man, Matthew Kyng [and John Gillyng, foresters,

John Rykot and John Hardy, verderers,

Thomas Chybunhurst, William Gillot, Adam atte Orchard, John John [sic] Bereford, John Baily, Gilbert Basset, Robert Eustas, Thomas Norton, John atte Wode, Thomas North and Robert Bradele, regarders,

John Dosyere, Richard Wyth, Henry Aynoulf, John Grace, Richard Fynian, Alexander Hereward, Robert Aylesbury, William Blessed, William Jaket [and] John Weston, free tenants within and without the bounds of the forest

1   Who say that on Sunday in the feast of branches [Palm Sunday] in the 36th year of the reign of the aforesaid Lord King [10 April 1362] William Wyke of Elsfield came by night within the bounds of the forest of Stowood with bows and arrows to do harm to the Lord King respecting his deer, and Henry Burstall, forester, attached him.

2   They also say that Robert Dorre of Forest Hill has dogs which, on the Friday next before the feast of Pentecost in the aforesaid year [3 June 1362], killed a fawn, and that the said dogs on the Friday following [10 June] killed another fawn, and that on Saturday in the feast of St. Barnabas the apostle in the aforesaid year [11th June] the aforesaid dogs took a third fawn; and that the said dogs took a fourth fawn on the feast of Holy Trinity in the aforesaid year [12 June].

3   And that John Harald of Forest Hill has a dog which killed a fawn on the Friday next after the feast of the Holy Trinity in the aforesaid year [17 June 1362].

---

[29]   Recorded also in E32/279, m. 8, and in the *Boarstall Cartulary*, No. 568.

[30]   In 1309 the keepership of Shotover and Stowood was bought from Philip Mymekan (see p. 86) by Sir John de Haudlo, Keeper of Bernwood: *Cal. Pat. 1303-13*, 152. He enfeoffed it to himself, his son Richard, Richard's wife Isabel, and their children: *Cal. Pat. 1330-34*, 30. Richard died five years before his father, so that when the latter died in 1346 the Forest passed to Isabel and her second husband, Sir Robert Hildesle (see **9**). Isabel's son Edmund de Haudlo died young, and on her death in 1361 Shotover and Stowood passed initially to her daughter Margaret, wife of Sir John Appleby: *Complete Peerage vi*, 398; *Cal. Inq. p. m.ii*, 70, No. 100.

4   And that John Shepherd of Over Horspath has a dog to the injury of the Lord King's forest, in driving out the same Lord King's deer from their haunts.
5   And that Thomas Cosyn has two dogs which killed three fawns in the forbidden month in the present year, the 37th.
6   They also say that the villages written below are outside the forest and do not have common in the forest, but put their pigs into the Lord King's woods against the assize of the forest, namely the vill of Noke, 12 pigs valued at 18s. And that [sic] the vill of Islip, 20 pigs valued at 12s., Woodeaton 6 pigs valued at 9s., Elsfield 8 pigs valued at 12s., Beckley 10 pigs valued at 15s., Forest Hill 12 pigs valued at 18s., Wheatley 10 pigs valued at 15s., Horspath and Horspath 18 pigs valued at 27s., Cowley and Cowley 12 pigs valued at 18s.
7   They also say that the Prioress of Littlemore wasted her wood in Shotover against the assize of the forest.
8   They also say that whereas the foresters used to have their refreshment at the Manors of the lords of Cuddesdon, Forest Hill, Cowley, Horspath and Horspath, Islip, Wood Eaton, Beckley, Elsfield and Noke, their food has been withdrawn, and they were accustomed to have it from antiquity.
9   They also say that in the time of Robert de Hildesle various trees were felled for the expenses of the Lord King's hospital for boys at Abingdon, and after the death of the said Robert the stumps of the aforesaid trees remained untouched until the time when John Appulby received the custody of the aforesaid forest, in which year, 35 [1361-2], he sold them for 26s. and received that money.

In testimony of which the aforesaid jurors affixed their seals. Given the day place and year written above.
[Nineteen seals remaining.]

E32/306/6 [31]

Inquisition held at Brill on the Thursday next after the feast of St. Lambert in the thirty-eighth year of the reign of King Edward the third after the conquest [19 Sept 1364] before Peter atte Wode, deputy for the keeper of the forest this side of Trent regarding the state of the forest of Shotover and Stowood in the county of Oxford, by oath of

John Appleby, keeper of the aforesaid forest,

Robert Gamage, Richard Forester, John Torton, William Dufield, Thomas Mann, Matthew Ryng [and] John Gillyng, foresters,

John Ruycote and John Hardy, verderers,

---

[31]   Also recorded in the *Boarstall Cartulary*, No. 569.

William Gilot, Walter atte Welle, Robert Bradele, Adam atte Orchard, John Bydowe, Thomas Bere, Gilbert Basset, John Bereford, Thomas North, John atte Wode, Thomas Bernard [and] Thomas Norton, regarders

Richard Fynian, Thomas Brayles, Alan atte Corner, John Collins, John Muleward, Henry Aynulf, John Woodewe, Alan Mayster, John Grace, John Benet, William Sherreve [and] Simon Aynulf, free tenants

1   Who say that on the Saturday next before the feast of St. Peter in Cathedra in the 38th year of the present Lord King [17 February 1364] Thomas of Williamscot while passing through the forest of Stowood with three greyhounds caught and killed a buck of the third year in the aforesaid forest.

2   They also say that the Prioress of Studley has made a certain high fence around her close of Westmoor next to the aforesaid forest where the Lord King's deer cannot enter nor return to the forest; which close is on the boundary of the forest and a great injury to the Lord King's deer.

3   They also say that the Abbot of Westminster[32] felled an oak in the forest of Stowood next to Croundlesepoul in the moor of the said forest in the 36th year of the reign of the aforesaid Lord King after the feast of the Nativity of St. John the Baptist [24 June 1362]; valued at 2s.

[Nineteen seals remaining.]

E32/306/7 [33]

Inquisition held at Brill on Wednesday in the feast of St. Lambert in the thirty-ninth year of the reign of King Edward the third after the conquest [17 September 1365] before Peter atte Wode, deputy for the keeper of the Lord King's forest this side of Trent, regarding the state of the forest of Shotover and Stowood in the County of Oxford, by oath of

Robert Gamage, deputy for John Applebey, keeper of the aforesaid forest,

John Torlton, William Duffield, Thomas Man, Matthew Ryng [and] John Gillyng, foresters,

John Ruycote [and] John Hardy, verderers,

William Gilot, Walter atte Welle, Robert Bradley, Adam atte Orchard, Thomas North, Gilbert Basset, Thomas Bere, John atte Wode, Thomas Norton, John Bidowe, Adam Uppe, John Bailyf of Ildesle, regarders,

John Muleward, John Colles [Collett], Simon Molden, John Joustere, William Frankeleyn, Thomas Clement, Ralph Gareford, Walter Godrich [and] John Peche, free tenants,

---

[32] The Abbey of Westminster held Islip and a manor in Noke: *V.C.H. Oxfordshire vi*, 209, 269-270.
[33] Also recorded in E32/279, dorse.

1   Who say on their oath that the Prioress of Studley has a certain high
wooden fence at Westmor which was enclosed against the assize of the forest.
2   They also say that Stephen Bydle [Biterle] of Thomley and Walter Pauw
of Worminghall used to put down vervain to catch the Lord King's deer in the
fields of Thomley and Worminghall within the aforesaid forest, to the injury of
the Lord King's forest.

In testimony of these things the aforesaid jurors have affixed their seals.
Given the day place and year written above.
[Twenty-seven seals remaining]

E32/306/8 [34]

Inquisition held at Headington on the Friday next after the feast of St. Benedict
in the forty-first year of the reign of King Edward the third after the conquest
[14 January 1368] before Peter atte Wode, deputy of William of Wykeham,
keeper of the Lord King's forest this side of Trent, regarding the state of the
forest of Shotover and Stowood in the County of Oxford by oath of

Thomas Man, deputy for Edmund atte Poule,[35] keeper of the aforesaid
forest,

Thomas Gamage, John Ranger, Richard Parker and John Gille, foresters

John Ruycote and John Hardy, verderers,

Thomas Norton, William Gilot, John Bereford, Walter atte Welle, Gilbert
Basset, Thomas North, Adam atte Orchard, Thomas Bernard, John Bailiff,
John Bidou, Thomas Bere [and] Ralph Gareford, regarders,

Richard Fynian, Richard Sporiare, Alexander Nicole, John Meleward, John
Colles, John Martyn, John Pirou, Robert Wouburne, William Thursteyn, John
Hickes, John Grace [and] Henry Aygnoulf, free tenants within the bounds of
the forest.

1   Who say [that] on the Wednesday next after the feast of the Apostles Peter
and Paul in the 41st year of the aforesaid Lord King [30 June 1367] a doublet
was found in the covert of the forest of Shotover, abandoned in the same place,
and by whom they do not know; value 6s.8d., wherefore John Hickes has to
answer for this, as forfeit to the King.

---

[34]   Also recorded in E32/279 m. 14d.
[35]   Edmund de la Pole was the husband of Elizabeth (de Haudlo), co-heiress with her sister Margaret to
the de Haudlo estates. In 1366 there was a redistribution of these and the keepership of Shotover and
Stowood was taken away from Margaret and her husband John Appleby (see fn. 1, p. 137) and given
to Elizabeth: *Cal. Pat. 1364-67*, 276-7.

E32/306/9 [36]

Inquisition held at Headington on the Sunday next after the feast of St. Bartholomew the Apostle in the forty-second year of the reign of King Edward the third after the conquest [27 August 1368] before John de Foxle, keeper of the Lord King's forest this side of Trent, regarding the State of the forest of Shotover and Stowood in the County of Oxford, by oath of

Richard Forester, deputy for Edmund atte Pole, knight, keeper of the aforesaid forest,

John de Thorlton, Thomas Man, Thomas Gamage, Richard Agace [and] John Gellyng, foresters,

John de Ruycote and John Hardy, verderers,

Robert Gamage, Edmund Giffard, Thomas North, John Bereford, Walter atte Welle, William Fauconere, Robert de Bradele, Thomas Bere, Thomas de Norton, John Baylyf, John Bydow and John atte Wode, regarders,

Thomas Freshwater, John Hauvill, Thomas Coworth, Hugh Squier, John Hatfield, Gilbert Basset, Richard Clerc, William Frankeleyn, John Ledhale, Robert Harpusham, Ralph Gareford and Walter Godrych, free tenants,

1   Who say that John Woderove of Temple Cowley was a habitual evildoer to the Lord King's venison by night, with ropes, in the 42nd year of the aforesaid Lord King.

2   They also say that that the same John felled and carried away green wood valued at 40d. in the bailiwick of Shotover in the aforesaid year.

3   They also say that in the 42nd year of the aforesaid King, within fifteen day's of the Lord King's last hunting in the aforesaid forest, Nicholas Damory, knight, with certain members of his household, hunted and caught a doe in grease in Richard Lyght's close; of which the said Richard had his share.

4   They also say that Alexander, chamberlain of Nicholas Damory, is a habitual leader of the same Nicholas' greyhounds in the forest by night, to do harm to the Lord King with respect to his venison, against the assize of the forest.

5   They also say that Robert of London commonly walks in the forest with bows and arrows by night to do harm to the Lord King with respect to his venison, against the assize of the forest.

In testimony of these things the aforesaid jurors have affixed their seals. Given the day place and year written above.

[Twenty-three seals remaining.]

---

[36] Also recorded in E32/270 m. 3.

E32/306/10 [37]

Inquisition held at Forest Hill on the Sunday next after the feast of St. Edward the King in the 46th year of the reign of King Edward the third after the conquest [21 March 1372] before John de Foxle, keeper of the Lord King's forest this side of Trent, regarding the state of the forest of Shotover and Stowood in the County of Oxford by oath of

Richard Forster, deputy for Edmund de le Pole, keeper of the aforesaid forest

William Wurth, John Ranger, John Pope, John Gillyng, Richard Agas, Thomas Man and Richard Cachero, foresters

John Ruycote and John Hardy, verderers,

Thomas Chybenhurst, William Gillot, Adam Atte Norchard, Robert Bradele, Walter atte Welle, John Hauvill, Thomas North, John Berford, Gilbert Basset, Thomas Norton, John Bailly and Roger of Thame, regarders,

John Benet, Alan Tornere, Robert Spogger, Richard Fynian, Thomas Brayle, Hugh Cok, John Martyn, John Colles, John Pyrou, John Drye, Henry Aynolf [and] William atte Mull, free tenants within the bounds of the forest,

William Webbe, John Fille, William Werin, John Gibbes, John Hauvill of Kirtlington, Thomas Galworth, John Hatfeld, Thomas Rolf, Thomas Sonier, John Stowforde, Walter Leche and Robert Harpesham, free tenants without the bounds of the forest,

1   Who say on their oath that Richard Cacheroo, Forester of Shotover, sold to Richard Basset of Forest Hill an oak valued at 40d. on the Saturday next before the feast of St. Martin in the 45th year [8 November 1371] in Whatelecleres within the aforesaid forest.

2   They also say that that the same Richard Cachero sold to John Lynere of Holton on the day and year stated above, in the same place, 2 oaks valued at 6s. 8d.

3   They also say that the same Richard Cachero sold to Richard Basset an oak valued at 3s. in the aforesaid forest on the Thursday next after the feast of the Birth of the Lord in the 45th year [1 January 1372]

4   They also say that the same Richard Cachero sold to John Chalenor of Oxford a cart-load of saplings at the feast of St. Michael in the aforesaid year [29 September 1371], valued at 6d.

5   They also say that John Raunger and Richard Cachero sold to Robert atte Brasenose of Oxford 2 oaks valued at half a mark, namely on the Wednesday next after Epiphany in the aforesaid year [8 January 1372]

---

[37]   Also recorded in E32/271 m. 9d.

6   They also say that Richard Cachero sold to John Frere of Cuddesdon an oak in Depeslades, valued at 12d., on the Thursday next before the feast of the Purification of the Blessed Mary in the aforesaid year [30 January 1371].

7   They also say that Richard Cachero and John Rengour felled and sold 2 cart-loads of wood, valued at 14d., with the assent of their associates in the aforesaid forest on the Monday next after Palm Sunday in the aforesaid year [31 March 1371].

8   They also say that Richard Cachero sold to John Kenyton one cart-load of wood in the aforesaid forest, valued at 8d., on the Wednesday next after the feast of Easter in the aforesaid year [9 April 1371].

9   They also say that John Ruycote, verderer, and Richard Forest gave to Thomas Wormenhale of Oxford a tree for firewood valued at 12d., namely on the Tuesday next after the feast of St. Matthew in the aforesaid year [23 September 1371].

10   They also say that Richard Forster gave to John Lovel of Horspath 2 cart-loads of firewood valued at 12d. in the aforesaid year.

11   They also say that Richard Cachero sold to Richard Rose green thorns valued at 4s. 6d. in le Shereveruydyng in the aforesaid forest the Friday next after the feast of St. Michael in the aforesaid year [3 October 1371].

12   They also say that Richard Cachero sold to John Style of Cowley 4 cart-loads of wood valued at 8d. on the Tuesday next before the feast of the Translation of St.E[dmund] archbishop in the aforesaid year [3 June 1371] by gift of Richard Forster.

13   They also say that John Raunger and John Style of Cowley felled 2 cart-loads of firewood valued at 2s. on the Tuesday next before the feast of St. Martin in the 45th year [4 November 1371].

14   They also say that John Rangour and Richard Cachero sold to Geoffrey Lowemoers of Oxford 4 oaks in the aforesaid forest towards Headington, valued at 3s., with the assent of all the foresters in the aforesaid year.

[Twenty seals remaining.]

E32/306/11 [38]

Inquisition held at Oxford on the Saturday next after the feast of St. Valentine in the 50th year of the reign of King Edward the third after the conquest [16th February 1376] before John de Foxle, keeper of the Lord King's forest this side of Trent, regarding the state of the forest of Shotover and Stowood in the County of Oxford by oath of

Richard Forester, deputy for Edmund de la Pole, keeper of the aforesaid forest,

---

[38]   Also recorded in E32/276 m. 2d.

John Hay, William atte Freth, Richard Bayly, Richard Agace and John Gillyng, foresters,

John Ruycote and John Hardy, verderers,

John Hauvyle, Thomas Chibenhurst, John atte Wode, William Gilot, John Bereford, Adam Up, William Thomele, Robert Bradele, Gilbert Basset, Thomas Norton, Thomas North and Roger Tame, regarders,

Thomas Darches, William Webbe, John York, Thomas Sybford, Thomas Colworthe, Walter Sawyare, Thomas Dawe, John Wrench, Thomas Prat, John Bidow [and] William Chyvele, free tenants,

1   Who say that William Man and John Harald, servants of Richard Baylif and Richard Fryth, foresters of Shotover, sold to John Thoky of Garsington [gap] three oak saplings valued at 6s. 8d., the said John Thoky knowing that the said saplings were from the timber and demesne wood of the Lord King, namely on the Thursday next after the feast of St. Martin in the 49th year of the aforesaid Lord King [15 November 1375]

2   They also say that Roger Pope, John Bayliff of Horspath and John Shaldewell [Chaldewell], shepherd, came into the aforesaid forest with three greyhounds to do harm to the Lord King in respect of his venison in the middle of the night on the Tuesday next after the Purification of the Blessed Mary in the 50th year of the aforesaid Lord King [5 February 1376]; however Roger Pope, John Bayliff of Horspath and John Chaldewell were attached by John Hay, Ranger in the same forest on the aforesaid night. And they say that Brother Richard Rodecote, warden of the Hospital of St. John of Sandford, master of the said Roger Pope, John Baylif of Horspath and John Chaldewell, shepherd, knew about this deed and afterwards received them and had [them] in his service. And the aforesaid greyhounds belonged to the said Richard.

In testimony of these things the aforesaid jurors affixed their seals. Given the day, place and year written above.

[Twenty-one seals remaining]

[Other inquisitions into the forest of Shotover and Stowood, which have not survived in the Public Records, are to be found in the Boarstall Cartulary. These are:

1337   BC p. 172, 565
1342   BC p. 173, 566]

Extracts from the rolls of the Keeper of the Forest
South of Trent

[Inquisitions which duplicate those in the E32/306 series, transcribed above, and those for Shotover and Stowood which have been published in the Boarstall Cartulary are not included. The extracts are in chronological order.]

E32/278
6-10th Edward III [1332-7]

m. 6] *Wychwood*
Inquisition held at Charlbury before John of Macclesfield, deputy of lord Robert of Ufford, keeper of the Lord King's forest this side of Trent, on Saturday in the feast of the Assumption of the Blessed Virgin Mary in the sixth year of the Lord King Edward third after the conquest [15th August 1332] regarding the state of the forest of Wychwood and transgressions committed in the same forest,

by Thomas of Langley keeper of the aforesaid forest
and by Richard Dobbe riding forester in the aforesaid forest
and by Richard Baker, William Mereman, Richard of Cogges, Nigel Mereman, Robert Lysours, John Stontesfeld, William Stontesfeld and Thomas of Eynsham walking foresters in the aforesaid forest,
and by Ralph Castilon, William de Leye and Robert Barton, verderers of the aforesaid forest,
and by Nicholas of Ascott, William Machin, Bartholomew Chamberlein, Thomas de Bitcheheye, Henry Bloxham, John Borians, Walter Gygour, Simon Hunte, John Pachon, James le Blount, Robert le Waller and John of Ludwell, regarders of the aforesaid forest
and by Roger de Nowers knight, Richard of Williamscot, John of Lewknor, Robert de Trillowe, Gilbert of Charlbury, William de Louches, Peter de Dodecote, John de Loundres, William le Blunt, Thomas in le Hale, John Merrymouth, Walter of Fifield, William Malyn, Walter Coke, Henry le Turnour, Reynold of Dean, John atte Thurne, William of Fairford, William of Overton, John Gibbes, Ralph le Mason, Richard de Whitefeld, William Walrond and William Austyn, 24 free and law-worthy men dwelling outside the forest and adjoining to it, sworn and bound by their oath;
1 all which aforesaid jurors say on their oath that on the Thursday next after the feast of St. Valentine the martyr in the 19th year of the King son of King E[dward] [20th February 1326] William Doucer and John Martyn of Shorthampton came into the Lord King's aforesaid forest of Wychwood and in the same they caught a buck of the third year and venison there at their will and

carried it away, and that the same John Martyn is a habitual evil-doer both to the vert and the venison in the aforesaid forest both by day and by night

2   and that on the Monday next after the feast of St. Nicholas in the aforesaid year of the above-mentioned King [9th December 1325] Thomas Faber of Shorthampton came into the aforesaid forest and in the same caused a large apple tree to be felled, which he took from there at his will

3   and that on the Monday on the morrow of the finding of the Holy Cross in the first year of King Edward third after the conquest [4th May 1327] Walter Pap of Leafield came into the aforesaid forest and in the same placed four ropes which were found blood-stained by the foresters and handed over to Thomas of Langley, keeper of the aforesaid forest, for keeping until the next Justice Eyre of the aforesaid forest

4   and that the Abbot of Winchcombe, the Abbot of Lettele [Netley], the Abbot of Eynsham and the Bishop of Winchester asserted large areas of their own soil which are now outside the forest by the perambulation,[39] by what warrant it is not known.

In witness to this the aforesaid jurors have affixed their seals.

E32/281
Roll of Bartolomew de Burgherssh
10-17th Ed III [1336-44]

m.4 d] *Shotover*

Inquisition held at Beckley before John of Macclesfield deputy of Bartholomew Burgherssh keeper in the twelfth year of the reign of King Edward third after the conquest [1338] regarding the forest of Shotover and transgressions, namely by

Philip de Baggesore deputy of John de Haudlo, keeper of the aforesaid forest

and by John Baroun, William Agar and Hugh de Kynedesleye foresters in the same forest,

and by John Symeon and John of Stowford[40] verderers in the same forest,

and by John de Bradelee, Richard atte Chaumbre, Robert son of Thomas Fraunkelyn of Cowley, John Eustas, John atte Norcherd, William Spileman, William Bernard and John Somer of Garsington, regarders of the forest,

---

[39] These were the perambulations of 1298 and 1300, see p. ii of the Introduction.

[40] Stowford was a hamlet on the boundary between Stanton St John and Headington, now represented only by Stowford Farm: *V.C.H. Oxfordshire v*, 283.

and by Thomas Giffard and John atte Wode of Arncott regarders chosen for the day[41]

and by Robert Dosiere, William Piroun, John Hereward, Richard Brid, Nicholas Brail, William Feutrier, Thomas Skot, William Hardekile, John Rottelen, Clement Martyn of Wick, Thomas Aynulf and John Beneyt, twelve good and free men dwelling within the aforesaid forest & adjoining to the same, sworn;

all which aforesaid jurors say that

1   on the Friday next after the feast of St. Gregory the Pope in the 12th year of the reign of King Edward third after the conquest [13 March 1338] master Richard de Risyndon, Walter his brother, Richard chaplain of Beckley, Robert brother of the same and Walter chaplain of Oddington [illegible] of the said Richard de Risyndon with seven unknown men came and entered within the covert of the forest of Stowood in a certain place which is called Abovethe-brevetonesboure and there made an assault on William Agar and Hugh de Kyneseteleye, walking foresters of the same forest, and shot at the same foresters and attacked the said foresters with great force, who on this raised a hue and cry, by which they were attached and put on bail of Edward of Ludlow rector of the church of Beckley [illegible]; but they took nothing of the Lord King's deer. In witness of this etc.

m. 6] *Wychwood*:

[The edge of the membrane is creased and torn and some words have been lost.] Inquisition held at Charlbury before Simon of Drayton, deputy of the lord Bartholomew de Burgherssh keeper of the Lord King's forest, held on the Tuesday in the feast of St. [illegible] Bishop in the 11th year of the reign of King Edward third after the conquest [1337], regarding the state of the forest of Wychwood and of transgressions, namely by

Thomas of Langley keeper of the aforesaid forest and by

Richard Dobbes riding forester in the same forest and by

William de la Legh and Robert of Barton verderers of the same forest and by

James le Blount, Bartholomew le Chaumberleyn, Henry [illegible], Josep of Woodstock, Reginald de Hurlee, Simon le Hunte, John Pachin, Nicholas of Ascottt, Walter le Gigour, John Boriens, John Denoten, Thomas Blakeman regarders of the same forest and by

---

[41] In the Ordinance of the Forest of 1306 it was stipulated that, if any forest official was prevented by death, illness or other cause from attending a court, the Justice was to choose a man to replace him on the day (with the exception of the verderers, who were still to be appointed by the county): *Statutes of the Realm 1*,148.

John de Hynton, Robert le Botiler, Adam de Coldurn, Henry le Turner, Reginald of Dean, John Gibbes, Thomas [illegible, ?Cham-] berleyn, William Barentyn, William Austyn, John Gerard, John atte Halle and John of Ludwell twelve good and free men dwelling within the said forest

Robert of St. Paul, John of Milcombe, Henry of Headington, William Steel, William Conqueraunt, John Godard, William Perreres, John Durwayn, William [illegible words] Rook, Nicholas Fynk, Richard de Deabere, Henry Stirthuppe, twelve true and law-worthy men dwelling outside the said forest and adjoining it, sworn,

1   Who all say that [illegible, the wood of?] the Lord King of Pynnesley was destroyed of 96 great oaks by Peter de Dodecote underbailiff of Woodstock[42] and that in the same wood 28 oaks were felled by the same Peter to the destruction of the aforesaid wood, and in the wood called Gunnildegrove 300 great oaks and 12 great oaks were felled by the same Peter and 12 great oaks similarly to the destruction of the wood, and that the said Peter de Dodecote destroyed 100 great oaks or more by estimation in the wood of Bladon to the destruction of the said wood

2   and that Peter Broune of Cornbury Margaret of the same and Andrew baker of the same are habitual evildoers to the King's deer in the park of Woodstock with ropes and other contrivances and that the said Peter Brunne is a habitual carrier of venison taken in the aforesaid manner in the same park to the towns of Oxford Witney and other neighbouring towns with great damage to the Lord King and to his beasts in the aforesaid park. In witness of this etc.

m. 7] *Shotover*

Inquisition held at Beckley on the Friday next after the feast of St. Luke the Evangelist in the 13th year of King Edward third after the conquest [22 October 1339] before John Verdon and John of Macclesfield, deputies of lord Bartholomew de Burgherssh, keeper of the forest this side of Trent of the King and also of the lady Philippa queen of England, regarding the state of the forest of Shotover and transgressions in the same forest, namely

by Philip de Baggesore deputy of the lord John de Haudlo, keeper of the aforesaid forest, and by

---

[42] Peter de Dodecote was clerk of the King's works for the manor of Woodstock and on 18 March 1337 it was ordered that he should receive as much money as necessary for "repairing the houses, walls, mills, ponds, palings and parks" there, while another grant on December 13th in the same year granted him an allowance for money spent in repairs to the parker's lodge in Woodstock Park and the lodge at Cornbury, amongst others: *Cal. Close 1337-1339*, 38, 220. Presumably the timber felled was used in these works. Pinsley Wood was in Hanborough, and Gunnildegrove belonged to Hordley, both of which were members of Woodstock manor (*Rot. Hund. II*, 850). The site of Gunnildegrove is probably now largely within Blenheim Park, although in 1298 it was outside the park walls: James Bond & Kate Tiller, eds., *Blenheim, Landscape for a Palace*, p. 29; *V.C.H. Oxfordshire xii*, 443.

John de Churchefeld and John Baroun walking foresters in Shotover and by

William Agar and Hugh de Kynsedle walking foresters in Stowood, and by John Symeon and John of Stowford verderers of the same forest, and by

Richard de la Chaumbre, John Fraunkelyn, William Spileman, John Eustaz, Thomas Fraunkelyn, Robert brother of Thomas, John atte Orchard, Thomas of Arncott, John Simon and William Bernard regarders in the same forest, and by

John de Falleye and Nicholas le Cleere, regarders chosen for the day, and by

John Hereward, Clement Martyn, Will le Veutrier, Robert le Dosiere, William atte Nelme, Richard Pyroun, Giles de Baggesore, Thomas Aynulf, John de Rottelee, Richard Simond, William Piroun and Robert Edward, free tenants dwelling within the aforesaid forest,

and by John Fraunkelyn of Stanton, Thomas le Cir, Henry de Codestow, John of Thomley, John of Hasley of Thomley, Thomas de Brymme, Thomas of Wheatley, Walter Belewe, Thomas son of William, John Odbright, Thomas Page and Hugh Brown, 12 good and free men dwelling outside the forest and adjoining to the same, sworn and bound by their oath:

all which aforesaid jurors say on their oath that

1 the Master of the Hospital of St. John at the East Gate of Oxford has a certain wood of the King's ancient demesne which is called SeyntJoneswode[43] and is within the metes and bounds of the forest of Shotover

2 and that the Prioress of Littlemore has a certain wood called Swalenhil and it is of the Lord King's ancient demesne and within the metes and bounds of the same forest

3 and that the Prior of the Hospital of St. John of Jerusalem in England has a certain wood which is called Purihale[44] and it is of the Lord King's ancient demesne and outside the bounds of the aforesaid forest by the perambulation

4 and that the same Prior of the Hospital has a certain wood called Acremele and it is of the Lord King's ancient demesne and outside the bounds of the aforesaid forest by the perambulation

5 and that the Abbot of Osney has a certain wood called Beyondthebrook[45] and it is of the Lord King's ancient demesne and outside the forest by the perambulation

---

[43] This wood had been granted to the hospital in 1246: *V.C.H. Oxfordshire v*, 279.

[44] This and Acremel (**4**) became the property of the Hospitallers of Jerusalem when the Order of the Templars was suppressed.

[45] Beyondthebrook was in Forest Hill and is recorded as a boundary point in the perambulation of Shotover and Stowood in 1300: *Eynsham Cart.* ii, 96, No. 652

6   and that the Prioress of Studley has a certain wood called Lynhale[46] and it is of the Lord King's ancient demesne and outside the bounds of the aforesaid forest by the perambulation

7   and that the Abbot of Westminster lord of Islip has a certain great wood called Islepeswode which is of the Lord King's ancient demesne and outside the forest by perambulation

8   and that the Abbot of Eynsham has a certain wood called Boydyneswode and it is of the Lord King's ancient demesne and outside the bounds of the aforesaid forest by the perambulation

9   and that Thomas of Stowford formerly servant of John of Stowford, verderer of the aforesaid forest, entered the aforesaid forest in the wood called Stowood and in a certain place called le Denizpiece within 3 weeks next after St. Barnabas the Apostle last interfered with a certain brood of sparrowhawks without warrant, took them and carried them away to the house of John himself, wherefore Agnes of Stowford, wife of the same John, gave a sparrow-hawk to a certain one of her damsels and another sparrowhawk to a certain serving man of lord John de St. John, for whose name inquiry is to be made; the same John of Stowford knowing of the aforesaid gifts.

10   and that the aforesaid John of Stowford and Henry brother of the same have and hold about 100 sheep grazing within the aforesaid forest at all times of the year both in the forbidden month and at other times, to the damage of the Lord King and the Lord King's tenants of Headington and its members, and harm to the beasts in the same.

11   and that William Agar habitually has 100 sheep grazing in Stowood within the aforesaid forest in the aforesaid manner

12   And that Richard le Forestier now parker of Beckley has 100 sheep grazing in Stowood at any time in the aforesaid manner.

m. 7] *Wychwood:*
Inquisition held at Charlbury on the Monday next after the feast of St. Luke the Evangelist in the thirteenth year of the reign of the Lord King Edward third after the conquest [25th October 1339] before John de Verdon and John of Macclesfield, deputies for lord Bartholomew de Burgherssh keeper of the King's forest this side of Trent, regarding the state of the forest of Wychwood and of the transgressions committed in the same forest, to wit
    by Thomas of Langley, keeper of the same forest and by
    Simon le Ridere lieutenant of the aforesaid Thomas and by
    Nigel le Mereman, Hugh le Botiler, Richard atte Lee, Thomas Janekyns, John Wodham, William atte Lee, William Blackwell, John le Versy and Nicholas Rose foresters in the same forest, and by

---

[46]   Lynhale was also in Forest Hill and a boundary point in 1300: *loc. cit.*, & *Rot. Hund. ii*, 717.

William de Leeghe, Stephen of Curbridge, Robert of Barton verderers of the same forest and by

Thomas Blakeman, John Denot, John Boriens, William Gigour, Simon le Hunt, Nicholas of Ascott, James le Blount, Joseph of Woodstock, Henry of Bloxham and Bartholomew Chamberleyn regarders of the aforesaid forest and by

John Gibbs and Reginald of Dean the regarders chosen for the day and by

John of London, Richard Dobbes, Robert le Botiler, Richard de Lettelton, John atte Halle, Thomas le Benes, Thomas Frankeleyn, John Reson, William atte Bury, William le Ridere, Richard Gibbes and John Gerard, twelve free tenants dwelling within the aforesaid forest and adjoining it, sworn and bound by their oath; all which aforesaid jurors say on their oath that

1 on the Monday next before the feast of the Nativity of St. John the Baptist in the aforesaid year of the King [21 June 1339] William Wylde of Crawley hunted a certain buck and killed it within the forest and because of this was arrested with the stolen goods and he was handed over to mainpernors until the next coming of the Keeper of the Forest [South of Trent] to the aforesaid forest. And because the flesh of the said buck was lean it was given to the poor. In witness of this the said jurors affixed their seals to this inquisition on the aforesaid day place and year.

E32/261
Roll of Bartholomew de Burgherssh
10-18th Edward III [1336-45]

m. 3] *Shotover & Stowood*
[A version of the inquisition recorded here is transcribed as No. 564 in the *Boarstall Cartulary*]

m. 5] *Wychwood*
[The right hand edge of the membrane is torn, creased and stained, and some words are illegible or lost]

Inquisition held at Charlbury before Bartholomew de Bourne and John of Macclesfield deputies on this occasion of the lord Bartholomew de Burgherssh, keeper, on the Sunday in the morrow of the translation of St. Thomas Martyr in the year of King Edward, of England 16th and truly of France third [7th July 1342] regarding the state of the forest of Wychwood and transgressions, namely by

Thomas of Langley keeper of the aforesaid forest and by
Simon le Rydere lieutenant of the same Thomas and by

Nigel Mereman, Thomas [illegible] John Wodehorn, William de Blakewell, William le Forester and John de Versy, walking foresters in the aforesaid forest and by

William de Leghe and Robert of Barton verderers in the same forest and by

James le Blount, John Denot, Nicholas of Ascott, John Boriens, Walter Gigour, Bartholomew Chaumberleyn, John Gibbes, Reginald of Dean, Henry of Quenewode, Nicholas de Luttestowe, regarders of the same forest and

Henry le Spicer & Richard Dounal regarders for the day and by

William Barentyn, John Resonn, William Perkyn, Thomas Fraunkelyn, John atte Berwe, John Free, John [illegible], Robert Chaunduyt, John atte Halle, John Gerard, Richard Gybbes, Henry de Cokeswell, twelve free tenants within the same forest and by

Richard Dobbes, John de Louwe, Edmund le Vycar, Nicholas Tewe, John Bernard, Walter Ive, John Ive, William le Symple, Richard Ladde, John of London junior, Thomas Under Wode, Richard le Pore of Eynsham twelve good and free men dwelling outside and adjoining the same, sworn;

1   all of whom say that Peter de Dodecote, bailiff of Woodstock under the lord William de Montagu, earl of Salisbury,[47] felled and carried away at Wottard three oaks, each worth 2s., for the house of Adam le Draper in the aforesaid year, and the same Peter acquired 15 oaks as a reward

2   and that the same Peter after that took away from Gunnildegrove as many, each of which is worth 2 s for the use of [illegible] without warrant in the aforesaid year

3   and that the same Peter felled [illegible] one oak worth 2s. in the wood of Bladon for the repair of the mill of Combe without warrant in the [illegible] year without warrant [sic]

4   and that the same Peter caused to be felled and delivered in the wood of Combe for the repair of the mill of Bladon [illegible] oaks each one worth 2s. in the aforesaid year without warrant

5   and that the said Peter felled and delivered to Walter de Hacche of [illegible] in the aforesaid year one oak worth 2s. in the wood of Gunnildegrove without warrant

6   and that the aforesaid Peter felled for the repair of the bridge of Bladon one oak worth 2s. without warrant

7   and that the aforesaid Peter felled and took away [illegible] 3 oaks each worth 2s in the aforesaid year for the repair of the bridge of Newynton

[47] William Montagu, earl of Salisbury, was then farmer of the manor of Woodstock and its members: *Cal. Close R.. 1337-1339,* 38.

8   and that Peter [illegible] caused to be delivered in the aforesaid year 3 oaks worth 2s each in the aforesaid year [sic] without warrant for the repair of the bridge of Hordley [illegible words]

9   and that the same Peter felled and took away for his own work in the wood of Pynnesle in the above-mentioned year 20 oaks each worth 2 s without warrant[48]

10   And that the Abbot of Eynsham made a certain coppice in his wood of Charlbury by estimation 30 acres in the above-mentioned year of the Lord King without warrant

11   and that the aforesaid Abbot made a coppice in his wood of Eynsham of 40 acres by estimation in the aforesaid year without warrant

12   and that the lord Hugh le Despencer made a coppice in his wood of Holworke containing by estimation 20 acres in the above-mentioned year without warrant

13   and that the lord [illegible, Bishop of Winchester?] made a coppice in his chace of Witney of 40 acres by estimation without warrant

14   and that lord ... Lovel [illegible] and made a certain coppice in his wood of Minster containing 10 acres by estimation without warrant

15   Lord Edmund of Cornwall made a certain coppice in his wood called Asthall of 20 acres [illegible words] without warrant

16   Master Elyas, Chancellor of Salisbury,[49] made a certain coppice in his wood of Stockley of [membrane torn] by estimation in the aforesaid year without warrant

17   and that lord Edmund de Bereford clerk[50] made a certain coppice [some words missing or illegible] 10 acres by estimation in the aforesaid year without warrant

18   and that John de Leghe made [a coppice] in his wood of Hensgrove of 10 acres by estimation in the aforesaid year without warrant

19   and that lord [some words missing or illegible] made a coppice in his wood called Smale Oke containing 5 acres by estimation in the aforesaid year

20   and that on the Friday next after the feast of the translation of St. Thomas Martyr [the remaining few lines of the document refer to an offence against the venison but the details are illegible].

[48]   Peter de Dodecote held ½ a knight's fee in Hanborough: *Feudal Aids* iv, 177.

[49]   Elyas de Sancto Albano, Chancellor of Salisbury 1340-?: *John Le Neve, Fasti Ecclesiae Anglicanae 1300-1540*, comp. Joyce M. Horn (1962) 17.

[50]   Edmund de Bereford held the Prebend of Shipton by royal grant of 1328: *ibid.*, 84. His wood was Priest Grove (Prestgrave).

m. 5d]　*Shotover*

Inquisition held at Beckley before Bartholomew de Bourne and John of Macclesfield, deputies of Bartholomew de Burgherssh, keeper of the forest this side of Trent of the Lord King and of the lady Philippa Queen of England on the Wednesday next after the feast of the translation of St. Thomas the Martyr in the year of the reign of King Edward third after the conquest 16th of England and truly third of France [10th July 1342], regarding the state of the forest of Shotover and transgressions in the same namely by

John de Louches, deputy of John de Haudlo, keeper of the aforesaid forest, and by

Richard le Forester, riding forester in the same forest, and by

John Baroun, William Agar, John de Cherchehull and Hugh de Kynnedesley walking foresters in the same forest, and by

John Symean and John of Stowford verderers of the same forest, and by

Richard of the Chamber, Thomas Giffard, Thomas of Arncott, John Eustaz, Nicholas le Clerk, John Fraunkeleyn of Holton, William Spileman, Thomas Fraunkeleyn of Cowley, John atte Norchard, Robert son of Thomas, John Somer and John Macy, regarders of the same forest, and by

Walter Belewe, John Notebem, John Odebright, Thomas son of William of Hampton, William Robyn, John son of Walter, Thomas son of William, Thomas Fraunkeleyn, Thomas Page, Richard Saundres, William Willes, and Henry of Cuddesdon, twelve good and free men dwelling outside the forest and adjoining to it, sworn and bound by their oath; all which say that

1 the Master of the Hospital of St. John outside the east gate of Oxford has a certain wood of the ancient demesne of the Lord King which is called SeyntJoneswode and is within the metes and bounds of the forest of Shotover

2 and that the Prioress of Littlemore has a certain wood which is called Swalewenehul and is ancient demesne of the Lord King and within the metes and bounds of the same forest

3 and that the Prior of the Hospital of St. John of Jerusalem in England has a certain wood which is called Purihale and it is of the Lord King's ancient demesne and outside the metes of the aforesaid forest by the perambulation

4 and that the same prior of the Hospital has a certain wood called Acremele and it is of the Lord King's ancient demesne and outside the forest by the perambulation

5 and that the Abbot of Osney has a certain wood called Byyondethebrok and it is of the Lord King's ancient demesne and outside the forest by the perambulation

6 and that the Prioress of Studley has a certain wood called Lynhale and it is of the Lord King's ancient demesne and outside the forest by the perambulation

7   and that the Abbot of Westminster lord of Islip has a certain large wood called Islepeswode which is of the Lord King's ancient demesne and outside the forest by the perambulation

8   and that the Abbot of Eynsham has a certain wood called Boydeneswode and it is of the Lord King's ancient demesne and outside the forest by the perambulation. In witness of these things etc..

E32/283
Roll of William of Wykeham
36-37th Edward III [1362-4]

m. 1d] *Wychwood*
Roger de Beauchamp, Edward de Spenser, Margaret Pereres had briefs whereby their woods were redeemed, given at Westminster.

   John Free, Walter Pap, John Jakelot, William Comyng, Thomas Perkyn, Henry Tymmes and William Crips had ...

m. 5d] [An inquisition into the state of Shotover & Stowood, a version of which appears as No. 568 in the *Boarstall Cartulary*]

E32/269
Roll of William of Wykeham
38th Edward III

[This roll contains one inquisition already transcribed (E32/306 /2) and two charters of the Abbey of Eynsham, which are calendared in *Cal. Pat. 1301-1307,* 493 and in the *Eynsham Cartulary* I, 322, No. 483]

E32/270
Roll of John de Foxle
42-43th Edward III [1368-70]

m. 1d] *Wychwood*
John atte Halle & John Underwood had a commission to sell 24 acres of underwood in the forest of Wychwood by order of the lord Roger de Elmerugge, keeper of the said forest, which was given at Charlbury on 24th August in the 42nd year [1368].

   John Mere had warrant for 1 tree of fee 3d given there in the above-mentioned year.

   Thomas Golafre has a warrant to take 1 buck in the forest which was given at Woodstock on the 26th day of August in the 42nd year.

The prior of Coldnorton has a warrant to take 1 tree in the aforesaid forest by gift of William of Wykeham, former keeper of the Lord King's forest this side of Trent, which was given at Charlbury on 24th August in the 42nd year.

Shotover
Thomas of Missenden had a warrant for 1 buck in the aforesaid forest, given at Woodstock 26th August in the 42nd year.

m. 3] *Wychwood*
Inquisition held at Charlbury on the Thursday in the feast of St. Bartholomew the apostle in the 42nd year of the reign of King Edward third after the conquest [24 August 1368] before Peter atte Wode, deputy of John de Foxle keeper of the Lord King's forest this side of Trent, regarding the state of the Forest of Wychwood in the county of Oxford by oath of the foresters, verderers, regarders and other ministers of the said forest

1   who say that Thomas of Williamscot made a coppice containing 6 acres in his wood of Kiddington in the 42nd year of the aforesaid Lord King, value of the acres 6s.8d.

2   They also say that Roger de Beauchamp made a coppice in his wood of Quenewode of 4 acres, worth 5s., in the same year.

3   They also say that the earl of Warwick made a coppice in his wood of Spelsbury of 6 acres, worth 6s.8d.

4   They also say that lord John de Grey and the lady de Grey felled 1500 oaks in their wood of Coggeswood.

5   They also say that John Appulby[51] made a coppice containing 4 acres in his wood of Estleyhull in the abovesaid year.

6   They also say that the lord John Golafre made a coppice containing 6 acres in his wood of Bikerugge in the 42nd year of the aforesaid Lord King .

7   They also say that the Chancellor of Salisbury[52] made a coppice containing 6 acres in his wood of Stockley in the aforesaid year.

8   They also say that the lord Edmund of Cornwall made a coppice containing 10 acres in his wood of Asthall Leigh in the aforesaid year against the assize of the forest.

9   They also say that John Herde on the Tuesday next after the feast of the Assumption of the Blessed Mary in the aforesaid year [22 August 1368] let loose a dog at a buck of the third year in the water of Bladen, and the same

---

[51] John Appleby held both the Wahull and Shippenhull manors in Chadlington, as part of the inheritance of his wife Margaret de Haudlo: *Cal. Pat. 1364-67,* 276-7.

[52] John Norton, Chancellor of Salisbury 1361-1402: *Fasti, (Salisbury Diocese)* 17.

John had the said buck and did with it as he wished, against the assize of the forest.

m. 6] *Shotover*
Roger Elmrugge former sheriff of Oxfordshire for money received from sale of underwood in the forests of Shotover and Stowood in the time of William of Wykeham, 41st year. [1367]   £10 14s 10d.

E32/271
Roll of John de Foxle
44-46th Edward III [1370-3]

m. 1] Memorandum of recognisances made by John de Foxley in the 44th year.

Shotover and Stowood
John of Stowford, agister, for money received from pannage of pigs in
   the 43rd year [1369]   15d.
Edmund de la Pole, value of one mare acquired as a stray in the same
   year   ½ mark
the same Edmund, value of 4 piglets acquired in the same year   8d.
the same Edmund, money received from pannage of pigs in the 44th
   year   8d.
John Bereford and Robert Gamage, money received for sale of
   underwood in the same forest of Shotover in the 43rd, 44th
   and 45th years   £13 3s.7d.

E32/273B
Roll of John de Foxle
45th Edward III [1371-2]

m1] *Bernwood*
Inquisition held at Headington on the Monday in the feast of St. Tiburtius and St. Valerianus in the forty-fifth year of the reign of King Edward third after the conquest [14th April 1371] before Peter atte Wode, deputy for John de Foxle, as to the state of the Forest of Bernwood in the county of Buckingham ... [this inquisition is followed immediately by]

Shotover

Inquisition held in the same place and year written above before the same P etc., as to the state of the forest of Shotover and Stowood in the county of Oxford by oath of the foresters, verderers, etc.,

1   who say that in the 43rd year of the aforesaid Lord King [1369] the Abbot of Westminster felled an oak worth 40d. in the aforesaid forest and stripped the bark from it.

2   They also say that in the aforesaid year Richard Russel of Woodeaton came with one of his dogs and killed a deer in the aforesaid forest and did with it as he wished.

3   They also say that lord Edmund de la Pole took one mare in the aforesaid forest, worth 6s.8d. and 4 pigs worth 8d., acquired as strays.

4   They also say that Thomas Lachford on the Friday next after the feast of the Annunciation of the Blessed Mary in the 45th year of the aforesaid Lord King [28 March 1371] came by night at Cowley and there met Thomas Gamage the Lord King's forester coming from his bailiwick and made an assault and wounded, assailed and ill-treated the same against the Lord King's peace, by which the same forester from the aforesaid time until now could not serve as a keeper in the aforesaid forest, in prejudice and contempt of him the Lord King. In witness of these things etc..

m. 5d] Sums arising from sale of underwood, pannage and agistment

Wychwood   16s.8d.
Shotover and Stowood   13s.1d. & vert 6s.8d.

E32/275
Roll of John de Foxle
49th Edward III [1375-6]

[The document consists of several membranes which have been sewn together into one long roll. Each membrane has been given a number at a later date]

m. 1] *Wychwood*

Inquisition held at Charlbury on the Thursday next after the feast of the Purification of the Blessed Mary in the 49th year [7 February 1375] before John de Foxle, keeper of the Lord King's forest this side of Trent regarding the state of the forest of Wychwood in the county of Oxford, by oath of the foresters, verderers, regarders & other ministers of the aforesaid forest;

1   Who say that John Hancock and Richard Botte on the Monday next after the feast of St. Andrew in the 46th year of the aforesaid Lord King [6 December 1372] killed a buck at Ascott in the aforesaid forest with dogs.

2   They also say that William Beauchamp, knight, felled four hundred oaks in the wood of Spelsbury at divers times in the 46th and 47th years without licence.

3   They also say that lord Thomas Soneye chaplain entered the forest with bow and arrows intending to do harm to the Lord King's hunting on the Monday next before the feast of St. Peter in chains in the 48th year, and he is a habitual malefactor in the aforesaid forest. In witness of these things etc.

m. 4] *Wychwood*
John de la Pole knight has a licence to fell 10 acres of underwood in his wood of Asthall and Fulbrook, given at Westminster on the 22nd day of November in the 49th year [1375]

m. 5] *Shotover & Stowood*
Robert atte Brasenose of Oxford had a brief as to transgressions of vert, given at Stanton on the 6th day of February in the 49th year.

William Prest had a warrant for one oak and one doe in Shotover which was given at Stanton on the day and year written above.

William Wanty had a warrant for 2 oaks which was given at Charlbury on the 8th day of February in the aforesaid year.

Thomas Golafre has a warrant for one doe which was given at Radley on the 10th day of February in the 49th year.

Gregory Bottele rector of the church of Headington had a warrant for 2 robors [dead trees] bearing neither fruit nor foliage, given at Radley on the day and year written above.

m. 5] *Wychwood*
John Hancock and Richard Botte had a brief as to transgressions of venison, given at Charlbury on the 12th day of February in the 49th year.

John de Norton chancellor of Salisbury had a licence to fell 30 oaks in his wood of Stockley, given at Charlbury on the above-mentioned day and year.

Brian of Cornwall had a licence to fell a hundred oaks in his wood of Asthall, the above-mentioned day place & year.

Nicholas Wagur had a warrant for one oak there, day & year as above

John de Foxle, clerk, had a warrant for one oak of fee, 3s., the aforesaid day place and year.

Thomas atte More and John Carswell, verderers, had warrants for 2 oaks for their good service, given at Charlbury 8th day of February in the 49th year.

Brian of Cornwall has a licence to fell 40 acres of underwood in his wood of Asthall, given the 4th day of April in the aforesaid year.

John Foxle, clerk, has a warrant for one buck given at Henley on the 12th day of July in the 49th year.

E32/276
Roll of John de Foxle
50th Edward III [1376-7]

m. 2d] *Wychwood*
Inquisition held at Charlbury on the Thursday in the feast of St. Valentine in the 50th year of the reign of King Edward III [14th February 1376] before John de Foxle, keeper of the Lord King's Forest this side of Trent, regarding the state of the forest of Wychwood in the County of Oxford, by oath of the foresters, verderers, regarders and other ministers of the aforesaid forest
1   who all say that on Tuesday in the Vigil of the Purification of the Blessed Mary in the 50th year of the aforesaid King [29th January 1376] Thomas Saron entered the aforesaid forest and there caught three bucks with ropes and carried away the flesh and hides, which hides were found in the house of Thomas himself, and it appears by the aforesaid inquisition that the vill of Shorthampton has to answer for 18d. In testimony of these things etc.
2   And that the keeper of the forest of Wychwood had a brief to take into the King's hand the wood of the Abbot of Nottele [Netley] called Northlegh wood [illegible words] Hirecourt [Harcourt] called Pirenho in the aforesaid Forest for defaults by the woodwards, so that they should answer for all revenue from them before the King's Bench at our next coming to the aforesaid forest. This given at Charlbury 14th day of February in the aforesaid year.

m. 4d] 50th year [1376]
John Pope and John Chaldewell had a brief, given at Bray on the 20th day of October in the previous year.
    Thomas Cob of Stonesfield and John atte Halle of Chilson had a commission to sell 12 acres of underwood in the park of Cornbury, given at Havering on the 17th day of November in the 50th year.
    John Chaloner, John Henyngton, Thomas Wormenhale and Robert Rose had a brief, given at Towcester 16th day of December in the aforesaid year.

m. 5d] Sums arising from sale of underwood, pannage and agistment
    Wychwood   16s.8d.
    Shotover & Stowood   13s.1d. and vert 6s.8d.

Survey of Wychwood Forest ?1609

[In the following transcript **f.** denotes the number of the folio in the original Survey and **p.** that of the page in the book into which the sheets have been pasted.

The document is in English. Some abbreviations have been expanded, but any Latin words and phrases have not been translated, and place-names and personal names have not been modernised.

The measurements are in acres, roods and perches.

The Survey was a working document and some entries have been marked with a cross or have 'compounded', 'comp.', asst (for assart) or other information written in the margin.

The lost first folio (see p. xviii) can be partly reconstructed from the contemporary index on ff. 45 and 46 [pp. 219-221] and from SP12/276, an associated document in which parcels of assart land in Wychwood are listed under their owner's name. Unfortunately neither of these is complete, so that the contents of folio 1 will remain largely unknown. It presumably described part of Hailey.

Names recorded in the index as being found on folio 1 are those of Henry Bringfeild, Leonard Boxe, Thomas Cornishe, John Clarke, [blank] Cullim, Thomas Crofts, Richard Dyer, Thomas Decine, [blank] Goddard, Richard Humphrey, Bartholomew Harris and John Martin.

Parcels of land described on fo: 1 as being in SP12/276 are:

Richard Humphrey	One close of pasture ground called Sarte Close lyinge between Thomas Croft's Sarte and Rushley	20-2-26
John Smithe	Tow closes of meadow and pasture lyinge betwene two lanes	14-1-18
Thomas Yate	One close of pasture lyinge neare Witney betwene the manor of Cogges and the Hyghe way leading from Witney towards Madley Well	4-3- 8
Leonard Boxe	Fowre closes of pasture whereof one is called Squyre close	27-3-17]

Whichwood Forest cum membris
[Edge of paper lost] [Adh]uc Witney   f. 2 (p. 25)

1
Walter Yate

One other close of pasture ground thereunto next adioyning and lying ut supra in the occupancy of George Stoute. Walter Yate freehold containing   6-3- 0

2
John Brooke

Two Closes of pasture ground thereunto next adioyning and lying ut supra in the occupancy of Robert Dawes. John Brooke of Southly freehold containing   7-1- 0

3
- Haines

One other close of pasture ground thereunto next adioyning and lying ut supra in the occupancy of [blank] Haines Freehold containing   11-3-13

4
Tho: Slaymaker

One cottage and one little close thereunto adioyning and lying at the Corner next to the Common or waste nere Northly: in the occupancy of Thomas Slaymaker Freehold containing   1-2- 0

5
Common

A parte of the heathe and waste lying betwene Madley Oke and Northly belonging to Witney containing   49-2-27

[gap]

6
Ric: Box

Three closes of pasture and arrable ground whereof one called Winchcroftes: lying betwene the Common field of Haley called the East Field and the said lane leading from Witney towards Northly: in the occupancy of Richard Box Freehold containing   16-0-29

7
Tho: Box

One other little close thereunto next adioyning in the occupancy of Thomas Box: Freehold containing   1-0- 0

8
Ric: Hunfrey

Three closes meadowe and pasture ground whereof one called Midlefeild lying ut supra: in the occupancy of Richard Humfrey: Freehold containing   44-0- 2

9
Walter Yate

One other close of pasture ground called Meryfeild thereunto next adioyning and lying ut supra: in the occupancy of Walter Yate Freehold containing   21-3- 0

10
Tho: Yate

One other close of pasture ground called Meryfeild extending in length betwene the lands of Leonard Box and Tho: Box: in the occupancy of Thomas Yate Freehold containing   16-1-34

11
Tho: Box

One other close thereunto next adioyning called Oxegrene: in the occupancy of Thomas Box Freehold containing   5-0-23

Adhuc Witney   **f. 2 (p. 25) dorse**
Haley

12
Robert Yate

One messuage with gardens and orchard and xj closes of meadowe pasture and arrable ground whereof one called Priest Close: one other Merifield, two other Lea Breach, <one> 2 other Spicers Hurne and the rest Old Breache: lying betwene Haley village and the said lane leading from Witney toward Northlye: in the occupancy of Robert Yate Freehold containing   157-2-28

13
Barth: Harries

Two other closes thereunto adioyning and lying ut supra: in the occupancy of Bartholomewe Harries freehold containing   5-0-35

14
John Brooke

Three little closes adioyning to the said Harries land: in the occupancy of John Brooke Freehold containing   2-1-11

15
Tho Yate

One close of pasture and arrable ground Called Stoney Rudge adioyning to the Old Breache in the occupancy of Thomas Yate Freehold containing   15-1-34

16
Leonard Box

One other close thereunto next adioyning and lying betwene the said Stoney Rudge and Swanhill Rudge: in the occupancy of Leonard Box Freehold containing   11-0- 4

17
Ric: Box

One other close thereunto next adioyning called Swanhill Rudge: in the occupancy of Richard Box Freehold containing   8-0-15

18 *- Russell*	One messuage and 2 closes adioyning to the land of Robert Yate called the Old Breache: in the occupancy of – Russell Freehold containing 4-3-26
19 *Wm Freeman*	One Cottage and one other close thereunto next adioyning: in the occupancy of Wm Freeman Freehold containing 1-2-20
20 *John Horne*	One other little close thereunto next adioyning: in the occupancy of John Horne Freehold containing 0-3- 0
21 *John Smith* *Jo: Horne* *et al.*	One close of pasture called the Common field adioyning to the lane in Haley leading from Witheridge Crosse to Hatfield Corner: in the occupancy of John Smith, John Horne and others Freehold containing 7-0- 2
22 *Bishop of* *Winchester* *Assart*	8 cottages with gardens and orchards and xvij Closes of meadowe pasture and woodland ground whereof one called Leazing Grove, another Hyde Crofte, lying betwene Witheridge Crosse, the East Field of Haley and Swanhill Ridge in the several occupancies of Barth Harries, Wm Porter, Edward Bowman John Horne [tear, at least one name and a forename lost] Box Stephen Brize Jerom Harries Tho: [tear, at least one name lost] Robert Foster and Tho Smyth containing 96-0-14

Adhuc Witney
Haley   **f. 3 (p. 26)**

23	The Greate Common field of Haley called the East Field containing 264-0-16
24 *Ric: Sherley*	One Cottage and one close lying at a corner of the said field next Witney: in the occupancy of Richard Sherley Freehold containing 2-1-25
25 *Wm Hunt*	One Cottage and two little closes lying betwene the said Sherley's land and the Comon Meadowe of Haley: in the occupancy of William Hunt Freehold, containing 1-2-25

26
Bushop
Winchester

One other long close of meadowe ground thereunto next adioyning and lying ut supra: in the occupancy of Wm Hunt. Bushop of Winchester Freehold
containing   3-0-24

27

One barne or [illegible] and a little close thereunto next adioyning and lying ut supra: in the occupancy of Hen: Hartshorne. Bushop Winchester Freehold
containing   1-0-20

28

The great Meadowe called Haley Common Meadowe and the homes, lying in length by the Water or Ryver of Wynrisse runninge throughe Witney.
containing   49-1-23

29

Five closes of meadowe and pasture ground whereof one called Bury Crofte, lying at one end of the said Comon Meadowe: in the occupancy of Tho Box. Bushop of Winchester Freehold
containing   52-2-24

30

One other greate Common field of arrable ground Called Haley West Field: containing   205-0-36

31
Jo: Smythe

One cottage and one close lying at one end of the said Common field next Crawley Bottome: in the occupancy of John Smyth containing   8-2-10

32

One other close thereunto next adioyning and lying ut supra: in the occupancy of Roger Werin:
containing   3-1-30

33

Three other little closes thereunto next adioyninge and lying ut supra in the severall occupancies of [blank]
containing   7-0-13

34

One other close thereunto next adioyning and lying ut supra: in the occupancy of Robert Horne:
containing   3-2-20

35
John Martyn

One close of pasture ground and one messuage thereunto next adioyning and abutting upon the Street in Haley: in the occupancy of Edw: Bowman: John Martyn Freehold, containing   11-3-0

Adhuc Witney
Haley

36

One messuage and 2 closes abutting upon Haley Street and lying betwene the said Martyns Close and Witheridge Crosse: in the occupancy of Henry Fitchoe
containing   4-1-18

37

One messuage and one close thereunto next adioyning and lying ut supra: in the occupancy of Robert Yate:
containing   0-3- 6

38

One little cottage and close thereunto adioyning : in the occupancy of Gilbert Maior containing   0-0-30

39
John Smythe

One messuage and 3 little closes lying ut supra: in the occupancy of John Smyth containing   2-0-38

40

One cottage and one close thereunto next adioyning: in the occupancy of [blank] containing   2-1-17

41

Two other closes thereunto next adioyning and lying ut supra: in the occupancy of [blank]
containing   3-3-36

42
Robert Foster

One messuage and one close thereunto next adioyning and lying by Witheridge Crosse: in the occupancy of Robert Foster Freehold containing   3-1-35

43

One other Close called Witheridge lying by the said Witheridge Crosse: in the occupancy of John Craftes
containing   1-3- 9

44

One other close thereunto next adioyning and lying ut supra: in the occupancy of Henry Ringe
containing   1-0-15

45	One other close thereunto next adioyning and lying ut supra: in the occupancy of Bartho: Harries: containing	1-0-10

46 One other close adioyning to the lane going from Witheridge Crosse to Hatfield Corner: in the occupancy of Bartholo Harries: containing   1-3-20

47 One messuage and one close lying ut supra: in the occupancy of [blank] Russell containing   1-3-34

48 One messuage and one close thereunto next adioyning and lying ut supra: in the occupancy of John Horne containing   0-3- 0

49 One other messuage and one close thereunto next adioyning and lying ut supra: in the occupancy of William Brooke containing   2-2-18

50 One messuage with gardens and orchards and three Closes thereunto next adioyninge and lying in Haley aforesaid: in the occupancy of Henry Ringe containing   8-3-38

Adhuc Witney   **f. 4 (p. 27)**
Haley

51 One Cottage and one close thereunto next adioyning and lying ut antea: in the occupancy of Jo Craftes containing   1-1-10

52
Edw: Craftes One other Cottage & close lying in Haley aforesaid: in the occupancy of Edw. Craftes Freehold containing   1-1-13

53
John Smyth One messuage with garden and orchard and one close of pasture and woodland ground lying ut supra: in the occupancy of John Smyth Freehold containing   16-0-14

54
John Horne One other messuage with gardens and orchard and one close of pasture ground lying ut supra and extending in length betwene two lanes there: in the occupancy of John Horne Freehold containing   6-1-35

55   One other close of pasture ground thereunto next
                      adioyning and lying ut supra: in the occupancy of William
                      Brooke containing   4-0- 6

56   One other close thereunto next adioyning: in the
                      occupancy of William Boobie containing   2-1- 9

57   One other close of pasture ground thereunto next
Wm Boobie   adioyning and lying ut supra called Charneys: in the
                      occupancy of Wm Boobie Freehold
                      containing   4-0-30

58   One other close thereunto next adioyning in the occupancy
Jo: Horne   of John Horne Freehold containing   1-2-25

59   One other close of pasture ground: called Pease Breache:
Jo: Smith et   lying ut supra betwene the said two lanes: in the occupancy
John Horne   of John Smith: Jo Horne Long Jo: Smyth [sic]
                      containing   7-1- 7

60   One litle long narrowe close thereunto next adioyning in
                      the occupancy of Edw: Bowman containing   1-2-31

61   Two other closes thereunto adioyning and lying ut supra in
                      the occupancy of [blank] Russell
                      containing   4-2-37

62   One other litle close thereunto next adioyning, called Oke
Jo: Smithe   Close: in the occupancy of John Smith containing   1-1- 9

63   One other close of pasture ground called Hatfield
Jo: Horne   thereunto next adioyning and lying nere Hatfield Corner:
                      in the occupancy of John Horne Freehold
                      containing   13-0- 3

64   Two closes whereof one called Hickrills lying ut supra: in
Jo: Crofte   the occupancy of John Craftes: containing   5-2- 3

65   One other close called Hatfield lying ut supra: in the
                      occupancy of Tho Smyth containing   4-2-20

Adhuc Witney   **f. 4 (p.27) dorse**
Haley

66   One other close of pasture ground called Hatfield lying
                       nere Hatfield Corner: in the occupancy of John Smith
                       containing   3-2-10

67   Fowre closes of pasture and meadowe ground whereof one
Thomas   called Cummyns Leaze lying ut supra: in the occupancy of
Cornishe   (Mr.) Darby of Crawley. Thomas Cornish of Witney
                       Freehold containing   36-1-21

68   One close thereunto next adioyning called Newe Close: in
Tho: Hawkes   the occupancy of Wm Wythers: Thomas Hawkes Freehold
                       containing   7-0-26

69   One other close thereunto adioyning called Delly Brache:
John Smyth   in the occupancy of John Smyth Jo: Horne Tho: Smyth
et al   Rich Smyth Wm Brooks and others
                       containing   10-1- 3

70   One other close thereunto adioyning called Delly Brache
Jo: Horne   Close: in the occupancy of John Horne Freehold
                       containing   8-2-30

71   One messuage with gardens and orchard and two Closes
Robert Yates   called Delly Brache Closes: thereunto adioyning and lying
                       in Haley: in the occupancy of Robert Yates Freehold
                       containing   17-2-28

72   One other messuage with gardens and orchards (and one
Rich: Russell   close) thereunto next adioyning and lying ut supra: in the
                       occupancy of Rich: Russell Freehold jure uxoris
                       containing   8-0- 0

73   One Cottage and close thereunto next adioyning in the
                       occupancy of Tho: Williams   0-3- 0

74   One messuage with gardens and orchard and one close
Hen: Fitchoes   Called Mobb Haies: thereunto next adioyninge and lying ut
                       supra: in the occupancy of Henry Fitchoes Freehold
                       containing   11-0- 6

75 Roger Werin	One other messuage with garden and orchards and three Closes whereof one called Dellyinge: one other Delly Brache: lying ut supra: in the occupancy of Roger Werin Freehold containing 9-2-25
76 Jo: Craftes	One other messuage with garden and orchard and one close thereunto adioyning and lying ut supra: in the occupancy of John Craftes Freehold containing 5-0-21
77 Edward Bowman[1]	Two messuages with backsides gardens and orchards and fowre closes of meadowe and pasture ground whereof two are called Rowles: one other Kinchams: the other Close End peece: thereunto next adioyning and lying ut supra: in the occupancy of Edward Bowman Freehold containing 25-3- 9
78 Ric: Russell	Two closes of pasture ground thereunto next adioyning and lying ut supra whereof one called Butt Close, thother Woodside Peece: in the occupancy of Richard Russell: Freehold containing 10-3-28

Adhuc Witney   **f. 5 (p. 28)**

79	Two cottages and two closes of arrable and pasture ground extending in length from the said Woodside Peece unto Wilcott[2] greene: in the occupancy of [blank] containing 39-0- 6
80 - Harte X	Two other Cottages and 4 closes of pasture arrable and woodland ground called Turleigh Sarte lying between Singeat Coppice and Dally Sarte: in the occupancy of – Harte Freehold containing 51-0- 6

[1]   Edward Bowman was one of the Under-keepers of Wychwood: *Cal. S. P. Dom. 1611-1618*, 22.
[2]   Wilcott greene is not in Wilcote, but is the place now known as Whiteoak Green.

81
Roger Werin
Edw: Bowman
Jo: Craftes sen
Jo: Craftes jun
Tho: Sparhauke

One Close of pasture ground thereunto next adioyning called Dally Sarte: in the occupancy of Roger Werin Edw Bowman Jo Craftes sen & jun and Tho Sparhauke: Freehold containing   16-1-14

82
Jo: Craftes

One Cottage or messuage with orchard and garden and one close called Home Close lying betwene the said Dally Sart and Kinchams: in the occupancy of John Craftes Freehold containing   7-2-35

83
Tho: Sparhauke

One other Cottage and little close thereunto next adioyning in the occupancy of Tho Sparhauke Freehold containing   0-1-20

84
Edw: Bowman

One little close abutting upon Dally Sarte: in the occupancy of Edward Bowman Freehold containing   1-3-28

85
Rich: Horne

Two closes of pasture ground lying betwene Dally Sarte and Gigley Sarte in the occupancy of John Craftes. Rich: Horne Freehold containing   22-0-24

86
Robert Horne
X

One close thereunto next adioyning Called Sarte Close: in the occupancy of John Croftes jun. Robert Horne Freehold containing   10-0-38

87
Fran: Darby
X

Two Closes of pasture ground called Gigley Sarte lying betwene Dally Sarte and Black pitt Sarte: in the occupancy of Francis Darby and Roger Werin: Francis Darby Freehold containing   35-0-14

88
Tho: Carter
X

Three closes of meadowe and pasture ground called Blackepitt Sarte, adioyning to Ramesden grounds: in the occupancy of [blank] Payne. Tho Carter Freehold containing   65-2- 5

89
Rich Busshoppe
X

Two closes of pasture and woodland ground whereof one called Cocks Wood Sarte: lying betwene Blackpitt Sarte and Wilcott field: in the occupancy of Richard Bushoppe Freehold containing   12-2-29

Adhuc Witney   **f. 5 (p. 28) dorse**

90
John Daie

One little close of wood lying betwene Blacke pitt Sarte and Wilcott field as aforesaid: in the occupancy of John Daie: John Daie Freehold containing   3-1-39

91
Edw: Bowman

One other close of pasture and woodland ground called Giglye thereunto next adioyning and lying ut supra: in the occupancy of Edw Bowman Freehold containing   25-1-29

92
Wm Hawkes
X

One other Close of pasture and woodland ground called Olde Sarte thereunto next adioyning and lying ut supra: in the occupancy of Wm Hawkes Freehold containing   11-2- 4

93
- Gunne
X

One other close of pasture ground called Old Sarte thereunto next adioyning and lying ut supra: in the occupancy of [blank] - Gunne Freehold containing   28-3-22

94
Edm: Pridie

Fowre closes of pasture ground thereunto next adioyning and lying ut supra: in the occupancy of Edm Pridie Freehold containing   59-3-26

95
Rich: Box

One other greate ground called Forsaken hooke thereunto adioyning and to Wilcott Field: in the occupancy of Richard Box Freehold containing   50-3- 9

[gap]

96
Barth: Harries

Two closes of pasture ground whereof one called Hatforde and thother Puttock Ditche joining to the lane at Hatfield Corner leading to Witheridge Crosse: in the occupancy of Bartholomew Harries Freehold containing   10-3-38

97 *Wm Boobie*	One little close lying ut supra: in the occupancy of William Boobie Freehold containing 0-1-20
98 *Jo Smith*	Fyve closes of pasture and arrable ground whereof two called Olde Breache, (one other Hatford): lying betwene Puttock Ditche and Caulkhill: in the occupancy of John Smyth Freehold containing 32-1-22
99 *Jo: Smith sen* *Jo: Smith jun* *Bar: Harries* *Joan Russell*	One other close lying ut supra: in the occupancy of John Smith sen. John Smith jun. Bartholomewe Harries & Joan Russell: Freehold containing 11-3-38
100 *John Horne*	Fyve closes of (meadowe) pasture arrable and woodland ground whereof one called Edkins Meade, one other Spicers Hurne and one other the Lopes: lying ut supra betwene Caulkhill and the said lane leading from Hatfield Corner: in the occupancy of John Horne Freehold containing 31-3-21
101 *Ric Brakspeare*	One close of woodland ground called Meryfield adioyning to Spicers Hurne and Caulkhill Copice: in the occupancy of Rich: Brakspeare Freehold containing 4-1-12

Adhuc Witney   **f. 6 (p.29)**

102 *[Blank]* *Waynman*	Foure closes of medowe pasture and woods whereof one called Caulkhill: one other Caulkhill Copice lying betwene Northly Waste and Hatfield Corner: in the occupancy of Mr. [blank] Waynman, Tho Handes and Wm Androwes. Mr. [blank] Waynman Freehold containing 67-3- 0

[gap]

103
Tho: Yate

Ten Cottages with gardens and backsides and 7 Closes of meadowe pasture and wood whereof one called Purtons Meadowe: another Purtons Grove, one other Purton Close: one other Furzie Close: adioyning to Northly and lying betwene Wilcott Field and Caulkhill Copice: in the severall occupancies of [blank]. Tho Yate Freehold containing   52-3- 3

104
- Saunders

One little close lying ut supra: in the occupancy of [blank] Saunders Freehold
containing   1-0-10

105
- Russell

One other little close called Merifeild Close lying ut supra: in the occupancy of - Russell Freehold
containing   5-0-21

106
Jo: Smyth

Two other closes called Merifield, thereunto next adioyning and lying ut supra: in the occupancy of John Smyth Freehold containing   6-0-27

107
Tho: Taylor

Two closes of pasture ground called Knaves Nolle: thereunto adioyning and to Hatfield Corner: in the occupancy of Tho Taylor Freehold
containing   59-3- 1

Northly

108
Leonard Box
(asst)

One peece of wood called Osney Wood alias Osney Hill adioyning to the waste or Common of Northly. Leonard Box Freehold containing   59-2-13

109
Common [the
word *not* added]

The waste or common belonging to Northly:[3]
containing   271-0-28

---

[3]   The Survey describes only the western half of North Leigh, but it seems to include the whole of North Leigh Heath: *V.C.H. Oxfordshire xii*, 215. This heath was continuous with that of Hailey, **5**, and Hanborough **276.**

110
Rex[4]

8 Cottages with gardens and backsides and 12 closes of pasture ground: lying in Northly: in the severall occupancies of Tho Ring, Philipp Brakspere, Richard Brakespeare, Richard Gardener, John Smith, John Kent, Jo Blakwell, Robert Erles, Margaret Ridley. Dominus Rex Freehold containing   23-0-33

111
Sir Wm Pope

12 messuages or Cottages with gardens and orchards and 34 Closes of meadowe and pasture ground lying in Northly aforesaid in the severall occupancies of John Kent, Widowe Collins, Tho: Franklyn, Widowe Saunders, Widowe Phippes, - Parrett, Widowe Sheriffe, Edw: Harte, Wyd: Bond, Henry Slatford, Tho Townsend and others. Sir Wm Pope Freehold
containing   88-3-37

Adhuc Northly   **f. 6 (p. 29) dorse**

112
Wm Robyns

One Close of pasture thereunto adioyning and lying in Northly: in the occupancy of Wm Robyns Freehold containing   1-2- 3

113
John Sheref

One cottage and one close thereunto next adioyning and lying ut supra in the occupancy of John Sheref Freehold containing   0-3- 0

114
Wm Fynlis

One other cottage and one close thereunto adioyning and lying ut supra in the occupancy of Wm Fynlis Freehold containing   0-3- 0

115
Tho Francklyn

One other cottage and a close thereunto adioyning and lying ut supra in the occupancy of Tho Francklyn Freehold containing   1-1-25

116

3 other cottages and 3 little closes thereunto adioyning and lying ut supra: in the severall occupancies of John Kepe John Pyne containing   4-3-28

---

4   In 1611 Sir William Pope claimed the whole of North Leigh and denied that it was in the Forest: P.R.O. SP14/195 No. 6.

117   One messuage with gardens and orchards and one close of
Wm Kinge   pasture ground thereunto adioyning and lying ut supra: in
                   the occupancy of John Dawson. Wm Kinge Freehold
                   containing   8-0- 0

118   One other messuage with gardens and orchards and two
                   Closes lying nere the church in Northlye aforesaid: in the
                   occupancy of Wm Kinge Freehold
                   containing   12-1- 7

119   One messuage and one close called the Parsonage lying ut
Parson   supra: in the occupancy of [blank]
                   containing   2-0- 8

120   2 other little cottages thereunto adioyning: in the
                   occupancy of Wm Karidge and [blank]
                   containing   0-1-20

121   The Town feild called Hey Crafte containing   44-1- 3

122   One other Common field called Cadwell field lying
                   betwene the Towne closes of Northly and Mousley Corner:
                   containing   60-3-32

123[5]   One other common field thereunto next adioyning and
                   belonging to Northly aforesaid: containing   201-3-15

124   Three closes of pasture and arrable grounds lying at the
Wm Kinge   further corner of the said common field: in the occupancy
                   of Wm Kinge Freehold containing   11-1-24

125   Three other closes thereunto next adioyning and lying ut
Sir Wm Pope   supra: in the severall occupancies of Tho Broughton,
                   Widowe Sherife and Mrs. Harte. Sir Wm Pope Freehold
                   containing   5-3- 6

---

[5] The un-named field is Edgings (Echenes) Field (see p. 130, **10**): *V.C.H. Oxfordshire xii*, 214
(map), 215. In P.R.O SP12/276 entries **121**, **122** and **123** are recorded as belonging to Sir William
Pope.

Ramesden

126
Tho: Taylor

One cottage and three closes of meadowe pasture and woodland ground called Tharmon Haies: in Ramesden nere Wilcott field: in the occupancy of Thomas Taylor Freehold containing   48-0- 3

127
Stephen Brises

One little close of wood or Copice thereunto next adioyning and lying ut supra: in the occupancy of Stephen Brises Freehold containing   3-3-24

128
Walter Larner

Two closes of pasture ground thereunto next adioyning and lying ut supra: in the occupancy of Walter Larner Freehold containing   7-2- 4

129

One messuage and one Cottage: with gardens and orchards and 6 closes of meadowe pasture and arable ground lying in Ramesden aforesaid: in the occupancy of Walter Larner Freehold containing   22-3-39

130
<Tho> Hen
Larner

One Cottage and one little close lying ut supra in the occupancy of Thomas Larner Freehold containing   1-3-17

131
Hen Larner
(Comp)
X

Two messuages with gardens and orchards and 7 closes of meadowe, pasture and woodland ground whereof one called Crockes Sarte lying ut supra: in the occupancy of Henry Larner Freehold containing   44-0-10

132
Leonard Pettie
(Comp)

One Cottage and one close of pasture and woodland ground lying ut supra: in the occupancy of Leonard Petty Freehold containing   52-3-15

133
- Joyner

One cottage and one close thereunto adioyning and lying ut supra: in the occupancy of Widowe Joyner Freehold containing   6-0-37

134

4 cottages and one Close of pasture ground lying ut supra called Shutley: in the occupancy of diverse containing   8-1-27

135
Paule Silvester

One other Cottage and one close thereunto adioyning and lying ut supra: in the occupancy of Paule Silvester Freehold containing   1-2-24

136
Sir Fra:
Fortescue

Two messuages with gardens and orchards and 4 closes of pasture and arrable grounds lying ut supra in the severall occupancies of Richard Joyner and Richard Greene. Sir Fra Fortescue Freehold containing   10-1- 6

137
Alexander
Crossley

One cottage and 3 closes of pasture ground lying ut supra: in the severall occupancies of Richard Joyner [sic]. Alexander Crossley Freehold containing   7-3-10

138
Sir Wa:
Harecourt

One cottage and 3 closes lying ut supra: in the occupancy of Wm Larner. Sir Walter Harecourt Freehold containing   8-0-28

139

One messuage and one close called Swinpie lying ut supra: nere Crockes Sarte: in the occupancy of Henry Larner, Walter Larner, Walter Kincham and Arthur Leeche and others. Freehold
containing   13-3- 4

Adhuc Ramesden   **f. 7 (p. 30) dorse**

140
Walter Kirbie

One long narrowe close of pasture ground lying in Ramesden nere Swinpie: in the occupancy of Walter Kirbye Freehold containing   3-0- 9

141
Sir Wa:
Harecourt

One other little close thereunto next adioyning and lying ut supra: in the occupancy of Wm Larner. Sir Walter Harecort Freehold containing   3-0-34

142
Paule Silvester

One other little close thereunto adioyning and lying ut supra: in the occupancy of Michael Grene. Paule Silvester Freehold containing   1-2-34

143
Wm Joyner

One other little close lying at a corner ut supra: in the occupancy of Wm Joyner Freehold
containing   3-0-11

144 *Walter Kincham* *alias Kerby* X	One close of pasture ground lying by it self nere Crockes Sarte: in the occupancy of Walter Kincham als Kerby Freehold containing	5-3-16

145 *Ric: Drinkwater*	One cottage and one close of pasture ground lying in Ramesden aforesaid: in the occupancy of Richard Drinkwater Freehold containing	3-1-33

146 *- Franchise*	One other Cottage and close thereunto next adioyning and lying ut supra: in the occupancy of Widowe Franchise containing	2-0- 3

147 *Wm Joyner*	One other Cottage and close thereunto next adioyning and lying ut supra: in the occupancy of Wm Joyner Freehold containing	1-0-30

148	One close of meadowe ground lying at the end of the street in Ramesden: in the occupancy of Edward Winter containing	4-3- 0

149	Two little closes abutting to one end of the said former close: in the severall occupancies of Rich: Grene: Wm Bushop and Rich: Joyner containing	1-1-18

150 *(Comp Walter* *Larner 5-0-0* *Walter Kincham* *2-2-0)*	One close of pasture ground called Harrolls Sarte: lying ut supra: in the occupancy of Richard Joyner Walter Larner Raphe Leeche Walter Kerby Freehold containing	10-2-14

151 *Wm Andrewes*	One little close of pasture ground lying at the side of the common field of Ramesden: in the occupancy of – Marshall: Wm Andrewes Freehold containing	2-0-35

152	One common field of arrable ground belonging to Ramesden containing	71-3- 1

153	One other greate common field[6] thereunto belonging containing	115-2-25

[6] This is the site of the assart ordered by Matilda, Countess of Gloucester. See p. 78, **88**.

Adhuc Ramesden   **f. 8 (p. 31)**

154 *Rich Greene*	One close of pasture ground adioyning to the same common field in the occupancy of Richard Greene Freehold containing 4-0-16

155
(Walter Kirby)

Two closes of arrable ground lying betwene the two said common fields: in the occupancy of Walter Kirby containing   6-2-34

156

One other close lying ut supra: in the occupancy of Owen Larner containing   2-3-10

157

Three other closes lying ut supra in the severall occupancies of [blank] containing   25-3-39

158

Two litle closes thereunto adioyning and lying ut supra: in the severall occupancies of William Bushoppe and [blank] containing   1-1-11

[gap]

(Parte of the Manor of Wytney)
The Chacewoodes

159
- Brice

One parcell of wood or sale called Singeat Coppice lying nere Ramesden grounds and adioyning to Wilcott Grene: in the occupancy of [blank] Bryce Freehold containing   86-0-15

160

Three cottages and one little waste called Wilcott greene thereunto adioyning containing   13-1- 1

161

One other Cottage and waste ground lying betwene the said Wilcott Grene and Barleyhill Copice: in the occupancy of – Brice Freehold containing   8-2-32

162
- Brice

One sale or coppice called Barley hill Coppice thereunto adioyning and to Ackman Street: in the occupancy of – Bryce Freehold containing   34-3- 8

163   One other parcell of wood or sale called Little Smaley
                thereunto next adioyning: in the occupancy of - Brice
                Freehold containing   21-3-13

164   One other wood called by the names of Greate Smalley
                Colletts Copice and Henley Coppice thereunto adioyninge
                and lying betwene Ackman Street and Deane Grene: in the
                occupancy of – Brice containing   83-2-12

[Adhuc] the Chace Wodes   **f. 8 (p. 31) dorse)**

165   One other great Wood called by the names of the Chace
- Brice   Woodes: Water Vynes Copice and Deane Coppice:
                adioyning to Ackman Strete aforesaid: in the occupancy of
                – Brice Freehold containing   211-0-39

166   One other coppes called Blindwell Copice and a little close
                or greene thereunto adioyninge: in the occupancy of – Brice
                Freehold containing   21-2-30

Crawley (Part of Witney)

167   One Water Myll and two little meadowes lying nere
                Crawley Bridge: in the occupancy of [blank]
                containing   4-0-20

168   The meadowe called the Common Meadowe thereunto
                adioyning and lying ut supra:
                containing   25-3-35

169   One messuage and one close of meadowe ground lying by
John Hampshire Crawley Bridge: in the occupancy of John Hampshire
                Freehold containing   3-1-14

170   One messuage and 3 closes of meadowe and pasture ground
Bishop of   wherof one called the Lynch, one other Worsell, thother the
Winton   Longe West: lying in Crawley aforesaid: in the occupancy
                of John Hampshire. Bishop of Winchester Freehold
                containing   29-0-19

171   One close of arrable (and pasture) ground called the
                                   Towne West thereunto adioyning and lying ut supra
                                   containing   13-2-16

172   One messuage and 3 closes of pasture ground lying in
Edw Bowman   Crawley aforesaid: in the occupancy of Edward Bowman:
                                   Freehold containing   11-3-35

173   One messuage and 2 closes of pasture ground lying ut
Adam Selman   supra: in the occupancy of Adam Selman Freehold
                                   containing   4-2-16

174   One messuage and 3 cottages and 5 closes of pasture
                                   ground lying ut supra: in the severall occupancies of
                                   [blank]. Francis Darby Freehold containing   5-3- 8

175   One cottage and one close adioyning to the Cross Waies in
                                   Crawley aforesaid: in the occupancy of [blank]
                                   containing   0-3- 6

176   One close thereunto adioyning·and lying ut supra: in the
Fra: Darby   occupancy of Edw Bowman and Richard Moppe
                                   containing   2-1-11

Adhuc Crawley   **f. 9 (p. 32)**

177   One messuage and One close of pasture ground lying in
                                   Crawley aforesaid: in the occupancy of George Box,
                                   containing   1-0-32

178   One messuage and one close of pasture ground lying ut
Peter Daie   supra: in the occupancy of Peter Daye Freehold containing
                                   6-0- 0

179   One messuage and two closes of arrable ground lying ut
Wm Brookes   supra: in the occupancy of William Brooks Freehold
                                   containing   10-3-37

180   One messuage with gardens and orchard and two closes of
Geo: Birdseye   pasture and arable ground lying ut supra: in the occupancy
                                   of George Birdseye Freehold containing   7-0-10

181 *Ric: Box*	One other messuage and one close of pasture ground lying ut supra: in the occupancy of Richard Box Freehold containing	2-0-20

182	One litle close thereunto next adioyning and lying ut supra: in the occupancy of Wm Brise containing	0-1-16

183 *Hen Ringe*	One messuage and one close lying ut supra: in the occupancy of Henry Ringe Freehold containing	2-1-17

184	One cottage and close thereunto next adioyning and lying ut supra: in the occupancy of [blank] containing	0-1-16

[gap]

185	Two great common fields of arrable ground lying on bothe side Crawley Bottome belonging to Crawley Containing	354-2-25

186 *Geo: Birdseie*	One little close at thend of the said common field: in the occupancy of Geo Birdseye Freehold containing	1-0-38

187 *(John Hampshire)*	Two closes of pasture and woodland ground called the Breaches adioyning to the common field and to Deane Greene: in the occupancy of John Hampshire containing	51-1-29

Here endeth one parte or plott of Whichwood Forest

188
Taston Sartes[7]
Robert Web
Robert Prentice
Christopher
Harries
Tho: Gey
Tho: Rooke

One field of arrable ground Called Taston Sartes: lying betwene Charlebury Field and Spelesbury Woodes: in the occupancy of Robert Webb, Robert Prentice, Christopher Harries, Thomas Gey, and Thomas Rooke Freehold containing   44-1-26

189

A parte of Charlebury Field called the Coate Field alias Pinckle Hill or Rawlins Crosse Field: thereunto adioyning and lying ut supra: in the occupancy of [blank] containing   53-2-14

[In the following entries, * indicates those where comp has been added, in a different hand]

190
Ledwell Sartes
John Pridie
Abraham Hedges
*Tho: Harries**
*Rich: Irons **
*Jo: Coates **
Tho: Gey
Tho: Brewer
*Geo: Tenant **
Antho: Tenant
Wa: Robinson

One field or ground called Ledwell Sartes adioyning to Rawlins Crosse and Grymesditch and belonging to Charlebury: in the occupancy of Tho: Harris Richard Irons John Coates Tho: Gey Tho: Brewer Geo Tenante Anthony Tenante Walter Robinson Abraham Hedges and John Prydie Freehold containing   65-0-18

191
Hopkins Sarte
*Geo Tenant **
*Tho Harries **
*Ric Irons **
*Wm Harris **
Antho: Tenant
*Jo: Coates **

One other ground called Hopkins Sarte in Charlebury Common Field adioyning to Sir Harry Lees Woods: in the occupancy of Geo: Tenant Tho: Harris Rich: Irons Wm Harris Anthony Tenant and Jo: Coats Freehold containing   17-0-21

---

[7]   **188** to **206** describe part of Charlbury and Fawler. In SP 12/272 plots 188-197 and 204 are listed together under the names of fourteen men described as "tenants of Sir Henry Lee".

192
Cockshute Sarte
Antho: Joyner *
*Abraham
        Harris* *
Jo: Coates *
John Shepheard
Jo: Priddie
Jo: Irons
Tho Harris *

One other ground called Cockshute Sarte: lying ut supra: in the occupancy of Wm Shepheard Anthony Joyner Abraham Harries John Coates John Shepheard John Priddie <John> Richard Irons Tho: Harris sen Freehold containing   17-1-25

193 Newe Sarte
Wm Shepheard
Jo: Priddie
Jo: Pointer
Ric: Irons
Jo: Coates
Tho: Harries
Giles Camden *
Antho Joyner *

One other ground of arrable land called Charlebury Newe Sarte lying ut supra: in the occupancy of Wm Shepheard John Priddie John Pointer Rich: Irons John Coats Tho: Harries Giles Camden and Anthony Joyner Freehold containing   19-1-13

194
Baldocks Sarte
John Roughes

One little close of pasture ground called Baldocks Sarte thereunto next adioyning: in the occupancy of John Roughes freehold containing   7-3-14

195
Abbots Wood

solo proprio

Lees Rest

Sir Hen: Lee

The greate wood called Abbots Wood (153-2-7) severally named Winter Slade Copice, Cockshute Coppice, New Sart Coppice (30-2-11) Maget Sarte Coppice (117-0-2) Olde Raules Copice Horsman Walles Copice London Sarte Copice Woodstocke Hatch Rushmore Copice Styquarter Copice with a faire howse called Lee's Rest lying all together betwene Charlebury Fields and Fawler Fields: in the occupancy of Sir Henry Lee freehold
containing   301-2-36

196

Charlebury Sarte

John Pridie
Tho: Harries *
Jo: Rough
Jo: Grey
Abraham Hedges
Antho: Joyner *
Tho: Brewer
Jo: Coates *
Rich: Irons *
Geo Tenant *
Abraham
*   Harris **
Wm Harries *

One greate Common field of arrable ground called
Dustfield and Abridge: belonging to Charlebury adioyning
to the said Abbott Woodes: in the occupancy of John
Prydie Tho: Harries John Rough John Grey Abraham
Hedges Anthony Joyner Tho Brewer John Coats Geo:
Tenant Abraham Harries Wm Harries and Rich: Irons:
Freehold
containing   156-1- 2

197

Geo Tenant

One little close adioyning to one side of the said Common
field: in the occupancy of Geo: Tenant freehold
containing   3-2-18

Fawlar

198

Leonard Pettie *
Tho: Harries
Rich: Irons *
Wm Shepheard
Jo: Hedges
Tho Bumpas
Giles Camden *
Ed: Priddie
Robert: Henton
Jo: Bumpas
Jo: Hunt

One greate common field called <Marden Field belonging
to> Fawler (Sarte) extending from Charlebury New Sarte
to Fawlars Slattpitts: in the occupancy of Leonard Pettie
<Tho> Alexander Harries of Charlebury Richard Irons
Wm Shepheard John Hedges Tho: Bumpas Giles Campden
Ed: Priddie Robert Henton Jo: Bumpas and John Hunt:
Freehold containing   167-3-22

[St. Johns Colledge and Westminster Colledge added in another hand, in the
margin]

199

One close of arrable ground called Fawlares Slattpitte
thereunto next adioyning: in the occupancy of [blank]
containing   15-1-25

200 *Wm Roffe*	One other close of pasture ground thereunto next adioyning: in the occupancy of Wm Roffe freehold containing 5-0-16
201 *<Tho>* *Alexander* *Harris* *(comp)*	Two closes of pasture called Horsman Walles adioyning to Sir Harry Lees Woods: in the occupancy of Thomas Harries Freehold containing 8-3- 4
202 *John Hedges*	Two other closes of pasture ground called Horseman Walles thereunto next adioyning: in the occupancy of John Hedges Freehold containing 9-1-23
203 *Tho Bumpas*	One other close of pasture ground thereunto also adioyninge: in the occupancy of Tho Bumpas Freehold containing 5-2- 3
204 Assart Fields *Jo: Hunt* *[blank] Pettie* *Jo: Dumpar* *Tho: Bumpas* *Jo: Hedges* *Ed: Prydie*	One greate common <field> assart field called Rushmore and the Slattpitts: belonging to Fawlar: in the occupancy of Jo: Hunt Leonard Pettie John Dumpar Tho: Bumpas John Hedges and Ed Prydie Freehold containing 362-0-12
205 *Ric: Hedges* *Ed: Priddie* *Jo: Hedges*	One other greate common assart field (called Abbots Side) thereunto next adioyning and belonging to Fawlar: in the occupancy of Richard Hedges [illegible superscription] Ed Prydie and Jo: Hedges Freehold containing 369-2-19

Adhuc Fawler   **f. 10 (p. 33) dorse**

206 *Leonard Pettie* *(comp)*	Three closes of pasture and woodland ground called Stakhey adioyning to the said Common field and lying betwene Nettleden Hill and Stuntesfoorde: in the occupancy of Leonard Petty Freehold containing 44-0-28

[gap]

207[8]
solo proprio
Sir Hen: Lee
X

The woods called by the severall names of Spelesbury Woods alias Saintley, Spanrydinge Wood Wardley Wood and Chilcott Wood: with a Cottage in Spanrydinge Lane: all lying together betwene Taston Sarts, Rorehill Lane and Sir Harry Lee's Sartes by Grimesditch: in the occupancy of Sir Henry Lee Freehold
containing   216-1-21

208
X

One close called Sarte Close lying at one corner of the said woods next Rawlins Crosse: in the occupancy of Sir Hen: Lee Freehold
containing   9-2-18

209

One other close of pasture ground lying at thother corner of the said woods called Wardley Close: in the occupancy of Sir Harry Lee Freehold
containing   5-1-20

210

One field of arrable ground called Broade Sartes lying betwene Rorehill Lane and Deadman Ryding: in the occupancy of Sir Harry Lee freehold
containing   68-1- 0

211

Two sales or parcells of wood whereof one called Rorehill thother Darnill: thereunto next adioyning and lying ut supra: in the occupancy of Sir Harry Lee freehold
containing   100-2-34

212

Two closes of pasture ground called Sarte Closes thereunto next adioyning and lying ut supra: in the occupancy of Sir Harry Lee: Freehold
containing   19-3-32

---

[8]   **207** to **216** record a stage in the making of the Ditchley estate. **207** to **212** were part of Spelsbury manor, which had been bought by Cromwell Lee in 1599 and inherited by his brother Sir Henry Lee in 1601. **213** to **216**, "Forest" or "king's soil", belonged to the king's manor in Bloxham and, as "the manor of Ditchley" were bought by Sir Henry in 1583: Elsie Corbett, *A History of Spelsbury*, 39, 158. The adjoining part of Enstone manor, **218** and **219**, was still owned by Sir William Pope although occupied by Sir Henry Lee.

213
Forest

One fair house called Ditchley House (with gardens and orchards) and 9 closes of meadowe pasture and arrable ground: whereof some called the Snossons, one other the Conygree, one other the Cunditt Close and another the Meadowe Close: lying together by Ditchley Howse: in the occupancy of Sir Harry Lee Freehold
containing   68-1-23

214
solo regis
(comp)
X

One greate field of arrable ground thereunto next adioyning called the Common Sartes: lying on bothe side Grymes-ditch: in the occupancy of Sir Harry Lee Freehold
containing   138-1-37

215
solo regis
(comp)
X

Three closes of pasture ground lying at one end of the said great field and adioyning to Woodstocke Rydinge whereof two called Dustfield Sarts & thother Bottome Close Sarte: in the occupancy of Sir Harry Lee Freehold
containing   73-0-25

Adhuc Sir Hen: Lee   **f. 11 (p. 34)**

216
solo regis
(comp)

Two parcells of wood whereof one called Ashe Coppes, thother Bottom Wood and 5 closes of meadowe pasture and arrable ground whereof one called Meadowe Close and another the Lammas Close: lying betwene the said Sarte grounds and Sir Wm Pope's land by Boxden Lake head: in the occupancy of Sir Harry Lee Freehold
containing   193-3-12

217
(Sheldon)
(comp)

One other wood called <Shere> (Sharswell) Coppes and three closes of pasture and woodland ground whereof one called Litle Wootton Sarte   65-0- 5
thereunto adioyning and lying ut supra: in the occupancy of Mrs. [blank] Dormer and (Ralph Sheldon)
containing   <176-0-14>111-0- 9

['Ralphe Sheldon Esq., belonging to Barton (Sharswell) parish' [9] added in a different hand]

[gap]

---

[9]   At the date of the Survey Sesswell's Barton was shared between Ralph Sheldon and the Dormer family, but it is not known how this piece of land became attached to the manor. In the 1298/1300 perambulation it is called 'the Erle's wood of Bloxham', the earl presumably being Edmund, Earl of Cornwall, who was overlord of Sesswell's Barton: *VCH Oxon. xi*, 63.

218 Winchcombe Sartes

Sir Wm Pope   One greate field of arrable ground and three closes of
                        meadowe and pasture ground called Winchcombe Sartes[10],
                        lying betwene Deadman Ryding and Asterley Grounds: in
                        the occupancy of Sir Henry Lee: Sir Wm Pope Freehold
                        containing   181-1-13

219   One messuage and two cottages with gardens and
Sir Wm Pope   backsides and six closes or grounds of meadowe pasture
                        arrable and woodland: whereof some called Ditchlie Sartes
                        alias Farme Sartes, one other Boxwood: lying together
                        betwene Ditchley House and Kiddington Sartes and
                        Boxden Lake: in the occupancy of Sir Harry Lee: Sir Wm
                        Pope freehold containing   464-3- 6

220 Kiddington Sartes

(Earle of   Two greate fields of arrable and warren called Kiddington
Montgomery)   Sartes (with a cottage): and three parcells of wood whereof
                        one called Hillwood one other Outwood and thother West
                        Coppice: lying together betwene the said Sartes of Sir Wm
                        Pope, Glimpton Fields at the bound, and Berins Lane: in
                        the occupancy of [blank]. (Earle of Montgomery Freehold)
                        containing   606-1-20

221   Two closes of meadowe and pasture ground called Berins
<Tho> (Rich:)   Close thereunto next adioyning and lying at Berins Lane
Askewe (comp)   End: in the occupancy of <Thomas> Richard Askewe
                        freehold containing   12-1-15

                                                              f. 11 (p. 34) dorse

222   Two closes of meadowe and woodland ground lying at
<Tho> (Rich:)   Beryns Lane end and adioyning to Glympton Sartes: in the
Askewe (comp)   occupancy of <Thomas> (Richard) Askewe: Freehold
                        containing   14-0-38

223   One other close of woodland ground called Harkwood
<Tho> (Rich:)   lying by Slape Bridge: in the occupancy of <Thomas>
Askewe (comp)   (Richard) Askewe: Freehold containing   11-3-38

---

[10] This land includes the assarts recorded on p. 109, **11** and **12**.

224 Glympton Sartes

Vincent Cowper   One cottage and one field of arrable ground called Glympton Sartes and two parcells of wood called Glympton Wood: thereunto adioyning and lying betwene Berins Lane and Boxden Lake: in the occupancy of [blank] Tisdale. Vincent Cowper freehold
containing   83-2-27

225   Two closes of pasture ground thereunto next adioyning and
- Pollard   lying ut supra: in the occupancy of - Tisdale. – Pollard freehold containing   23-2-35

[The following nine entries are bracketted together and have *Forest* and *Assarts* written in the margin]

226[11]   One close of pasture ground called the Slape lying nere
Collegium   Slape Bridge: in the occupancy of Arthure James. Mawdlin
Magdalen   Colledge Freehold containing   28-1-36

227   One other close of pasture and woodland ground called the
Wm Horne   Slape: adioyning to Wootton Field: in the occupancy of Tho Fortie: Wm Horne freehold
containing   14-3-11

228   One close of pasture ground called Cowpers Sarte abutting
- Pollard   onto the Slape: in the occupancy of Tho: Tisdale. – Pollard Freehold containing   39-3-14

229   Two closes of pasture and arrable ground called Greene
(Vincent) –   Sarte lying betwene Cowpers Sarte and Boxden Lake: in
Cowper   the occupancy of Thomas Tisdale. [blank] Cowper
[three illegible   Freehold containing   78-3-18
words]
(Worcester)

230   One close of pasture ground adioyning to Wm Hornes
Tho Fortie   Slape Close: in the occupancy of Tho Fortie Freehold containing   10-1-27

[11] The survey is not consistent in indicating when another manor or parish has been reached. **226** to **231** are in Glympton, but **232** to **236** in the royal manor of Wootton.

231 *Wm Castill*	Three closes of pasture ground thereunto next adioyning: in the occupancy of Wm Castill Freehold containing 14-3-22

231
Wm Castill

Three closes of pasture ground thereunto next adioyning: in the occupancy of Wm Castill Freehold
containing 14-3-22

232
(Rex)
X

One ground or waste of sarte land called Wootton Wood Leaze: thereunto next adioyning
containing 55-3- 0

233
(Rex)
X

One parcell of wood called Wootton Wood thereunto adioyning and lying nere Woodstocke Parke: The Kinge Freehold containing 73-1-30

f. 12 (p. 35)

234
Jerome Nash
Sartes
(compound)

Two closes of pasture ground and Sarte land (called Old Woodstock Sarte) thereunto adioyning: in the occupancy of Jerom Nashe Freehold
containing 78-2- 1

235
(Rex)

One parcell of waste lying betwene the said Sarte and the kings wood called Ambrose Copps. The Kinge Lo: [illegible words crossed out]
containing 96-0-13

236
(Rex)

Two parcells of wood thereunto next adioyning whereof one called Fewden and the other Ambrose Coppes. The Kinge Freehold containing 246-3-34

Stuntsfield

237

One common or waste called Stuntsfield Grene extending from the said woods towards Stuntsfield
containing 105-0-19

238

One close of pasture and arrable ground called the Callowe belonging to Stuntsfield containing 45-0-37

239

One other close at Rudden Well adioyning to Stuntsfield grene containing 46-2-21

240

One other close of meadow ground thereunto next adioyning called Tennetts Sarte containing 25-1-37

241   The messuages Cottages backsides gardens orchards and Towne Closes of Stuntsfield: in the severall occupancies of Richard Drinkwater, James Larner, John Osburne, Robert Chamberlen, Richard Hicks, Edm: Hollowaye, Robert James, James Loughton, Wm Hedges, John Huggins, Richard Waste, Rich: Meades, John Meades, Thomas Hayward, Richard Keate, Richard Bunne, Francis Robinson, Geo: Owen, Wm Larner, Robert Weston & James Drinkwater

containing   37-1-26

242   One common field called the Churche Field lying betwene the Towne and Nettleden Valley

containing   40-3-24

243   One other common field called Homefield lying at the other side of the Towne containing   219-0-12

Coome

244 Wootton Sartes

Sir Hen: Lee
Ric: Sadler
Ric: Hickes
Wm Hickes
James
Drinkwater
James Larner
Jo: Osborne
Rich: Keate
Fra: Robinson
Geo Owen

One greate common field called Wootton Sartes next adioyning to Stuntsfield field: in the occupancy of Sir Harry Lee, Rich: Sadler, Rich: Hicks, Wm Hicks James Drinkwater James Larner John Osborne, Rich Kate, Francis Robinson & George Owen of Stuntsfield and Henry Blagrave Wm Seacole Walter Payne, Wm Yate William Todman Rich: Hill Geo: Warden John Maye Ro: Warde Wm Booton, Nicholas Bucknor John Hurst, Ro Chamberlen James Wamsell, Wydowe Hawkyns and Henry Newman of Coome Freehold

containing   222-1-32

Hen: Blagrave
Wm Seacole
Wa: Payne
Wm Yate
Wm Todman
Ric: Hill
Geo: Warden
Jo: Maye et al.

[The first ten names in the margin are separated from the rest by a line and have *Stuntsfield* written beside them, the others have *Coome* written beside them.]

Adhuc Coome **f. 12 (p. 35) dorse**

245
Stevens Sarte
Wm Woodward
Tho: Brewer
Lewis Pollard

One other greate Common field called Stevens Sartes: thereunto next adioyning and to Woodstocke Parke: in the occupancy of William Woodward, Tho Brewer & Lewis Pollard (and others). Freehold
containing   123-2-12

246 (Newe Sarte
Hartsoare)

One other greate common field called (Hartesore et New Sarte alias) Coome Homefield lying betwene Coome Green and Woodstock Park
containing   231-2- 8

247 Coome
Old Sartes
Lewis Pollard
Hen: Blagrave
Ric: Hill
Ro: Chamberlen
Hen: Newman
Wm Bootun
Wa: Payne
et al.

One other common field called Coome Old Sartes thereunto adioyning and lying ut supra: in the occupancy of Lewis Pollard, Henry Blagrave, Rich Hill, Robert Chamberlen, Henry Newman, Wm Booton, Walter Payne, Jo: Maye, Hen Jackson, Robert Warde, Wm Seacole, Tho Rappingale, John May sen, Nicholas Bucknor, Tho Forres Freehold
containing   140-1-34

248
(Rex)

The greate waste or common called Coome Greene extending in length from Stuntsford to Woodstocke Parke:
containing   242-2-34

249
<Lewis> (Jo:)
Pollard

One close of wood or copice called Nottoakes, lying nere the end of the said Coome Grene next Stuntsfoord: in the occupancy of <Lewis> Jo: Pollard: Freehold
containing   18-2- 0

250

One little close of meadowe ground lying at Stuntsfoord: in the occupancy of [blank]
containing   0-2- 4

251

One other meadowe thereunto next adioyning called Wignam Meadowe: in the occupancy of [blank]
containing   10-0- 3

| 252 | One greate common field thereunto adioyning called (Westfield alias) Coome Home Field |
| | containing 194-0- 0 |

| 253 | One meadowe called One Acre Meadowe lying at the narrowe corner of the said common field: in the occupancy of [blank] |
| | containing 10-3-17 |

| 254 | One other meadowe called <Cleame> (Clayme) Meadowe lying betwene the said Common field and Robertsfoord: in the occupancy of [blank] |
| | containing 14-3-10 |

| 255 | One other meadow (called Clayme) lying at the end of the same and by the waterside: in the occupancy of [blank] |
| | containing 11-2-36 |

| 256 | One other meadow thereunto next adioyning called (Colenam alias) Coome Meadow: in the occupancy of [blank] containing 30-1-10 |

257
John Gregory   One messuage and 3 closes of pasture ground whereof one called the Fallowe Close and one other the Wyer Close: lying in Coome: in the occupancy of John Gregory
containing   13-1-13

Adhuc Coome   **f. 13 (p. 36)**

258
Robert   One messuage and two closes lying in Coome in the
Newman   occupancy of Robert Newman Freehold
containing   4-3- 3

259
Ric: Keene   One cottage and one close lying ut supra: in the occupancy of Rich: Keene Freehold
containing   4-1-27

260
Walter Payne   One messuage with gardens and orchard and one close thereunto adioyning and lying ut supra: in the occupancy of Walter Payne Freehold
containing   6-3-33

261 *Ric: Hill*	One messuage and 2 cottages and 10 little closes thereunto adioyning and lying ut supra in the occupancy of [blank]. Rich Hill: freehold containing	16-2- 6

262 *Rex*	Fowre cottages and 5 closes of pasture ground lying ut supra in the severall occupancies of Henry Blagrave John Carver Tho Hurst (free) and Tho Smyth. The Kinge Freehold containing	15-2-37

263	One faire house with gardens and orchards lying ut supra: in the occupancy of John Pollard freehold containing	8-0-27

264 *Other inhabitants in Coome*	Other messuages Cottages backsides gardens orchards and little Towne closes in Coome aforesaid in the severall occupancies of Henry Blagrave, Nicholas Bucknoe, Geo: Warner, Tho: Bucknoe, Edw: Duke, Wm Yates, Ric Keyes, Wm Woodward, John Maye, Robert Chamberlen, Widowe Hawkins (and Reade), John Pollard, Robert Warde, Wm Booton, John Newman, Tho Forres, Walter Forres, Lawrence Betts, Wm Boulton, William Seacole and the parson containing	151-0-10

265	One close of pasture ground called Frogden abutting upon Berry Field: in the occupancy of John Pollard gent. freehold containing	14-2-13

[**266** and **267** are bracketed, with *asst* added in the margin]

266 *Tenants of Coome*	One greate field called Berry Field thereunto adioyning and belonging to Coome aforesaid containing	86-0-16

267	One common meadow called Chaw Crafte belonging to Coome containing	20-2-22

268 *John Johnson*	One Water Myll and 3 little meadowes lying betwene the said meadowe and Coome Bridge: in the occupancy of John Johnson Freehold containing	8-3- 9

269	Two fields of arrable ground thone called Over Est End Field: thother Est End Field belonging to Coome containing	58-1-25

270	One meadowe thereunto adioyning called Coome Towne Meade containing	15-2-37

Adhuc Coome   **f. 13 (p. 36) dorse**

271 *John Pollard*	Two closes of pasture ground whereof one called Perfumes and thother Harcotts: adioyning to Over Est End Field and Est End Field: in the occupancy of Jo: Pollard and [blank] Butler. John Pollard freehold containing	18-2- 5

272 *Jo: Newman* *Jo: Seacole* *Wm Booton* *Jo: Amsden*	5 Cottages and 7 little closes of pasture ground lying betwene the said two closes of Mr. Pollards in the severall occupancies of John Newman Jo: Seacole Widow Hollowey Wm Booton and Jo: Amsden. Freehold containing	5-2-33

Woodstocke Parke

273 *Rex*	The Greate Parke called Woodstocke Parke so much thereof as is within the Forest:[12] with the King's Majestie's house there: containing	1629-0-11

274	That parte of the said parke which is without the bound of the Forest: containing	452-0- 0

275	One Water Myll called Bladen Myll and one greate meadowe called King's Meadowe and two other litle meadowes whereof one called Bladen Meadowe: lying betwene Bladen <Mill> Water and Woodstocke Parke: in the occupancy of [blank] containing	110-2-21

[12] The river Glyme, which flows through Woodstock (Blenheim) Park, formed the boundary of the Forest. The royal palace was on the northern bank, therefore within the Forest.

Long Hanborowe

276 *Rex*	That parte of the Kings Heath which is within the Forest lying betwene Wottwell well, Gospell Oke and Hanborowe containing 193-3-38
277	One parcell of wood thereunto adioyning called <illegible words> Mill Woode[13], the king Freehold containing 18-0-38
278	One little meadowe called Spratsham lying betwene the said wood and the Ryver of Bladen and belonging to Hanborowe containing 3-3-26
279	Two closes of meadow ground called the Rydings lying nere the said ryver of Bladen: in the occupancy of [blank] containing 15-1-33

Adhuc Hanborowe   f. 14 (p. 37)

280 *Rex*	One parcell of wood called Myll Wood: adioyninge to the said Rydings: in the occupancy of [blank]. The Kinge Freehold containing 22-2-15
281 *<Tho:> John Culpepper*	Two closes of pasture and woodland ground: called Bodies Hill, abutting on the said Mill Wood: in the occupancy of Tho Bodies. <Tho> John Culpepper freehold containing 7-0-25
282	Two common fields of arrable ground: whereof one called Bushey Hide: lying betwene Coome Bridge and Hanborowe Towne Closes: containing 88-3-11
283 *Foelix Carter*	One litle meadowe by Coome Bridge: In the occupancy of Christopher Booth: Foelix Carter freehold containing 3-2- 0
284 *Ric: Irons*	One other litle meadowe thereunto next adioyninge: in the occupancy of Ric: Irons Freehold containing 1-3-35

---

[13] The name must be incorrect (see **280**). This wood is now known as Abel Wood.

| 285 | One long narrowe meadowe called Coomebrowe meadowe, lying in length by the Ryver of Bladen containing 28-2-32 |

286
John Culpepper
Ric: Irons
Ric: Stutter
Moris Mericke
Tho:
Lymborowe
and others
Inhabitants
in Long
Hanborowe

The messuages Cottages backsides gardens orchards and Towne closes in Long Hanborowe in the severall occupancies of Richard Meades Wm Wrighte Bryan Bradford John Wray Rich: Deane John Lord, Rich: Kennar Ja: Woollridge, Tho: Prior Philip Dasby, Rich Rowland, Tho: Lymborowe, Moris Mericke, Tho Bodies, John Terry Tho: Hicks, Ed: Slowe, Tho Keene John Brooke John Astoll Christopher Boothe, Morris Cappe Hughe Deane - Hollyman, John Gobbett John Fawler Tho Haynes, John Culpepper, Oliver Carter, Richard Stutter, Wm Wray, Ja Wrath Geo: Hitchcocke, John Kerton Rich Irons, Henry Horne, Rich Frons, John Wollom, - Hillman Rich Weller Henry Salter Jerom Sibith John Gardiner - Dizendou, Tho Butcher, Tho Ives - Rooke Jo: Ede Jeffrey Hichman - Shipton, Wm Fletcher Wm Bale
containing   247-2- 6

287
Mr. Fletcher
(Comp)

One close of arrable ground and two closes of meadowe ground, lying by Bladen Bridge: in the occupancy of Wm Fletcher Freehold
containing   41-0-13

288

Two other little meadowes called Common Meadowes lying ut supra:
containing   10-0-33

289
Edw Johnson
[illegible note
added]

One watermyll and 3 litle meadowes thereunto adioyning and to the water of Bladen: in the occupancy of Edward Johnson freehold
containing   8-0- 2

Adhuc Hanborowe   **f. 14 (p. 37) dorse**

290
John Culpepper

Two closes of arrable ground called Old Copice lying next to the greate heath: in the occupancy of [blank]. John Culpepper freehold
containing   8-1-20

291
- Cole

One other close of arrable ground with a barne thereon sett: thereunto next adioyning and lying ut supra: in the occupancy of John Gregory. – Cole freehold
containing   2-2-32

292

One cottage and one litle close thereunto next adioyninge: in the occupancy of Wm Colegrave freehold
containing   1-2- 0

293
Jo: Culpepper

One other cottage and litle close thereunto next adioyning. John Culpepper freehold
containing   1-1-10

294
Moris Mericke

One other cottage and one close called Blowen thereunto next adioyning: in the occupancy of [blank]. Moris Mericke freehold
containing   6-2- 5

295

One other close of pasture ground thereunto next adioyning: in the occupancy of Stephen Ringe
containing   6-0- 7

296
Wm Fletcher
(comp)

One other close of pasture ground called Blowen, adioyning to the greate heathe: in the occupancy of Wm Fletcher Freehold
containing   15-0-25

297
(John)
Culpepper

One cottage and two closes of pasture ground called Blowen thereunto next adioyning and lying ut supra: in the occupancy of [blank]. – Culpepper freehold
containing   19-1- 0

298
Wm Good

One litle close thereunto next adioyning and to the Oke in Foule Lane: in the occupancy of Wm Good Freehold
containing   1-2-39

299
Wa: Culpepper

One other close of pasture ground called Musley thereunto next adioyning and to Foule Lane: in the occupancy of [blank]. Walter Culpepper freehold
containing   8-0-18

300
- Culpepper
Wm Good

Three other closes called Lamas Closes thereunto next adioyning and to the great Common field: in the severall occupancies of – Culpepper and Wm Good: Freehold containing   10-3-34

301

One greate common field of arrable ground called Middle Field lying betwene Long Hanborowe and Church Hanborowe containing   288-1-12

Churche Hanborowe

302
Rex

One peece of wood thereunto next adioyning called Pynsley Wood the Kings land containing   108-1-10

303

One other great Common field of arrable ground called the Milne Field lying betwene the said Pynsley Wood and the Ryver of Bladen containing   295-1- 2

Adhuc Hanborowe   f. 15 (p. 38)

304

Two meadowes whereof one called Hanborowe South Meadowe and thother Hanborowe Nye Meadowe: lying betwene the said Mylne Field and Cassington Fields containing   96-3-22

305

One greate common field of arrable ground called the South Common Field containing   314-0-13

306

Two meadowes whereof one called Stone Acres: adioyning to the said Common field, and extending in length by the Ryver of Bladen towards Eynsham Mylne
containing   36-3-32

307
Hen: Salter

One litle meadowe called Ferretts Meadowe lying by the bound next to Sir Wm Spensers meadowe: in the occupancy of Henry Salter Freehold
containing   3-0- 2

308
Sir Wm Spencer

One other meadowe thereunto next adioyning: in the occupancy of Sir Wm Spencer Freehold
containing   8-3-25

309
Jo: <Wynnishe>
Willis

One close of meadow ground, lying betwene the said meadows and the Town closes of Church Hanborowe: in the occupancy of John Wynnishe

containing   15-0-33

310
Collegium
Corpus Christi

Three closes of pasture ground called Musley: thereunto adioyning and to the bound of the Forest near Eynsham Heath: in the occupancy of Wm Good: Collegium Cor. Christi Freehold containing   10-3-12

311
Roger Broakes

Two closes of pasture ground thereunto next adioyning in the occupancy of Roger Brookes freehold

containing   6-3- 6

312

One other close of pasture ground thereunto adioyning and lying betwene the Towne closes and Fowle Lane: in the occupancy of Jeffrey Hichman containing   4-2-15

313
Felix Carter
Ric Stutter
- Cole
Jo: Gregory
and others

5 messuages or cottages with gardens and backsides and 14 closes of meadowe pasture and arrable ground thereunto adioyning and lying ut supra: in the severall occupancies of Thomas Watson, Tho Humfrey, Wm Ball Wm Harries, Raphe Cox, Richard Stutter, Felix Carter, - Cole, John Weller, Wm Colegrove, John Gregory and Wm Hollyman containing   49-2-38

Adhuc Hanborowe   **f. 15 (p. 38) dorse)**

314
Wa: Culpepper
- Clarke
Stephen Ringe
Ric: Kenner
Roger Broakes
Hen: Salter
Wm Good
Ric: Townsend
et al.

The messuages, Cottages, backsides, gardens orchards and Town closes in Church Hanborowe: in the severall occupancies of Walter Culpepper, Wm Good, Hugh Weller, Justinian Symons, Humfrey Johnson, Richard Weller, John Westley, John Weller, Roger Brookes, - Clarke, Richard Townesend, John Salter, Henry Salter, Richard Kenner, Stephen Ringe, Wm Townsend containing   63-3-28

[gap]

315
Sir Wm Spencer
One peece of wood called Burley Woods[14] and one meadowe called Burley Meadowe: adioyning to the River of Bladen but without the bounds of the forest which is the said Ryver there: in the occupancy of Sir William Spencer
Freehold containing   92-2- 7

316
One litle meadow thereunto adioyning called Greate Burham: in the occupancy of Mr. – Greneway
containing   4-1-33

317
One other litle meadowe called Cassington Meade lying ut supra: in the occupancy of [blank]
containing   1-0-28

Here endeth one other of the plotts of Whichwood Forest

---

14 See fn, p. 76.

III   **f. 16 (p. 39)**

Extra Forest

Walcott	One faire house with gardens, backsides and orchards and
318	one Water myll and 27 closes of meadow pasture
- Fitzhughes	woodland ground and arrable fields whereof some called

Walcott Leaze, one other Charlebury Meadowe, one other
Stepdells Close, one other Reynolds Close, one other
Hoggs grove, one other the great grove, one other Myll
Grove, one other Calves close, one other Cowe Marsh, one
other Milkings Close, one other Midle Marshe, one other
Marshe Meadowe, one other the Oxe Marshe, one other
the further Marshe and the rest Walcott fields lying
together betwixt Cornebury Parke and the fields of
Shortehampton and without the bounds of the forest: in the
occupancy of – Fitzhughes Freehold
containing   423-0-7

Shorte Hampton   The messuages Cottages gardens and orchards and the
319   Common fields and Closes of meadowe pasture and
Sir Fra: arrable ground belonging to Shortehampton: whereof one
Fortescue[15]   called the Kings Meadowe, one other Chadwells one other
- Hoskins   5 Acres, one other 12 Acres, and other Hellman Hatchett,
- Blagrave   one other Spinidge and another Brownes Peece: in the
Rich: Browne   occupancy of Sir Fra: Fortescue, - Hoskins, - Blagrave and
Rich: Browne Freehold: adioyning to Walcott grounds
aforesaid and lying betwene the same and Silson fields,
and without the bounds of the Forest
containing   366-3-14

Silson   The messuages Cottages backsides gardens and orchards
320   Towne closes and Common fields of arrable pasture and
meadow ground: in Chilston alias Silson: lying betwene
Shortehampton and Askott: and also without the bounds of
the forest in the severall occupancies of [blank]
containing   410-0-14

---

[15] Sir Francis Fortescue was the Lieutenant (Keeper) of Wychwood. *Cal. S. P.Dom. 1595-97*, 314, 566.

Ascott	The messuages cottages backsides gardens and orchards (in
321	Ascott) the common fields and Closes of meadowe pasture
Sir Fra: Fortescue	and arrable ground, belonging to Ascott lying betwene

Silson and Shipton common fieldes and also without the bounds of the Forest: in the severall occupancies of Wm Peasley Roger Poole, Edw: Norcott Bartho: Hunnyborne Christopher Whitinge, Foulke Chony, Gilbert Peasley, - Box, Edward Winchester, Peter Fletcher - Dunsford, Wm Seeley, Widowe Cooke, - Hudston, Tho Whitinge, Geo: Peasley, Wm Whiting, - Perry, Tho Waldron, Anthony Williams, Rich: Fletcher, Tho: Hicks, - Bond, Robert Hicks containing   890-3- 3

f. 16 (p. 39) dorse

322[16]

Sir Fraunces
Fortescue's
Woodes

One lodge Called Bowmans Lodge and one Close of pasture ground and greate Woods lying about the same Lodge called by the severall names of Easewell: Rowburrowes, Blackwell and Studley Coppes: adioyning to the Forest nere Studley Gate, and lying without the Bounds: in the occupancy of Sir Frauncis Fortescue Freehold containing   319-3- 7

The Field [Leafield]

323
One part
without the
forest
another parte
within

One Common field of arrable ground called Broade Sarte belonging to the village called the Field and lying nere the said woods without the forest Bounds
containing   101-2-27

324

One close of pasture ground called Studley Sarte lying next Studley Gate: in the occupancy of [blank]
containing   9-2-26

325
Drue Larner

One cottage and one close of pasture ground thereunto next adioyninge: in the occupancy of – Bennett. Drue Larner freehold containing   5-2- 0

---

[16] The woods named in this entry belonged to the manor of Shipton-under-Wychwood and are recorded as such in a Survey of 1552: P.R.O. LR2/189 f.84.

326
Rich: Hedges

One messuage and two Cottages with gardens and orchards and 8 closes of meadow pasture and arrable ground lying in Field aforesaid: in the severall occupancies of Richard Fitzhu... Tho: Harries, Roger Goodman, Ralphe Hitchman Tho: Grymes James Honnyborne John Hix and Richard Hedges. Richard Hedges freehold
containing   83-0- 2

327
Ro: Waysye

Two cottages and one close lying ut supra: in the occupancy of Ro: Waysye and Wm Randoll. Ro: Waysye freehold
containing   3-0-10

328
Ro: Sampson

One cottage and one close thereunto next adioyninge: in the occupancy of Ja: Cobel. Ro: Sampson freehold
containing   1-3-26

329
Wm Odey

Two cottages and two closes lying ut supra: in the occupancy of Jo: Dix and Tho West: Wm Odey freehold
containing   6-1-27

330
Sir Fra:
Fortescue

Two cottages and 3 closes of pasture ground lying ut supra in the severall occupancies of Ed: Eeles, James Clarke and Leonard Martyn. Sir Fran: Fortescue freehold
containing   19-2-29

331
Ric:
Underwood

Three closes of pasture and woodland ground lyinge ut supra: in the occupancy of Rich: Underwood: Freehold
containing   11-2-34

332
Church-Land

Two little narrowe closes thereunto adioyninge: in the occupancy of Ri: Varny and Ed: Rawlyns.The Churche Land containing   2-3-35

333
Hen: Rawlyns

One messuage with garden and orchard and one close of pasture ground thereunto adioyninge and lying ut supra: in the occupancy of Henry Rawlyns:
containing   8-3-34

334
James Clarke

One close of pasture and woodland ground lying ut supra: and adjoyning to Broad Sarte: in the occupancy of James Clarke freehold
containing   11-2-29

| 335
Edw Rawlyn | One other close thereunto next adioyning: in the occupancy of Edward Rawlyn Freehold
containing | 3-2-30 |

Adhuc the Field **f. 17 (p. 40)**

[On this page there are a number of erasures and interlineations. A line of unknown significance had been drawn down the margin beside entries **336** to **347**, and brackets have been placed coupling Nos. **336** and **337**, and **342** and **343**.]

| 336
John Neate
(compound) | One messuage and <three> two closes of pasture and woodland ground, lying in Field aforesaid and extending to Studley gate: in the occupancy of John Neate Freehold
containing <39-1-12>24-0- 6 |

| 337 | (One close of pasture called Hollow Oke: in the occupancy of <illegible name> Neate
containing | 15-1- 2 |

| 338
Richard Irons
(compounded) | One close of pasture ground (called Barrowe Hill) lying ut supra and abutting on the Town greene: in the occupancy of John Harries: <Wm> (Richard) Irons freehold
containing | 13-0-38 |

| 339
William
Whitinge
(comp)
X | One other close thereunto next adioyning and abutting ut supra: (called Barrowe field): in the occupancy of Wm. Whyting Freehold
containing | 6-3-15 |

| 340
Forest | The Towne greene containing | 5-1-35 |

| 341 | One cottage and little close within the same greene: in the occupancy of Ed Colyn containing | 0-1-12 |

| 342
<*John Harries*>
(Sir Francis
Fortescue)
(comp) | Two closes of pasture ground called Cowe Close and Claye Cose lying betwene the Towne grene and Gateley Coppes: in the occupancy of <John Harries> (Sir Francis Fortescue) Freehold
containing | 26-0-12 |

343
Sir Fra:
Fortescue

Two other closes thereunto next adioyning: in the occupancy of John Harries: Sir Fra: Fortescue freehold containing   13-0-36

344
<Sir Edward
Cooke>
John Harris

One other close thereunto next adioyninge Called Lowbery: in the occupancy of John < Walter: Sir Edw Coke freeh> (Harries freehold) containing   18-2-21

345
<Richard>
John Hodges

One close of pasture next adioyninge to the close called Hollow Oke: in the occupancy of <Rich:> John Hodge: Freehold containing   27-1-38

346
Sir Rowland
Lacy

<One coppice called Lowbery: in the occupancy of Sir Rowland Lacy containing   41-2- 0>

[This whole entry is crossed out; see **431**, p. 218. The following entry is also crossed out, after several erasures and substitutions, many of them being illegible.]

347
Sir Rowland
Lacy, (comp)
Richard Langley
and Ann White
his daughter at
the court at the
Bar ....at
Whithall

Three closes of pasture ground called The Sartes adioyning to Astall Sartes Greene: in the occupancy of John Neate and John Harries, <[illegible] Whistler> (illegible name) freehold containing   41-1-10

348

Two little common fields belonging to the Field lying betwene the said Sartes and Broade Sarte containing   15-3- 2

349
Sir Fra:
Fortescue

One close of pasture ground called Longe Sarte abutting upon Broade Sarte in the occupancy of John Tomes John Neate et al. Sir Frauncis Fortescue freehold containing   26-2- 2

350
Hunfrey Griffith

One other close of pasture ground thereunto next adioyning and abutting ut supra: in the occupancy of Hunfrey Griffith Freehold containing   7-0- 6

351
Rich: Irons

Two closes of pasture and woodland ground adioyning to the said Long Sarte: in the occupancy of Wm Hitchman. Richard Irons freehold containing   11-2-29

352

One other close of pasture and woodland ground therupon abutting and adioyning ut supra: in the occupancy of Richard Harwell containing   · 3-3-20

353
Anthony
Belcher

Two little closes of pasture ground thereunto adioyning: in the occupancy of Anthony Belcher Freehold containing   3-1-38

Adhuc the Field   **f. 17 (p. 40) dorse**

354
Antho:
Hitchman

One little close of pasture ground adioyning to the said Belchers Closes: in the occupancy of Anthony Hitchman: Freehold containing   [blank]

355
Jo: Tomes

One messuage and 4 closes of pasture ground lying in the Field aforesaid: in the occupancy of John Tomes Freehold containing   13-1- 2

356
Jo: Harries

One messuage and three closes of pasture ground (one called 15 lands) lying in Field aforesaid: in the occupancy of John Harries Freehold
containing   15-2-23

357
Hen: Maior

One litle long narrowe close thereunto adioyning: in the occupancy of Hen Maior: Freehold
containing   1-0-35

358
Giles Fitchet

One other litle close lying ut supra: in the occupancy of Giles Fitchett Freehold containing   2-0- 0

359
Sir Fra:
Fortescue

One other close of pasture ground lying ut supra in the occupancy of Giles Fitchett. Sir Fra: Fortescue freehold containing   6-1-37

360
Edw:
Winchester

xj closes of pasture arrable and woodland ground: whereof one called Lowbery: lying in Field aforesaid: in the occupancy of Edw: Winchester Freehold
containing   59-3-29

361
Rich:
Underwood

Three closes of pasture and woodland ground thereunto adioyning and lying ut supra: in the occupancy of Richard Underwood Freehold containing 11-2-34

362
Giles Fitchet

Two other closes thereunto next adioyning of woodland and pasture ground: in the occupancy of Giles Fitchet Freehold containing 9-2-23

363

One Cottage and a little close thereunto next adioyning: in the occupancy of John Serman
containing 1-3-19

364
(Matthew
Payne)
X

One messuage and one Cottage and two closes of pasture ground lying betwene Sarte grene and the lands of Edw: Winchester: in the occupancy of Matthew Payne: Freehold containing 19-1-22

365[17]
Wm Andrewes

Two Cottages and one close of arrable ground (adioyning to Sarte grene) called Astall Sartes alias Purrens: in the occupancy of Rich: Figures and Wm Morris. Wm Andrewes freehold containing 12-2-37

366
Sir Edw: Coke

One other close of arrable ground thereunto next adioyning and to Sarte Grene: in the occupancy of John Hicks. Sir Edw: Coke freehold containing 3-0-13

367

One common field called Purrens lying betwene Sarte grene and the lands of Edward Winchester:
containing 17-1-22

368
Sir Edw: Coke

One waste or common called Sarte greene abutting upon Astall Sarts grene: Sir Edw: Coke freehold
containing 15-2-10

369

The (other) messuages Cottages backsides and litle closes adioyning to those howses in Feld aforesaid in the severall occupancies of [blank]containing 4-1- 0

[17] Entries **365** to **369** describe the hamlet of Field Assarts which lies on both sides of the boundary between Asthall and Leafield, and include Purrens, site of the wood of Purveance (see p. 103 fn.). The survey does not make it clear to which vill the fields and houses belonged.

Astoll   **f. 18 (p. 46)**

370	One great Common or waste called Astoll Sarte grene,	
Wm Andrewes	adioyning to Minster Woods without the bounds of the	
	Forest: Wm Andrewes freehold	
	containing	113-0-20

371	Three closes of woodland ground called Astoll Woodes,	
Sir Edw: Coke	thereunto adioyning and lying ut supra: in the occupancy of	
	Sir Edward Coke Freehold containing	208-0-39

372
Two closes of meadowe ground thereunto next adioyning: in the severall occupancies of Thomas Silvester and Wm Andrewes containing   3-2-38

373
One waste called Lyehare belonging to Astoll and adioyning to the bounds of the Forest containing   26-0-2

[gap]

374
Sir Anthony
Cope
One copice called Fosgrove Copice[18], and one close of pasture ground, lying without the Bounds of the Forest and adioyning to Swynbrooke Closes: in the occupancy of Sir Anthony Cope Freehold containing   39-0-18

375
Samuell Cox,
- Johnson
One Long narrowe plaine of pasture ground called Johnson's plaine and Weedell Waste, with a Cottage therein: in the occupancy of Anthony Tasker: extending in length from Swinbrooke Closes By Fulbrooke fields and Shipton Downes to Farrington Slade. – Johnson and Samuell Cox freehold containing   185-0- 1

376
Sir Rowland
Lacy
One copice thereunto adioyning and lyinge betwene the said plaine and Taynton Woodes: in the occupancy of Sir Rowland Lacy Freehold containing   129-3-28

377
Sir Anthony
Cope
Two other copices thereunto adioyning Whereof one called Small Okes, thother Farrington Copice: in the occupancy of Sir Anthony Cope Freehold containing   60-1-38

[18] Fosgrove (Fawsgrove) Coppice, with Small Okes and Farrington (**377**), Westgrove (**429**), and Lowzie Grove (**430**) belonged to Fulbrook. See p. 83.

378
Samuell Cox

One messuage and one Cottage and one Close of pasture ground lying betwene Fosgrove Coppice and Taynton Woodes: in the occupancy of Samuell Cox freehold containing   62-3-22

379
Sir Fra:
Fortescue

A decaied grange somtyme belonging to the pryorie of Dearhurst and one parcell of wood called Taynton Woodes and Gun Grove: and one Copice called Farrington Copice[19], lying in length betwene the said Mr. Cox his Land and Farrington Sladd, and adioyning to the Forest but without the bounds thereof: in the occupancy of Sir Frauncis Fortescue Freehold containing   197-2- 1

380

One peece of pasture and woodland ground lying betwene Farrington Copice and Shipton Gate and at the end of Weedell Waste: in the occupancy of [blank] containing   70-3-34

[gap]

Forest

Cornbury Parke
381
Rex
X

One greate parke called Cornebury Parke, with a faire howse and a (water) myll in the same, and one meadowe adioyning to Charlebury field: in the occupancy of Gabriell Matthewe and Sir Fra: Fortescue. Kinge freehold containing   652-3-29

Finstocke[20]
382
Giles Camden
(comp)
X

One messuage with garden and orchard and 17 closes of meadowe pasture arrable and woodland ground whereof one called Hawkswell, one other Squire peece, one other Nether West Field, one other Broade Close, another Upper West Field, one other West Field, one other Hillcott, one other Wilkins Coppice: lying betwene Cornbury Parke and the bounds at Finstocke: in the occupancy of Giles Camden Freehold containing   <161-1-26> (142-3-30)

---

[19] Farrington Coppice was shared between Taynton and Fulbrook manors (see **377**) which explains the dispute recorded on p. 79, **89**.

[20] Only half of Finstock is recorded, the area corresponding to that included in the Forest by the 1298/1300 Perambulation.

383 *Jo Priddey* *(comp)*	One little meadow adioyning to Nether West Field and lying ut supra: in the occupancy of John Priddey Freehold containing 1-2-18
384 *Rich Wykins* *(comp)* X	One messuage with gardens and backsides and 5 closes of meadowe pasture and \<arr\> woodland ground whereof one called Hawkwell: two others Lurden Field: thereunto adioyning and lying ut supra: in the occupancy of Richard Wykyns Freehold containing 27-0-16
385 *John Hunt* *(comp)*	One little close of meadow ground lying ut supra nere Fawler Myll: called Deane Close in the occupancy of John Hunt Freehold containing 3-0-34
386 *Giles Camden* *(comp)* *Ric Wykins* *John Hunt*	One other close thereunto next adioyning and to Fawler Bridge: called Litle Downe Field: in the occupancy of John Hunt, Richard Wykins and Giles Camden. Freehold containing 8-0-13
387 *John Durle* *(comp)* X	One Cottage and one Close of pasture and woodland ground lying ut supra: in the occupancy of John Durle Freehold containing 7-2-33
388 *Ellis Day* *Edw Snap* *et al*	Two Cottages and one Close of pasture ground thereunto next adioyning and lying ut supra: in the occupancy of Ellis Day, Edw Snap and others Freehold containing 6-2-28

[The bottom of the sheet has been cut off, obscuring another word in the margin]

[tear in membrane,? **Adhuc] Finstocke**   **f. 19 (p. 42)**

389 *Jo: Day* *Giles Camden* * *Ri: Wykins* * *Wm Coelyn** *Tho: Camden* * *(compound)*	One close of pasture ground called Sarte Close thereunto next adioyning and lying ut antea in the occupancy of John Day, Giles Camden, Richard Wykins, Tho: Camden and Wm Coelyn: containing 17-0-18

[* = *(compound)* or *(do)*]

390
<Martin> Snap
(comp)

One little close adioyning to Finstocke Common: in the
occupancy of Edw Snap. – Martin freehold
containing   1-2-20

391
John
Honnybourne
(comp)

Fyve closes of pasture and woodland ground whereof some
called Paradice and others Wadbury: lying betwene
Finstock Common and Cornbury Parke: in the occupancy
of John Honnyborne freehold
containing   19-0- 0

[*Quer for John Saunders for Paradice Closes* added in margin]

392
<Ro> Thomas
Harries

One other close of woodland ground thereunto adioyning
and lying ut supra: called Paradice in the occupancy of
<Ro> Thomas Harries Freehold containing   4-1- 8

393
Jo: <Worcus>
Workhouse
(comp)

Two closes of pasture ground called Damase Leaze lying
ut supra: in the occupancy of John <Worcus> Workhouse
freehold containing   8-0- 3

394
Ric: Joyner
(comp)

Two other closes of pasture ground whereof one called
Lurden Field adioyning to Finstoke Common: in the
occupancy of Ric Joyner Freehold containing   9-3- 2

395
Tho Hedges
(will not agree
to the comp)

One messuage and three closes of pasture ground Called
Lymepitt field and Beninge, lying betwene Finstock
Common and Gattwell: in the occupancy of Tho: Hedges
Freehold containing   26-0- 2

396
Wm Coelyn
(comp)

One other messuage and three closes thereunto next
adioyning and lying ut supra: in the occupancy of Wm
Coelyn Freehold containing   19-3-17

397
Ric Hunt
(comp)

One other messuage and two Closes of pasture ground
thereunto next adioyning and lying ut supra: called
Lymepitt Field alias Beninge: in the occupancy of Rich:
Hunt Freehold containing   19-2- 5

398

Finstocke Common, being parte of the waste
containing   41-0- 8

[gap]

| 399
Rex | One coppice called Five Oaks Copice lying by it self in the waste nere the said Finstocke grounds. The Kinge freehold containing   56-3- 5 |

Woods

| 400
Rex | One coppes called Bucke Leape Copice lying nere Cornbury Parke: containing   64-3-17 |

| 401 | One other coppes called Eveden Copice thereunto adioyning: containing   74-2-28 |

| 402 | One other coppes called Haselwood Copice thereunto adioyning: containing   150-0-35 |

| 403 | One sale called Cranehill Sale extending from Cornbury Parke towards Mr. Batten's Lodge: containing   71-2- 2 |

| 404 | One close of pasture ground called Lea Crofte, lying within the said sale: in the occupancy of - Batten: containing   26-3- 2 |

| 405 | One inclosure rayled about called the Laund with a fair Lodge and garden in the same: in the occupancy of Mr. Batten[21]: containing   50-1-18 |

| 406
* | One great wood thereunto adioyning called Knighton Coppice containing   324-0- 7 |

[* in the margin the names *Sir Anthony Cope* and *Mr. Walter* have been added in one hand, *Parochia de Sarsden in Com. Oxon.* in another]

| 407 | One copice called Lankridge Copice thereunto adioyninge containing   121-2-28 |

| 408 | One other copice called Slatpitt Coppice thereunto adioyninge containing   95-0- 9 |

| 409 | One other copice called Cockshuthill Coppes thereunto adioyning containing   106-0-11 |

[21] Richard Batten was Ranger of Wychwood: *Cal. S.P.Dom. 1603-1619*, 564. The Lodge is now known as Ranger's Lodge.

410   One lodge called Hills Lodge (Kodsholl) and one close of
                              pasture ground, thereunto adioyninge in the occupancy of -
                              Fountaine <freehold> containing   3-3-16

411   One coppes called Layfridge[22] Copice lying nere the same:
                              containing   67-1- 7

412   One other copice called Boynhall Copice[23] adioyning to
                              Ascott Common Fields: in the occupancy of Sir Fra:
                              Fortescue. The Kinge freehold containing   85-0-12

413   One other copice nere the same called Forsakenhoe
                              Copice: in the occupancy of Sir Fra: Fortescue. The Kinge
                              freehold containing   50-1-22

Little Langley   **f. 20 (p. 43)**

414   One fair howse called Little Langley Howse and 4 closes of
Rex   pasture and woodland ground called the Farthinge and
                              Litle Langley: lying betwene the said Forsakenhoe Copice
                              and Langley Mannor: in the occupancy of Sir Fra:
                              Fortescue: The Kinge freehold
                              containing   59-3-34

Langley Manor

415   One faire howse called Langley Manor Howse and 14
Sir Francis   closes of meadowe pasture and woodland ground, called
Fortescue   Langley Mannor, by the severall names of Cuthatch,
(Compound)   Quernshill, Over Leaze, Norgrove Copice, Langley Parke,
                              Tyles Close, Barne Close, Mayes Close, the Wood Closes,
                              Burnete Close, Grasse Close: thereunto next adioyninge in
                              the occupancy of Sir Francis Fortescue Freehold
                              containing   336-1- 5

416   One coppes called <Putters> Pollard Hill Copse thereunto
Rex   next adioyning
                              containing   98-3-34

---

[22] Layfridge later became merged with Kingswood coppice, since there was "no certain known
division" between them: BL Add. MS 6027. Kingswood and Smallstones coppices, recorded on pp.
222-4, have been omitted from the Survey.
[23] Boynhall Coppice belonged to the manor of Ascott. See pp. 123, **7**, and 131, **5**.

417 *Part Sir* *Rowland Lacy* *thother The* *Kinge*	One other Coppes called Gateley Coppes, lying betwene Lillies Crosse and the Field containing	115-2-31

418

One other little wood called Potters Hill with a Cottage therein, called Potters Quarre: thereunto next adioyninge
containing   31-2-25

419

One peece of waste called Wastidge Hill Waste thereunto next adioyninge: containing   42-1-37

420

One wood thereunto next adioyninge called Wastidge: containing   139-0-36

421

One other wood[24] lying betwene Wastidge Hill Waste, and South Laund Waste:
containing   81-0- 8

422
<Sir Fr:
Fortescue>

One lodge and one ground rayled about called the Laund: thereunto next adioyninge: in the occupancy of - Ardes[25]. (Rex dominus) Freehold
containing   45-3-19

423
(Rex)

One waste called South Laund Waste thereunto next adioyninge: containing   81-1-36

424
Sir Edm:
Fettiplace

One peece of wood thereunto next adioyninge called Hengrove and one Waste called Swynbroke Waste: in the occupancy of Sir Edmond Fettiplace Freehold
containing   114-3- 0

425
Rex

One wood or copice called Upper Stockley[26] thereunto next adioyninge <illegible name> (Rex dominus)
containing   86-1-13

---

[24] Thomas Pride's definitive map of the forest, made in 1787 (P.R.O. MR288) shows two coppices in this area of which the larger one is Nottridge (Nuttridge, Natterigge) Coppice and the smaller Wastage. See also the acreages on pp. 222. The Jacobean surveyor has confused the two.

[25] John Ardes was an Under-keeper of Wychwood: *Cal. S.P. Dom 1611-1618,* 122.

[26] In other documents this wood is called Roustage (Roustede, Rustich).

426
Rex

One copice called Hawks Coppice adioyning to Wastidge Hill Waste: containing   85-3- 4

427

One other wood thereunto next adioyning called Broad Quarter: containing   141-2-18

428
Personage
Shipton
Swynbrooke
(asst)

One other wood called Nether Stockley adioyning to the bound next Astoll field; and belonging to the parsonage of Shipton and Swynbroke containing   127-0- 8

429

One other wood called Westgrove thereunto next adioyning and lying ut supra: in the occupancy of Sir <Fra: Fortescue> Anthony Cope containing   21-2-24

430
(asst)

One little Waste or Woodland ground called Lowzie Grove, adioyning to Astoll Woods containing   6-0-35

431
Sir Rowland
Lacye (comp)
(vid. ant. fo. 17)

One other parcell of wood called Lowberry adioyning to the said Astoll Woods: in the occupancy of Sir Rowland Lacy: Freehold containing   41-2- 0
[see fo. 17, earlier]

432

The wastes conteyned in this plott   [blank]

Here endeth the 3 and last plott of the Forest of Whichwood.

433   **Whichwoods Index**   **p. 45 dorse**

H				**C**		
Hicks	Richard	fo: 12		Coolin	William	fo: 19
Hicks	William	fo: 12		Camden	Tho:	fo: 19
Hill	Rich	fo: 12, 13				
Hickman	Jeffrey	fo. 15				
<Hodges	Richard	fo: 16>				
Harris	John	fo: 17				
Hichman	Anthony	fo: 17				
Honnyborne	John	fo: 19				
Harris	Roberte	fo: 19				
Hedges	Tho	fo: 19				
Hunt	Richard	fo: 19				
Hampshire	John	fo: 9				**p. 46**

A				**D**		
[tear]drowes	William	fo: 7, 17, 18		Dyer	Richard	fo: 1
[tear] ewe	Rich	fo: 11		Decine	Thomas	fo: 1
Amsden	John	fo: 13		Darby	Francis	fo: 5, 8
Ascott		fo: 10		Daye	John	fo: 5, 19
				Drinkwater	Richard	fo: 7
B				Daye	Peter	fo: 8
Bringfeild	Henr	fo: 1		Dumpar	John	fo: 10
Boxe	Leonard	fo: 1, 2, 6		Drinkwater	James	fo: 12
Brooke	John	fo: 2		Daye	Ellis	fo: 18
Boxe	Richard	fo: 2, 5, 9				
Boxe	Thomas	fo: 2		**E**		
Booby	William	fo: 4, 5				
Bowman	Edw	fo: 4, 5, 8				
Bishope	Richard	fo: 5				
Brakspeare	Richard	fo: 5				
Brises	William	fo: 7				
Bishop	William	fo: 7				
Brice	-	fo: 8				
Broke	William	fo: 9				
Birdesey	George	fo: 9				
Brewer	Thomas	fo: 9, 10, 12				
Bumpas	Thomas	fo: 10				
Blackgrave	Henry	fo: 12				
Booton	William	fo: 12, 13				
Brooke	Roger	fo: 15				
Belcher	Anthony	fo: 17				

C

Cullim		fo: 1
Crofte	Thomas	fo: 1
Cornishe	Thomas	fo: 1, 4
Clarke	John	fo: 1, 15
Crofte	Edw	fo: 4
Crofte	John	fo: 4, 5
Carter	Thomas	fo: 5
Crosley	Alexander	fo: 7
Coates	John	fo: 9, 10
Camden	Gyles	fo: 9, 8, 19
Cowper		fo: 11
Castile	William	fo: 11
Chamberlayne Roberte		fo: 12
Culpeper	Thomas	fo: 14
Carter	Felix	fo: 14, 15
Culpeper	John	fo: 14
Cole		fo: 14, 15
Culpeper	Walter	fo: 14, 15
Collegium Corpus Christi		fo: 15
Churchland		fo: 16
Clark	James	fo: 16
[tear]		fo: 17, 18
[tear]		fo: 18, 19

F

Freman	William	fo: 2
Foster	Roberte	fo: 3
Fitches	Henry	fo: 4
Finlis	William	fo: 6
Frankline	Tho	fo: 6
Fortescue	Frances, *miles*	fo; 7, 16, 17, 18, 20
Franchys		fo: 7
Fortye	Thomas	fo: 11
Fletcher	William	fo: 14
Fitzhughes		fo: 16
Feilde		fo: 16
Fitchet	Giles	fo: 17
Finstock		fo: 19
Fetyplace	Edm:	fo: 20

p. 46 dorse

G

Goddard		fo: 1
Gune		fo: 5
Grene	Richard	fo: 7, 8
Gey	Thomas	fo: 9
Grey	John	fo: 16
Gregory	John	fo: 12, 17
Good	William	fo: 14, 15
Griffiths	Humphry	fo: 17

K

Kinge	William	fo: 5
Kirby	Walter	fo: 7, 8
Kinge	Henry	fo: 9
Keate	Rich	fo: 12
Keene	Rich	fo: 12
(OXON)		

H

Humphrey	Richard	fo, 1, 2
Harris	Bartholomew	fo: 1, 2, 5
Haynes		fo: 2
Horne	John	fo: 2, 4, 5
Hunt	William	fo: 3
Hawke	Tho:	fo: 4
Harte		fo: 5
Horne	Roberte	fo: 5
Horne	Richard	fo: 5
Hawke	William	fo: 5
Harecort	Walter, *miles*	fo: 7
Hampshire	John	fo: 8
Harris	Christopher	fo: 9
Hedges	Abraham	fo: 9, 10
Harris	<Thomas> Alex	fo: 9, 10
Harris	William	fo: 9, 10
Harris	Abraham	fo: 9
Hedges	John	fo: 10
Hunt	John	fo: 10, 18
Hedge	<Rich> John	fo: 10, 16, 17
Horne	William	fo: 11

J

Joyner		fo: 7
Joyner	William	fo: 7
Joyner	Richard	fo: 7, 19
Irons	Richard	fo: 9, 10, 14, 17
Joyner	Anthony	fo: 9, 10
Irons	John	fo:9
Joyner	Anthony	fo:9
Johnson	John	fo: [blot], 13, 14
Johnson	Edw:	fo: 14
Irons	William	fo:17

L

Larner	Walter	fo: 7
Larner	Thomas	fo: 7
Larner	Henry	fo: 7
Leeche	Ralphe	fo: 7
Lee	Henry *miles*	fo: 9,10,11,12
Larner	James	fo: 12
Lacy	Rowlande, kt.	fo: 18 <20>
Langley		fo: 20

M

Martine	John	fo: 1, 3, 19
Montgomery	*comes*	fo: 11
Maye	John	fo: 12
Merick	Morris	fo: 14
Maior	Henry	fo: 17

434   **Forest of Whichwood**

A briefe of the Survey of the Kinges Majesties Coppices withyn the Forest of Whichwood taken by Mr. Hersey and Mr. Batten Anno 1609

	The Coppices		Whereout deducted			Remayn -ing	Every acre valet per annum	Every coppice valet per annum
Names		Contents at 18ft the Perch	ye Bow acre	Waste acre	for fenc- ing			
		a. r. p.	a	ac	a.r	a. r. p.	s.d	L. s. d
(Smalestones	11	124-2-14	1	15	15-1	93-4-14	2.6	11.13. 0>
Kinges Wood	20	96-1-11	1	16	14-3	64-2-11	2.0	6. 9. 0
Leyfridge	20	52-2-23	1	6	8-3	36-3- 3	4.0	7. 7. 0
(Fernehill)	20	44-2-19	1	10	6-3	26-3-19	2.0	2.13. 6
Wastage	18	65-3-28	1	8	9-3	47-0-28	3.4	7.17. 0
Hasellwood	15	124-0-23	1	8	14-3	100-1-28	4.0	20. 1. 6
Gateley	15	61-0-39	1	7	10-3	42-1-39	3.0	6. 7. 6
6 Slatpitts	12	81-1-28	1	12	10-1	56-0-28	2.0	5.16. 8
<Churchill	12	76-1-29	1	-	11-2	37-3-29	0	3.16. 0>
7 Nottridge	11	115-0-29	1	15	14-3	84-1-29	2.6	10.11. 0
8 Smalestones	10	124-2-14	1	15	15-1	93-1-14	2.6	12.13.0
9 Hawkes	9	69-2-23	1	4	10-2	54-0- 3	3.4	9. 0. 0
{ Cranwell	8	59-0- 1	1	10	12-2	35-2- 1	4.0	7.2. 0
Pollardes	8	78-3-18	1	10	12-1	55-2-18	3.0	8. 6.10
{ Gt Lankridge	7	86-0-22	1	12	10-0	63-0-22	3.4	10.10. 0
Little Lankridge	7	18-1- 7	1	5	3-0	9-1- 7	3.4	1.10.10
Five Oake	6	48-3- 3	1	4	8-2	35-1- 3	2.6	4. 8. 0
Evenden, Eveden	5	60-2- 7	1	7	11-2	41-0- 7	3.4	6.16.8
Broadequarr	4	116-2-39	1	10	12-3	92-3-29	2.6	11.12. 6
Cockshuthill	3	88-1-27	1	12	12-0	63-1-27	3.4	10.11. 0
Rowstage	2	74-0- 2	1	8	11-1	53-3- 2	3.4	9. 0. 0
Shakenhoofe	2	42-2-34	1	6	10-0	25-2-34	4.0	5. 3. 0
Buckleape	1	54-0-38	1	10	10-0	33-0-38	4.0	6.13. 0
<Shakenhoofe	2	42-2-34	1	6	10-0	25-2-34	4.0	5. 3. 0>
		a. r. p.				a. r. p.		li s d
Summa Total		1639-2-24				1155-0-24		173. 5. 4

435 Whichwood Forest

I Eveden Coppice	51-1- 1
I Lankeredge Coppice	126-0- 0
I Hasley Coppice	129-2- 0
I Cranehill Coppice	57-2- 0
I Buckleape Coppice	56-1- 0
I Pollard Coppice	84-0- 0
I Gateley Coppice	72-3- 0
I Shakenhowe Coppice	47-3- 0
Churchill Coppice	70-0 -0
I Smallstone Coppice	130-0- 0
I Kingswood Coppice	91-1- 0
I Cockshoothill Coppice	94-2- 0
I Leafridge Coppice	95-1- 0
I Slatpitt Coppice	82-0- 0
I Five Oake Coppice	49-0- 0
I Hawkes Coppice	72-2- 0
I Nuttridge Coppice	113-0- 0
I Rustich Coppice	62-0- 0
I Broadquarter Coppice	118-1- 0
I Wastwood Coppice	68-2- 0

1671-1- 0

436   p. 50

47- 3	Shakenhoofe	22
190- 3	Hawkes Copice ⎫	104-3
	Broadquarter ⎭	
062	Roustede	026-2
068-12	Wastwood	061 –
Non est inventa	Wasted Copice	052
113-	Nottridge	064
92-3	Gately and ⎫	034-1
non est inventa	Slyquarter ⎭	
91-1	Kinswood	052-2
95-1	Leverich	029
130	Smalestone Le Grove	063
94-2	Cockshoothill	048-2
	Eveden ⎫	
177	Great Langridg ⎬	065-1
	Little Langridg ⎭	
129	Chasewood	068
84	Pollard alias Cranehill	020
	[*Cranehill 57* in margin]	
56-1	Buckleape	<033> 025
49	Five Oke	016
82	Slackpitts	086

	his shreddings	835

4 loads of browse £4 keeper

[Writing on the dorse of this sheet has been obscured in the binding]

INDEX OF PERSONS AND PLACES

References to Wychwood, and to the County of Oxford, are so numerous that they have not been indexed.

No attempt has been made to differentiate between individuals with the same name, nor is it indicated when the same name occurs more than once on a page.

Names with the form *A filius B* have been indexed under *B* except for FitzEllis (of Ledhale) and FitzNigel (forester of Bernwood) as these definitely were surnames.

Persons with an occupational description (such as clerk, miller, parson, reeve) but no other surname, have been indexed under that description.

The names of kings have been indexed if they occur in the text but not when they occur in dating clauses.

The following abbreviations have been used: Alex., Alexander; Anth., Anthony; bro., brother; d., daughter; Edm., Edmund; Edw., Edward; Geof., Geoffrey; Gil., Gilbert; Greg., Gregory, Humph., Humphrey; Herb., Herbert; Mat., Matthew; Mic., Michael; mo., mother; Nic., Nicholas; Phil., Philip; Reg. Reginald; Ric. Richard; Rob. Robert; s., son; ser., servant; sis. sister; Step., Stephen; Tho., Thomas; w., wife; wid., widow; Wal., Walter; Wm., William.

Dawe:
John, 59, 72
Tho., 144
Dawes, Rob., 162
Dawson, John, 176
Daye, Daie:
Ellis, 213, 219
John, 172, 213, 219
Peter, 182, 219
Deabere, Ric. de, 148
Deadman Ryding, 188, 190
Dean (e), Dene:
Alan de, 62
Hugh, 199
Ric., 199
Reg./Reynold of, 145, 148, 151-2
Roger atte, 65
Dean (Oxon.), 8, 43
Deane Close, 213
Deane Coppice, 181
Deane Green, 181, 183
Decine, Tho., 161, 219
Deerhurst, Prior/Priory of, 47, 79, 128, 132, 212
Delly Brache, 169-70
Delly Brache Close(s), 169
Delly End (Hailey), 63fn
Delly Sarte, 170-1
Dellyinge, 170
Dene, see Dean(e)
Den(e)le, Denlegh, Den(e)leye :
Henry of, 116
Ric. of, 63, 79
Tho., 132, 134
Wm. bro. of Ric., 63, 79
Denizpiece, le, 150
Denot(en), John, 147, 151-2
Depeslades, 143
Dere, Reg. of, 152
Derneford, Wal. de, 48
Despencer, Despenser, de Spenser:
Edw., 129, 132, 155
Hugh le, 101-2, 108fn, 153
John le, 71
Step. s. of Roger, 88
Devereus, Deverews, de Evereux, de
Everewes:
Henry, 5-6, 9-11, 42, 57
John, 10, 11, 43
Wm., 5, 9-11, 42
Dey(e), Hugh de la, 121
Rob. atte, 124
Dirra see Dyrray

Dissinton, Simon de, 65
Ditch, Diche, *de Fossato*
Hugh, 17-18, 33
Wm. atte, 112, 114
Ditchley, Dichele:
Adam of, 2
Henry of, 65, 71, 110
Hugh of, 14
Peter of, 106
Ralph of, 15, 20, 25, 34, 56, 65
Tho. of, 123
Wal. of, 10
Ditchley (Oxon.), 1fn, 2, 7-8, 10, 14, 20, 22, 24fn, 34-6, 56-7, 64-5, 66fn, 67, 69, 109, 115, 123-4
Ditchley estate, 188fn
Ditchley House, 189-90
Ditchlie Sartes, 190
Dix, John, 206
Dizendou, -, 199
Dobbe(s), Ric., 145, 147, 151-2
Doberal, Step, 63
Dod(de):
Agnes, 77
John, 75-6
Wal., 58, 75
Dodecote, Peter de, 145, 148, 152, 153fn
Dodershulle, 96
Dogge, Wal., 26
Dolneye see Olney
Donecrondles, 109
Dormer, Mrs., 189
Dornford, Derneford:
Wal. of, 48
Wm of, 2-3, 41
Dornford (Oxon.), 1fn, 23, 35
Dorre, Rob., 137
Dosiere, Dosyere:
John, 137
Rob. (le), 147, 149
Doucer, Wm, 145
Dounal, Ric., 152
Douwe, Rob., 108-9
Dover (Kent), 93
Doyley, Douly, Doyli, Doylly, de Oyla,
d'Oilly, de Oylly
Henry, 48fn, 51
Roger, 36-7, 46, 76, 94
Wm., 57-8
Draper, Adam le, 152
Drayton, Simon of, 147
Drinkwater, Drynk(e)water:
James., 193, 219

\

SELECTIVE INDEX OF SUBJECTS